Accession no.
36199243

Early years foundations

D0533522

Early years foundations

Critical issues

Second edition

Edited by

Janet Moyles, Jane Payler and Jan Georgeson

LIS LIBRARY

Date	Fund
7.3.2014	e -War

Order No
02483300

University of Chester

36199243

Mc Graw Hill Education Open University Press

Open University Press
McGraw-Hill Education
McGraw-Hill House
Shoppenhangers Road
Maidenhead
Berkshire
England
SL6 2QL

email: enquiries@openup.co.uk
world wide web: www.openup.co.uk

and Two Penn Plaza, New York, NY 10121-2289, USA

First published 2007
First published in this second edition 2014

Copyright © Janet Moyles, Jane Payler and Jan Georgeson, 2014

All rights reserved. Except for the quotation of short passages for the purposes of criti-cism and review, no part of this publication may be reproduced, stored in a retrieval system, or transmitted, in any form or by any means, electronic, mechanical, photo-copying, recording or otherwise, without the prior written permission of the publisher or a licence from the Copyright Licensing Agency Limited. Details of such licences (for reprographic reproduction) may be obtained from the Copyright Licensing Agency Ltd of Saffron House, 6–10 Kirby Street, London, EC1N 8TS.

A catalogue record of this book is available from the British Library

ISBN-13: 978-0-335-26264-9
ISBN-10: 0-335-26264-3
eISBN: 978-0-335-26265-6

Library of Congress Cataloging-in-Publication Data
CIP data applied for

Typeset by Aptara, Inc.

Fictitious names of companies, products, people, characters and/or data that may be used herein (in case studies or in examples) are not intended to represent any real individual, company, product or event.

Praise for this book

"*Early Years Foundations: Critical issues is a timely and valuable edition for the early childhood bookshelf, offering high quality scholarship combined with deep understanding of early childhood practice. This is a book that values early childhood practitioners as critical partners and experts in young children's learning and development. At a time of fluctuating policy, the authors remind us of the need to advocate for what matters in early childhood and they suggest ways that we can provide excellent experiences for young children with potential to enhance their lives for the long term.*"
Jane Murray, PhD. is a Senior Lecturer at the University of Northampton

"*There seems to be a proliferation of publications currently in the field of early years education and care but this book stands out amongst the crowd for a number of reasons. In particular, the status of the three editing authors means that the content of the book is to be trusted to be both informed and thorough in its attention to detail, and this second edition has been carefully updated to incorporate recent reforms and initiatives. The editing authors' insistence on the creation of an early years text that centres on a critically reflective review of contemporary policy and research can only help to build the argument for a better future for young children's care and education.*

This is a book in which there are many chapters worthy of recommendation and which will form the basis for future debates and publications but Rogers' scholarly work on Enabling Pedagogy encapsulates some core research, essential to our understanding of our work with children, and is a strong and refreshing contribution, while Katz' notion of 'standards of experiences' for young children should give us all food for thought."
Dr Kathy Goouch, Reader in Education,
Canterbury Christ Church University

"*This book is not another bland 'how to do it' manual to accompany the EYFS, it goes much further in offering a truly challenging critique. Helpfully contextualised within the changing policy and political context, each chapter focuses on a different aspect of the curriculum framework and is written by someone with recognised expertise in the field. The strengths of the current EYFS are recognised but the issues and tensions are also made explicit with arguments backed up by theory and research evidence. This should be essential reading for experienced practitioners as well as Early Childhood Studies students.*"
Denise Hevey, Professor of Early Years, University of Northampton

Contents

Contributors

Sue BINGHAM ran a nursery school in Bedford for ten years, following her training as a Montessori early years teacher in California and London. Currently, she is a tutor on the Early Years and Primary PGCE course at Cambridge. Her interest in young children's emotional and social development led her to study for a Masters, then PhD, at the University of Cambridge, investigating ways of assessing and supporting young children's emotional and social knowledge and regulation in classrooms. As an early years adviser and a Pre-School Learning Alliance supporter, she has advised and coached practitioners in best practice. Recent research interests include 'School Readiness: Making schools ready for children' (TACTYC, 2012) and developing play-based early education programmes for kindergartens in China.

Gill BOAG-MUNROE is currently a tutor on the Masters in Learning and Teaching at the University of Oxford, where she was part of the team that carried out the National Evaluation of the Early Learning Parenting Partnerships programme. Her recent research has focused on hard-to-reach families and how they may be drawn into engagement with appropriate services. Her research into how language and concepts assist in the construction of identity is undertaken within an Activity Theoretical frame, while working from a Systemic Functional Linguistics perspective. She has collaborated with Jan Georgeson in developing a way to 'read' the buildings and spaces used in early years settings.

Liz BROOKER was an early years teacher for many years before returning to higher education. Her interest in the transitions to school of ethnic minority children stemmed from her own classroom experience and was the subject of the book, *Starting School: Young children learning cultures* (Open University Press, 2002). Liz continued to study transitions, including those of young babies into their first group-care settings, producing a book, *Supporting Transitions in the Early Years* (Open University Press, 2008). In the last few years, her work has focused on play, using a socio-cultural perspective to describe how the contexts and contents of children's play shape their own development and that of the communities they share with others. Her *Handbook of Play and Learning in Early Childhood* will appear in 2014.

Helen CLARKE is a Senior Lecturer at the University of Winchester teaching undergraduate and postgraduate programmes. She has particular expertise in learning and teaching science in the early years and primary phases, and her doctoral research explored young children's ideas about materials. She was co-researcher for the AstraZeneca Science Teaching Trust project, 'Young Children and their Teachers Exploring their Worlds Together'. Committed to celebrating the energy and enthusiasm that children, students and teachers bring to their learning, her current research interests include children's early exploration and enquiry, environmental education and teacher development, both in the UK and overseas.

Anne COCKBURN is a Professor of Early Years Education at the University of East Anglia. As a teacher, teacher-educator and researcher, she has spent many years working with colleagues from around the world investigating the teaching and learning of mathematics. She is also very interested in teacher well-being and enhancing the quality of working life and classroom performance. Recent books include *Mathematical Misconceptions: A guide for primary teachers* (with Graham Littler; Sage, 2008), *Understanding Mathematics for Young Children* (with Derek Haylock; Sage, 2013) and *Headteachers, Mediocre Colleagues and Educational Leadership: Reflections on teacher quality* (Palgrave Macmillan, 2013).

Rosie FLEWITT is a Senior Lecturer in Early Years and Primary Education at the Institute of Education, London, and a member of the London Knowledge Lab (http://mode.ioe.ac.uk/). Her research focuses on the complementary areas of young children's communication, language and literacy development in a multi-media age and inclusive practices in early education. Rosie uses principally ethnographic and multimodal approaches to the study of early learning, particularly how children use combinations of modes, such as spoken and written language, gesture, images, sounds and layout, as they engage with written, oral, visual and digital texts as part of their everyday literacy practices.

Jan GEORGESON (Editor) is Research Fellow in Early Education Development in the Institute of Education at Plymouth University. After working as a teacher of children with special educational needs in a range of secondary, primary and preschool settings, Jan developed a strong interest in the diversity of early years settings while working as an inspector of educational provision in the non-maintained sector. In 2006, she completed an EdD in Educational Disadvantage and Special Educational Needs at the University of Birmingham. Since then she has worked on research projects, as well teaching on Early Childhood Studies courses at undergraduate and master's level.

Michael JONES has a background in Speech and Language therapy and teaching. Michael was head of Luton's Traveller Education Support Service, and later became the town's first advisory teacher for children with speech and language difficulties. For three years he led the Every Child a Talker (ECaT) projects in Luton, Bedford and Thurrock, working with hundreds of children, practitioners, childminders and parents. Michael is an experienced trainer and has published widely on the subject of children's communication. He is co-author of *Let's Get Talking!* and *Supporting Quiet Children*, both published by Lawrence Educational. For more information, visit www.talk4meaning.co.uk.

Lilian G. KATZ is Professor Emerita of Early Childhood Education at the University of Illinois (Urbana-Champaign) and is a member of the Clearinghouse on Early Education and Parenting (CEEP). Lilian served as Director of the ERIC Clearinghouse for 33 years and is Past President of the National Association for the Education of Young Children. As well as all the states of the USA, Australia and Canada, she has lectured in 55 countries internationally. She is editor of the first on-line peer-reviewed, open-access, bilingual early childhood journal, *Early Childhood Research and Practice*.

Caroline LEESON is Associate Professor, Senior Lecturer and joint programme leader on the BA (Hons) Early Childhood Studies degree at Plymouth University. She has particular interests in the welfare of looked-after children and children with a parent in prison; safeguarding; early years leadership; and reflective practice. Her PhD looked at the involvement of looked-after children in decision-making processes. Before working in higher education, she worked as a local authority social worker in safeguarding, fostering and adoption and managed a family centre for a period of time.

Paulette LUFF is a Senior Lecturer in the Department of Education at Anglia Ruskin University where she leads the MA in Early Childhood Professional Studies and teaches on other early years degree courses. For the past ten years, much of Paulette's research has focused on the topic of child observation and its role in the planning, implementation and evaluation of early childhood curricula. She has co-authored two books and is now engaged in a project examining understanding and use of pedagogical documentation in different types of early years settings. Paulette has worked in the field of early childhood throughout her career, as a teacher, foster carer, school-home liaison worker, nursery practitioner and advisor.

Janet MOYLES (Editor) is Professor Emeritus, Anglia Ruskin University and a play/early years specialist. She has worked as an early years teacher and head and has written and edited widely, including *Just Playing?* (Open University Press, 1989), *The Excellence of Play* (Open University Press, 2009) and *Effective Leadership and Management in the Early Years* (Open University Press, 2007). She has directed several research projects including *Jills of All Trades?* (ATL, 1996), *Too Busy to Play?* (Esmee Fairbairn Trust/University of Leicester 1997–2000), *Study of Pedagogical Effectiveness in Early Learning (SPEEL)* (DfES, 2002) and *Recreating the Reception Year* (ATL, 2003).

Jayne OSGOOD is Professor of Education at London Metropolitan University. She is a sociologist of education focusing specifically on the early years and is particularly concerned to research issues of inequality relating to gender, social class and 'race' and to critically engage with policy as it affects the workforce, families and children in this context. As a feminist, she is committed to developing and applying critical feminist theorizations to her work.

John PARRY is a Lecturer in Education (Early Years and Primary) at the Open University. He has many years' experience as a practitioner working in the early years sector, primarily as a teacher and coordinator of a Portage service. From 2003 until 2009 he was Chair of the National Portage Association in the UK. His research interests include: the development of inclusion in schools and early years provision; early intervention; and social interaction in inclusive settings.

Jane PAYLER (Editor) is a Senior Lecturer in Early Years Education at the University of Winchester and Chair of TACTYC, Association for the Professional Development of Early Years Educators. Jane has taught, examined, researched, published, and practised in early years education and care for over twenty years. She has taught early years students from college vocational courses to university doctoral level. Prior to that, she worked in the NHS as a Health Education Officer. Since 2006, she has been closely involved in delivering and assessing the Early Years Professional Status. Her publications and research interests include inter-professional practice, professional development, and young children's learning experiences.

Karen PHETHEAN is a Senior Lecturer in Teacher Education at the University of Winchester. She teaches on the BA Primary Education and PGCE courses for Primary Science. She has a strong interest in research-informed practice and is module leader for the undergraduate dissertation. Prior to joining the university, Karen was a class teacher, science coordinator and Leading Science Teacher. She has been involved in a research/CPD project at the University of Winchester, *Teachers and Young Children Exploring Their Worlds Together.* She is currently undertaking an MPhil/PhD into the relationship between play, anxiety and learning within the context of primary science.

Linda POUND has worked in three universities and was an LEA inspector responsible for the early years for almost ten years. In addition, she has been head of a nursery school and deputy head of a primary school. In her current role as an education consultant, she provides training for early years practitioners around the country and beyond. Linda writes extensively for a range of audiences on a range of topics related to early childhood care and education.

Anne RAWLINGS is an Early Years Fellow at Kingston University. Anne began her career as a nurse and then trained as a teacher as a mature student. She is a founder member of the much praised Institute for Child Centred Interprofessional Practice (ICCIP) at Kingston and currently leads the ICCIP cross-disciplinary programmes and research. Anne is Vice Chair of the SEFDEY network. Recent publications include a widely read textbook on work-based learning and she has recently contributed to a book on *Interprofessional Working in Practice: Learning and working together for children and families* (Open University Press, 2011).

Jonathan RIX is a Senior Lecturer in Inclusion, Curriculum and Learning at the Open University (UK). His research interests focus upon: policies, practices and language that facilitate inclusion within the mainstream; capturing diverse perspectives; and developing models to facilitate our thinking about the form and function of education. He has recently researched parental perspectives and children's experiences of early intervention, and special educational provision in fifty countries. Jonathan spent five years on both the committee of Tiggers Playgroup, Balcombe and the National Portage Association Executive. He was also an advisor for the DFES/DOH Early Support programme and the DfE Pathfinder Project.

Sue ROGERS is Head of the Department of Early Years and Primary Education at the Institute of Education, London. Her research interests include play, curriculum and pedagogy in early childhood, young children's perspectives and child–adult interaction. She has published widely in the field of early childhood education, including three recent books: *Inside Role Play in Early Childhood Education: Researching children's perspectives* (with Julie Evans; Routledge, 2008), an edited collection on play pedagogy entitled *Rethinking Play and Pedagogy in Early Childhood Education: Concepts, contexts and cultures* (Routledge, 2011) and *Adult Roles in the Early Years* (with Janet Rose; Open University Press, 2012).

Anita SONI currently works as an independent Educational Psychologist working with clusters of Children's Centres and primary schools in the West Midlands. Anita is particularly interested in children's personal, social and emotional development, the Key Person approach, the use of group supervision with professionals from the children's workforce and supporting children with English as an additional language. Anita also works at the University of Birmingham as a tutor on the Educational Psychology Programme and teaches for the Open University.

Suzy TUTCHELL is a Senior Lecturer in Education at the University of Winchester, specializing in Early Years and Art and Design. Having taught for many years in inner-city London schools, she then worked as Community and Outreach manager for Discover, a hands-on children's museum in East London. She continued to champion the expressive arts in her subsequent role as early years and creativity consultant for a LEA as well as extensive work as a freelance trainer and consultant. Her most recent book on young children as artists is due for publication in 2014.

Judith TWANI qualified as a Junior teacher in the days of discovery learning and topic webs. When the National Curriculum arrived she moved to South Africa to teach in a small rural school that was a pioneer of multi-racial education. A return to teaching in England took Judith first to Year 2 and then to Reception where she discovered her passion for early years. She now works part-time for Early Excellence and as a development consultant for Christian Initiatives in early years education. She also has experience as a childcare assessor, OfSTED Inspector and as an independent consultant with *SMAR+PD*, *Talk4Meaning* and *Future Creative*.

Jane WATERS is the Director of Primary Initial Teacher Education and Training in the South West Wales Centre of Teacher Education at UWTSD: Swansea Metropolitan. Having worked initially as a primary classroom teacher and, more recently, as Director of an undergraduate Early Childhood Studies programme, she now works most closely with students training to be teachers. Jane lectures in outdoor play and learning, adult–child interaction, early years education and the ethics of research with young children. Jane's research interests lie in young children's experiences of outdoor spaces, interaction in early childhood education, and young children's agency and voice.

David WHITEBREAD taught as a primary school teacher for 12 years and is now a Senior Lecturer in Psychology of Education at the University of Cambridge. He is a developmental cognitive psychologist and early years specialist with a particular research focus in children's development of metacognitive awareness and strategic control in relation to a number of areas of learning. These have included children's problem solving and reasoning, mathematical strategies and road safety skills. Other interests include children learning through play, early years ICT, the education of the gifted and talented, children's drawings, and the application of cognitive neuroscience to education.

Figures, tables and photographs

Introduction

Janet Moyles, Jane Payler and Jan Georgeson

There is a continuing dilemma for practitioners in the current climate between doing what we know is essentially 'right' for young children from all backgrounds and conforming to the demands made by government and policy-makers, especially through the new Early Years Foundation Stage (EYFS) (DfE, 2012) – not always a happy alliance. The complexity for early years practitioners is in trying to make sense of all the legislation and policy documents in a climate of increased government intervention; *as well as* meet the obligations laid upon them, never mind continuing to do their best to ensure children have playful learning and development experiences. It is as well for practitioners to remember that they are '[n]ot only receivers of but also mediators of policy' (Ball, 2011), and that '[d]uring the interpretation process a policy can take on a different form from what was intended as practitioners will redefine it to accommodate the narratives of and within the setting' (Clandinin and Connelly, 1996: 26).

Dealing with children from birth to five years of age from diverse family backgrounds and cultures and with differential learning needs understandably challenges many practitioners – a role that is still not well understood, and significantly undervalued, both in society at large and politically. Such is the positive nature of early years practitioners that they continue trying to implement the early years curriculum and make learning fun and interesting. The need for being a reflective and analytical practitioner has clearly never been greater or more urgent than it is at present (Moyles, 2010).

This is definitely not a 'how to' book: the contributors instead use relevant contemporary research to make their points and encourage practitioners to challenge unnecessary imposed pedagogy and ask relevant 'why' questions. We agree with Alexander (2009: 20) that 'principles should guide the work of everyone who works in education, from school hall to Whitehall', but practitioners need to be able to articulate their principles and explain why particular pedagogy seems inappropriate. Edgington (1998: 6) argues that practitioners 'whose work is not underpinned by principles which they can back up with research evidence are less likely to be able to see a clear direction for the development of their practice, and more likely to fall victim to the many pressures which currently exist'. This book seeks to support practitioners to clarify their own principles and learn about some of the research evidence that supports their thinking about practice.

Readers are asked to consider how the concept of the 'capable young child' can emerge and be developed within (and sometimes despite) the prescribed curriculum content. By offering ways of critiquing the new EYFS, we wish to encourage early years educators to interrogate their practices and conceptualize the experiences they offer our young children from the perspective of the child. It is all too easy to get drawn into concerns about conforming to inspection demands and other politically based pressures, that the children's needs are sometimes unwittingly overlooked and the curriculum they experience is narrow and lacking in meaning (Moyles and Worthington, 2011).

The contributors have been asked, essentially, to set their focus and then, within that focus, outline the critical issues and challenges facing practitioners in England and beyond. They then examine some of the background to each topic, offering opinions on why the situation is as it is and how it might move forward within the new EYFS and similar prescribed curricula frameworks. Owing to the complexities already highlighted, we felt it appropriate to begin the book with a thorough analysis of the current context of early years education and care. Thus in Chapter 1, Liz Brooker writes about the opportunities and the challenges that the new early childhood 'landscape' presents, and describes how the developments and legislation of the last few years have brought about new ways of thinking and working that we need now to embrace if we are effectively to promote the interests of young children and their families.

While adhering to the overarching principles of provision as described in the new EYFS (DfS, 2012: 2: ii) – quality and consistency; a secure foundation; partnership working; and equality of opportunity – we aim, through the sections and chapters of this book, to ensure that early years educators are made aware of the many challenges the formulation and implementation of the new curriculum presents. Please note our use of 'implementation' for one cannot 'deliver' a curriculum to young children as if it were bottles of milk or they merely empty vessels. Delivery suggests, too, a deficit model in the way children are perceived, for example in 'working towards' goals and in need of 'being ready' rather than viewed as developing individuals who have a right to a childhood in which their learning makes sense, is fun and develops positive dispositions. Indeed, several writers argue that we must start from where the child is physically, emotionally, socially and intellectually rather than work to unachievable goals in this high stakes performance culture. In Chapter 16, David Whitebread argues that settings should consider how 'ready' they are to receive the whole range of backgrounds and capabilities of children who enter the setting. While play, for example, is mentioned in the new EYFS (paras. 1.9, 1.10), it is in the context of children investigating and experiencing things and 'having a go', or as being 'planned and purposeful' rather than any conceptualization of play as child-initiated, generating deeper and meaningful learning experiences: Sue Rogers (Chapter 4), among others, takes up the issue of play and enabling playful pedagogies, a topic that also permeates other chapters, including that of Linda Pound (Chapter 2).

The concept of reflective practice is well established (e.g. Moyles, 2010; Teaching Agency, 2012; Brock, 2014). But how can this evolve and develop in a climate where governments insist on dictating everyday practices, essentially removing the onus of responsibility and professionalism from practitioners and undermining the agency of the child? A recent example is the requirement that young children should be tested on synthetic phonics, a practice strongly challenged by those who know about young children's language and communication capabilities; they realize that all children learn differently and multiple methods are better employed (see Rosie Flewitt, Chapter 9). Boys, in particular, can suffer in relation to early writing skills, finding it physically difficult, as many of them do, to use writing implements readily enough to form fluent marks (Clarke and Featherstone, 2008). The expectations on mathematics are similarly flawed: Anne Cockburn takes up these challenges in Chapter 10, particularly in relation to the vital topic of young children's understanding of the concept of zero.

And then there's assessment and the EYFS Profile (Standards and Testing Agency, 2013), which, although slimmed down, still makes demands that most children may well not be able to meet, as they are unrealistic and do not take account of the diversity of children's background experiences or their development. The fact that children in the UK begin school several years earlier than their counterparts internationally heightens unrealistic expectations of them; other countries are far more realistic in relation to formalized learning, which, in most cases, does not begin until children are at least six years of age. This means that sensitive observation, assessment and documentation of children's abilities, capabilities and dispositions becomes a vital feature in working with such young children. A continual source of concern to early years educators, however, is that effective assessment means that individual children's learning and development must be taken into account in developing plans for the next potential areas of learning. Paulette Luff takes up this important topic in Chapter 3, while Jane Payler and Jan Georgeson focus on qualifications and quality in routes into early years (Chapter 5). They trace the development of issues in relation to qualifications and quality, raising questions about the evidence that is variously misused, ignored or over-used.

In Part 2, contributors cover specific areas of learning, including communication and language (Michael Jones and Judith Twani, Chapter 6), physical development and outdoor play (Jane Waters, Chapter 7), personal, social and emotional development (Anita Soni, Chapter 8), early literacy development (Rosie Flewitt, Chapter 9), mathematics (Anne Cockburn, Chapter 10), understanding the world, including ICT (Karen Phethean and Helen Clarke, Chapter 11), and expressive arts and design (Suzy Tutchell, Chapter 12). Part 3 moves on to explore partnership working and includes chapters by Caroline Leeson on leading early years services (Chapter 13), Gill Boag-Munroe on the new politics of parenting (Chapter 14), and Anne Rawlings on the integration of health and education (Chapter 15). Part 4 – Equality of Opportunity – examines school readiness (David Whitebread and Sue Bingham, Chapter 16), gender issues (Jayne Osgood, Chapter 17), and difference and diversity (Jonathan Rix and John Parry, Chapter 18).

It is the editors' intention that the book should also 'speak' to an international audience whom we feel can learn from our critique of the current English system, which can be facilitated by emphasizing the issues and challenges rather than the content of the EYFS. To this end, we have asked a respected author with an outside perspective (Lilian Katz, Chapter 19) to write a critical international overview of the new EYFS as a conclusion to the book. This view from afar helps us to reconsider how the dilemmas we face are grappled with in other countries. For instance, there are national challenges that have parallels in other parts of the world: China, for example, has only recently realized the need for young children to play and to be individually creative, and that it is possible to provide a curriculum based on play that nonetheless enables children to achieve the kinds of outcomes desired by parents, practitioners and policy-makers and become creative individuals (Zhu and Zhang, 2008; Vong, 2013). Also, across the world, the issue of what constitutes a 'teacher' is still explored, and since the Nutbrown Review (2012), in England in particular.

All our contributors are experienced writers and avid early years advocates who have written on topics about which they are both knowledgeable and passionate. They each lay out their specific focus and outline, within that focus, the challenges, issues and dilemmas facing practitioners in the UK and sometimes beyond. Each chapter starts with a brief abstract so that readers can 'tune-in' quickly to the contents. There is then an examination of some of the background issues to each topic, offering a critique of the EYFS expectations and how practitioners must reflect carefully and diagnostically if they are to best serve the learning and developments needs of the babies, infants and young children in their care, as well as their families. Each chapter offers points for reflection and discussion. Commendable books, articles and websites are highlighted (in **bold**) in the accompanying references and further reading lists.

With its particular reflection and discussion points section, we believe that all those involved in early years courses in initial and continuing professional development will find this book invaluable in supporting and challenging thinking about the issues underpinning the EYFS and its implementation. Early years educators are notorious for being mainly non-political in their passion for working – and playing – with young children. Only when we can argue authoritatively and knowledgeably about the most appropriate curriculum for birth to age five, offering evidenced critique from research and a valid professional stance, will our views be taken seriously by those who determine policy. We are keen that this book should support that process.

References

Alexander, R. (2009) *Children, Their World, Their Education: Final Report and Recommendations of the Cambridge Primary Review*. London: Routledge.

Ball, S.J. (2011) Teachers as actors/teachers as subjects: dealing with policy contradictions and contradictory policies. PowerPoint presentation, University of Exeter Seminar Series, 22 February.

Brock, A. (2014) *The Early Years Reflective Practice Handbook*. London: Routledge.

Clandinin, J.D. and Connelly, F.M. (1996) Teachers' professional knowledge landscapes: Teacher stories–stories of teachers–school stories–stories of school, *Educational Researcher*, 25(3): 24–30.

Clarke, J. and Featherstone, S. (2008) *Young Boys and Their Writing*. Market Bosworth: Featherstone Publishing.

Department for Education (DfE) (2012) *Statutory Framework for the Early Years Foundation Stage: Setting the standards for learning, development and care for children from birth to five*. Available at: http://www.foundationyears.org.uk/wp-content/uploads/2012/07/EYFS-Statutory-Framework-2012.pdf.

Edgington, M. (1998) *The Nursery Teacher in Action*. London: Paul Chapman.

Moyles, J. (ed.) (2010) *Thinking about Play: Developing a reflective approach*. Maidenhead: Open University Press.

Moyles, J. and Worthington, M. (2011) *The Early Years Foundation Stage through the Daily Experiences of Children*. Occasional Paper No. 1, TACTYC, The Association for the Professional Development of Early Years Teachers (http://www.tactyc.org.uk).

Nutbrown, C. (2012) *Foundations for Quality: The Independent Review of Early Education and Childcare Qualifications, Final Report*. London: DfE. Available at: www. education.gov.uk/publications/standard/EarlyYearseducationandchildcare (accessed 25 March 2013).

Standards and Testing Agency (2013) *Early Years Foundation Stage Profile Handbook*. Available at: www.education.gov.uk/eyfsp (accessed 25 March 2013).

Teaching Agency (2012) *Review of Early Years Professional Status Standards*. London: Teaching Agency. Available at: www.education.gov.uk/publications (accessed 25 March 2013).

Vong, K. (2013) China: pedagogy today and the move towards creativity, in J. Georgeson and J. Payler (eds.) *International Perspectives on Early Childhood Education and Care*. Maidenhead: Open University Press.

Zhu, J. and Zhang, J. (2008) Contemporary trends and developments in early childhood education in China. *Early Years: An International Journal of Research and Development*, 28(2): 173–82.

1 An overview of early education in England

Liz Brooker

Abstract

The decade of rapid change that preceded the first edition of this book has been followed by a further period of turbulent times for early childhood in England. As a consequence, both practitioners and providers face 2014 with a new – and still shifting – landscape in front of them. This chapter discusses some of the events and debates that have led to our current situation, and the challenges which these present to those working in the field. It is evident that political pendulum-swings can send shock waves through our services that have a direct impact on the experiences of young children and their families. As ever, it is providers and practitioners who act as buffers between the upheavals occurring on the national stage, and the experiences and environments offered to the children and parents for whom they are responsible. The chapter begins with a reminder of the 'state of play' in 2007 and then reviews the key changes in early childhood policy and curriculum, legislation and qualifications, which educators have been absorbing and managing in the subsequent period. It concludes that with a robust and dedicated workforce, it is still possible to build better futures for children in challenging times.

Introduction

The last few years have brought sweeping political changes in the education sector in England and early childhood policy-makers, providers and practitioners have had to adapt swiftly and sensitively to a new political environment and new conditions of service. In 2007, those working in services for young children were taking stock after a period of rapid reform and innovation, culminating in 'Every Child Matters' (DfES, 2003) and the Early Years Foundation Stage (DfES, 2006) and were hoping for a period of stability in which to consolidate their practice and provision. The most that was hoped for was small changes to current regulations to remove a few of the stresses practitioners were experiencing. Previous major policy shifts were bedding down, and qualifications levels in the childcare workforce were steadily rising. Many more educators were enrolled in continuing

professional development programmes, including those involving leadership qualifications and the sector could view itself, after a decade of change, both as more
professional and as more widely recognized.

Since 2007, however, economic crises and political changes have transformed
a service that was relatively well resourced and well regulated into a site of financial cuts and political contestation. This chapter traces these developments by
reviewing the key themes that continue to underpin our services: the quality and
appropriateness of our early childhood services; the qualifications and professionalism of the workforce; the research-based practice which prioritizes play and
relationships in provision for children; and the respect for young children as people who are human 'beings' in their own right, rather than human 'becomings' in
preparation for later life (Uprichard, 2008). As the United Nations launches its new
'General Comment' on children's right to play (UNCRC, 2013), practitioners need
to continue to defend these rights both locally and nationally.

Establishing the foundations: from research to practice, 1997–2000

A key reason for the sense of excitement and optimism that prevailed in early
childhood services around the turn of the present century was that government-
funded investment into early childhood research was being translated, almost
for the first time, into national policy. For more than a decade, research into
the quality of early learning had been demonstrating the distinctive factors that
made early childhood education and care different from all other phases of
education (Rumbold, 1990; Ball, 1994; Moss and Pence, 1994; Sylva *et al.*, 2001;
Siraj-Blatchford *et al.*, 2002). Now, the government of the day appeared intent on
putting these findings into action by a massive investment into the expansion of
preschool provision.

The events of 1997–2000 were driven by a specific political ideology and
agenda: a belief that investment in services for young children – both 'childcare'
and 'early education' – would lead to an array of benefits for individuals, families,
communities and the nation (Pugh, 2005). Accessible and affordable *childcare* – as
provided in the Nordic countries, for instance (Einarsdottir and Wagner, 2006) –
would enable parents of young children to get into training or employment, with
beneficial impacts on family poverty and on the social exclusion and isolation
that results from unemployment; higher levels of employment and earnings would
bring economic improvements through both increased tax revenues and increased
consumption of goods and service. Universal *early education*, meanwhile, would
tackle the historic social class differences in children's attainment and outcomes
(Feinstein, 2003), leading to a future generation of well-educated adults who would
in turn become competent workers, adequate earners and good parents. According to this model, investment in young children and their families was the best possible use of the nation's resources (Pugh, 2005).

The model was applied through a succession of initiatives: free and universal
preschool provision for children aged from three to five years; a huge expansion
of childcare places, especially across the private sector; tax credits for working

families as a contribution to childcare costs; a programme of Early Excellence Centres, along with the first wave of Sure Start local programmes, which were intended to offer universal access to integrated services for young families (Sure Start Unit, 2003); and the development of a curriculum framework for the newly named 'Foundation Stage' to apply to children in every kind of preschool provision, from individual childminders to large integrated centres.

The 'Curriculum Guidance for the Foundation Stage' (QCA, 2000) set out six areas of learning that have continued to underpin subsequent curricula, and suggested how a largely play-based environment could support children's progress across all the areas. A balance was sought between allowing a diversity of provision, to meet different needs, and ensuring an equal entitlement for all children across that range of options. 'Quality' was the watchword in research as well as in policy-making, and was beginning to be consolidated by means of research-based instruments such as the ECERs (Harms and Clifford, 1998) and Effective Early Learning (EEL) (Pascal and Bertram, 1997) programmes. Already, however, some critique of this 'universal quality' or 'what works' agenda (Dahlberg *et al.*, 1999) was emerging, with a warning that in applying 'research evidence' across a diversity of settings, families and children, we might be failing to respect and support difference.

Building on the foundations: 2000–2007

In the early years of this century, the underlying conceptions of the new Foundation Stage were rapidly revised as a framework for working with children under three years, and 'Birth to Three Matters' (DfES, 2002) was introduced. Educators welcomed the new guidance, pointing out that provision for children under three was grounded in a more holistic view of the individual – as a 'strong child', 'a skilful communicator', 'a competent learner' and a 'healthy child' – rather than as a learner progressing through the levels of a subject-based curriculum. Practitioners also highlighted the absurdity of dividing children into sectors based on their third birthday, and consultation continued towards the introduction of a combined and integrated framework for children from before birth to the end of the Reception Year. To their credit, the government of the day also commissioned extensive literature reviews on young children's learning and development (David *et al.*, 2003; Evangelou *et al.*, 2009) as the basis for the evolving curriculum frameworks.

The new Early Years Foundation Stage (EYFS) (DCSF, 2008) was piloted in 2006–2007 and implemented in full in 2008. While retaining the six 'areas of learning' from earlier curricula, it was structured on a far more holistic matrix of themes: 'a unique child', 'positive relationships', 'enabling environments', and 'learning and development'. It utilized the findings of the Effective Provision of Pre-School Education (EPPE) study (Sylva *et al.*, 2004) to recommend key principles for good practice, including a balanced offer of educator-led and child-led activities, and a strong partnership with parents and other caregivers.

The EYFS, however, was only one element in a network of initiatives that presented a continuing vision of the power of early childhood services to change society. The expansion of Sure Start from a locally based programme into a nationwide programme of Children's Centres was accompanied by the publication of the

Green Paper Every Child Matters (DfES, 2003) and, following consultation, its implementation in the Children Act (2004), the 'Ten Year Childcare Strategy' (HM Treasury, 2004) and The Children Act (2006). This ambitious statutory framework aimed to protect and provide for children from birth to eighteen, and to support parents and communities in creating nurturing environments for children. The five goals of Every Child Matters for children and young people – staying safe, being healthy, enjoying and achieving, making a contribution, and avoiding poverty and adversity – required a well-trained workforce working together in imaginative ways across administrative and disciplinary boundaries (Siraj-Blatchford *et al.*, 2007). Within early childhood, the EYFS was intended to promote these goals, and the new qualification of Early Years Professional was created to lead change in settings as they took on the new framework.

Early Years Professional Status (EYPS) was a product of the newly created Children's Workforce Development Council (CWDC, 2006), which itself had the specific remit of supporting the successful implementation of Every Child Matters. The EYPS was designed to equip practitioners from a range of backgrounds with the resources needed to carry forward both the EYFS and the Every Child Matters agenda in settings of varying types and quality. To lead change in practice, they required both a deep understanding of play pedagogies, and excellent skills in leadership and management.

Consolidate or change?: 2007–2010

From September 2008, the EYFS was implemented in all early childhood settings. Despite early responses that it was overwhelmingly complex to manage – and opposition from some special interests – many of its features made immediate sense to practitioners and parents. It created a continuous framework of care, education and welfare for all children from birth until the end of their Reception year, while underpinning the goals of Every Child Matters, which already received widespread support. In schools and settings, it rapidly became the 'new normal' for many practitioners, as a series of research reports demonstrated (BAECE, 2009; Brooker *et al.*, 2010), while an exploration of children's experiences within the new framework (Garrick *et al.*, 2010) gave many positive indicators.

Children and Young People Now (www.cypnow.co.uk) described the broad and positive consensus on the EYFS that emerged from surveys by the Pre-school Learning Alliance (PLA), National Day Nurseries Association (NDNA) and the British Association for Early Childhood Education (BAECE). Despite practical difficulties, respondents consistently mentioned child-led learning and user-friendly planning, good practice guidelines and improved record keeping as particularly strong aspects of the framework. BAECE's survey of its members reported that almost 70 per cent of respondents referred to the guidance for their planning, and around 90 per cent believed that most of the Early Learning Goals were pitched at the right level. Over 90 per cent of respondents confirmed that they felt 'very confident' or 'confident' in their understanding of the EYFS.

A stratified inquiry among practitioner groups – consulting seven types of practitioner in each of six English regions – found many respondents already attached to, and defensive towards, the framework (Brooker *et al.*, 2010). While each of the practitioner groups, including primary headteachers and childminders, had a different experience of working with the framework, the most frequently heard comment was that the EYFS was 'play-based' and 'child-led', and encouraged practitioners to do what they felt was right for children. A significant minority said that they did not want the framework to change – 'It's our Bible!', 'It's our bread and butter!' – although the majority suggested modifications in particular aspects of the assessment, paperwork or inspection regimes.

The EYFS did not constitute a shift in direction from earlier frameworks, but did try to situate its six 'areas of learning' within a holistic context that prioritized relationships, including with a Key Person, partnership with parents, and outdoor learning as essential elements. By extending the Foundation Years until the end of Reception, it appeared to stake a claim for play-based and child-initiated learning into the first year of school. As many commentators pointed out, however, there was an inherent tension in the proposal for a child-led learning programme that was assessed, after five years, against a set of prescribed learning goals and statements of achievement. This underlying tension came to the surface in the Reception Year, and was expressed most strongly by Reception teachers (Brooker *et al.*, 2010). By this time, however, the political landscape was undergoing a further seismic shift.

Shifting the foundations: a new world order from 2010

In 2010, two years after the full roll-out of the EYFS framework, a government review was commissioned, based on a wide range of evidence specially gathered (Tickell, 2011a, 2011b). This coincided, however, with a change of government, a continuing financial crisis, and a powerful new ideological stance towards children and families. Overnight the Department for Children, Schools and Families (DCSF), which had driven the expansion of services and the focus on qualifications, and developed the EYFS, was re-named the Department for Education; and almost the entire output of the previous administration was removed from the government's website. Even Every Child Matters became inaccessible, as if its aspirations were no longer officially sanctioned. From 2010 to the present, many aspects of early childhood provision have been reduced or dismantled, although the need for this provision has continued to rise as the nation's families have experienced increasing financial and social difficulties. Subsequent revisions of the EYFS have to be seen in this context.

Tickell's review of evidence (2011b) drew on research reports, surveys, workshops, expert consultations and thousands of submissions to an online consultation. It placed its priorities squarely in the 'New Labour' agenda of harnessing early childhood services to bring about social and economic change, arguing that, 'The return on public investment in high quality early years education is substantial, leading to decreased social problems, reduced inequality and increased productivity and GDP growth' (Tickell, 2011b: 4). This argument brings together evidence on the importance of narrowing the social class gap in the UK (Springate *et al.*, 2008), on the place of quality in shaping children's outcomes (Melhuish *et al.*, 2010), on the impact of parenting behaviours (Gutman and Feinstein, 2007) and on the determining role of early language exposure and communicative competence on later achievement (Hart and Risley, 1995).

Tickell's report on the EYFS was largely positive, demonstrating that around 80 per cent of practitioners and parents were more than satisfied with the impact on children's experiences and outcomes, and citing statistics to support this 'improving' trend. The Office for Standards in Education (OfSTED), for instance, described a positive impact on outcomes, and gave improved inspection ratings to nurseries and preschools (OfSTED, 2011), while official figures showed a reduction in the achievement gap (DfE, 2012c), as the scores of disadvantaged children improved while the median score for all children remained stable.

In her final recommendations, Tickell (2011a) outlined a 'slimmed-down' EYFS, which placed greater emphasis on three 'prime' areas of learning – personal, social and emotional development; communication and language; and physical development – with the other subject areas sitting alongside them. She suggested a more flexible framework, with a reduced number of challenging hoops and targets for practitioners, as well as children, to achieve. And she prioritized the role of parents as co-educators and partners with practitioners, insisting that they should be far more involved in the assessment and planning for their children's learning. The revised Early Years Framework became statutory in September 2012.

The Foundation Years revisited: EYFS 2012

In many respects, the new EYFS (DfE, 2012a) seems to be an attempt to make the original EYFS 'work', by simplifying its remit and removing some of the most difficult goals to achieve. Much of its text replicates the language as well as the principles of the 2008 framework. The presentation, however, sends strong messages about the political and ideological context within which the framework is situated – a context that was prefigured from the first day of the new government, when the education website was revamped.

Until May 2010, early childhood services were provided within a Department for Children, Schools and Families, whose cheerful rainbow logo and munchkin decorations were deliberately designed to be both child- and family-friendly. The first version of the EYFS was encased in a colourful folder embellished with photos of babies and young children. The folder included the statutory framework document and a much fatter volume of non-statutory 'practice guidance' with ideas for how practitioners should implement the statutory areas. Each of the learning strands was illustrated with examples of activities and assessments ('Look, listen and note') for every age band. Also included were a wall poster setting out the four principles and illustrating the strands which contributed to them; a set of coloured laminated cards with further discussion of the commitments which lay within each major theme; and a CD-ROM full of video clips showing the principles being enacted in a range of settings. This bundle of materials was initially criticized by some practitioners as being too complex to comprehend, but once in use it was described as user-friendly and clear (Brooker *et al.*, 2010).

Like the new Department for Education's website, the 2012 EYFS abjured any positive images of childhood in its presentation. The statutory framework is contained in one short, sombre booklet, and presents its message in a continuous text covering the learning and development requirements, assessment requirements, and safeguarding and welfare requirements. The content carries some mixed messages for providers, practitioners and parents, as other chapters will indicate. The Introduction, for instance, includes an explicit avowal of the value of childhood to the child *in the here and now*, rather than as future capital: A secure, safe and happy childhood is important in its own right (DfE, 2012a: 2).

This statement is soon forgotten, however, as the document makes clear its overriding imperative: to 'ensure children are ready for school' and to give them the basic knowledge and skills 'to benefit fully from the opportunities ahead of them'. Early childhood, then, has as its real goal the preparation of children for their future roles as learners and earners.

A similar tension emerges between the 'guiding principles' and the goals of the framework. The former state that:

- every child is a *unique child*, who is constantly learning and can be resilient, capable, confident and self-assured;
- children learn to be strong and independent through *positive relationships*;
- children learn and develop well in *enabling environments*, in which their experiences respond to their individual needs…; and
- *children develop and learn in different ways and at different rates.*

The principles affirm that practitioners should respect and respond to the fact that children grow and develop in different ways, at different paces and even in different directions. They imply a view of children as strong and competent learners, in their own individual ways, during the preschool and early school years. Unfortunately, the learning goals tell a different story. As in the 2008 framework, goals such as those for literacy are an affront to practitioners conscious of the different learning trajectories of younger children in the age group, of boys, and of children learning English as a second language (all assessments of language and literacy are to be conducted in English):

> *Reading*: children read and understand simple sentences. They use phonic knowledge to decode regular words and read them aloud accurately. They also read some common irregular words. They demonstrate understanding when talking with others about what they have read.

> *Writing*: children use their phonic knowledge to write words in ways which match their spoken sounds. They also write some irregular common words. They write simple sentences which can be read by themselves and others. Some words are spelt correctly and others are phonetically plausible.

'Goals' like these, with their requirement for early phonics training, are aligned with some of the subtext of the key themes. The EYFS provides, for instance, 'quality and consistency in all early years settings, so that *every child makes good progress and no child gets left behind'*. The final phrase in this statement is an uncomfort-able reminder of the much-criticized 'No Child Left Behind' legislation in the USA, commonly described by educators as 'no child left untested'. The EYFS should also secure 'equality of opportunity and anti-discriminatory practice, ensuring that every child is included and supported'. This laudable aim may be interpreted in many ways, but in the context of a 'no child left behind' agenda, it appears to leave no room for diversity in development and learning. All in all, the new framework reflects a subtle hardening of the stance towards young children and families, in accordance with the new political climate.

The new landscape

The EYFS 2012/13 is being implemented in a far harsher social, economic and political context than earlier curricula. The conservative government responded to the financial crisis of 2008, and to subsequent periods of recession, by cutting or reducing funding to all public services, including early childhood services. An initial hope that early childhood funding might be ring-fenced and protected has evaporated, as Sure Start Children's Centres have cut their services, or introduced fees for them, or in many cases closed. For practitioners, the task of maintaining high levels of quality with reduced levels of resource has created continual stress and difficulty. For parents, the closure of many aspects of the 'one-stop-shop' that children's centres were intended to provide, has created further hardship while many struggle with significant cuts in personal and family benefits.

The realignment of services represents more than simply a 'shrinkage' result-ing from financial difficulties. Rather, it is a conscious ideological turn away from the goal of 'universal' services, which were intended to bring together families from all sectors of society, to avoid stigmatizing and marginalizing the poor and disad-vantaged (Pugh, 2005). In the new climate, resources and services are targeted, somewhat punitively, at families whose children or parenting have already been identified as inadequate (among them, the '120,000 troubled families' identified by the Prime Minister, without any information on how this figure was constructed). Parents whose children are falling behind developmental standards at the age of two years are now obliged to bring them to be remediated in special two-year-old provision; if they decline, they risk having their remaining welfare benefits removed. This targeting of 'deficient' parents is described as a policy of 'fairness'.

It is for practitioners to struggle to make these new systems work: by using their knowledge, skills and leadership qualities to turn unhelpful policies into gen-uinely helpful provision; by calling on their understanding of the importance of play to compensate for early rote learning of phonics and 'regular and irregular words'; to ensure that children's diverse routes to development really are respected and supported; to treat children as individuals with rights *in the present*, rather than as material for future successful learning and earning.

There is courage to be gained from the vast increase in practitioner qualifica-tions over the last ten years: the 2011 provider survey (DfE, 2012b) shows almost 80 per cent of the workforce with at least a Level 3 qualification, and more than 15 per cent with Level 6, including a growing group of Early Years Professionals.

Following the Nutbrown Review of qualifications (Nutbrown, 2012), these numbers should continue to rise, and the EYFS requirement for continuing professional development should enable all practitioners to develop their ability to implement policies reflectively and critically, with the needs of children and families in mind, rather than slavishly.

In 2006, the United Nations Committee on the Rights of the Child (UNCRC) published an important and influential General Comment (General Comment 7, 'Implementing child rights in early childhood'), which insisted that children's rights must be safeguarded from before birth. In 2013, an equally important General Comment was launched, on the child's right to play. This document makes clear that children's right to play in early childhood must not be threatened by academic pressures, any more than by economic labour. Practitioners will need to use this new tool in their armoury as they continue to take up the struggle for young children.

Conclusion

This chapter has traced the evolution and continuous revision of early childhood policies in England over the last 15 years and their embodiment in curricular and welfare frameworks. It has indicated the many macro-level forces and influences that shape the work of practitioners and the experiences of young children in everyday classrooms and play-spaces. Despite current adverse circumstances, it argues that highly qualified practitioners can continue to support children's right to experience an early childhood that is free from the pressures of becoming-adult.

Points for reflection and discussion

1. What skills do practitioners require in order to accept and accommodate continual change in their policies and working conditions?
2. What degree of freedom can practitioners exert in interpreting and implementing curricular frameworks?
3. How can practitioners plan for the needs and preferences of children and families while meeting inspection requirements and achievement targets?

References and further reading

Ball, C. (1994) *Start Right: The importance of early learning*. London: Royal Society of Arts.

British Association for Early Childhood Education (BAECE) (2009) *Response to the QCA Consultation on the First Year of the Implementation of the Early Years Foundation Stage (EYFS) in England*. London: Early Education.

Brooker, L., Rogers, S., Ellis, D., Hallet, E. and Roberts-Holmes, G. (2010) *Practitioners' Experiences of the EYFS*. London: DfE.

Children's Workforce Development Council (CWDC) (2006) *Early Years Professional Prospectus*. Leeds: CWDC.

Dahlberg, G., Moss, P. and Pence, A. (1999) *Beyond Quality in Early Childhood Education and Care: Languages of evaluation*. London: Routledge.

David, T., Goouch, K., Powell, S. and Abbott, L. (2003) *Birth to Three Matters: A literature review*. London: DfES.

Department for Children, Schools and Families (DCSF) (2008) *Early Years Foundation Stage: Everything you need to know*. London: DCSF.

Department for Education and Skills (DfES) (2002) *Birth to Three Matters: A framework to support children in their earliest years*. London: DfES Sure Start Unit.

Department for Education and Skills (DfES) (2003) *Every Child Matters* (Green Paper). London: HMSO.

Department for Education and Skills (DfES) (2006) *Early Years Foundation Stage* (Consultation Document). London: HMSO. Available at: www.teachernet.gov.uk/publications (accessed 2 February 2013).

Department for Education (DfE) (2012a) *Statutory Framework for the Early Years Foundation Stage: Setting the standards for learning, development and care for children from birth to five*. Available at: http://www.foundationyears.org.uk/wp-content/uploads/2012/07/EYFS-Statutory-Framework-2012.pdf.

Department for Education (DfE) (2012b) *Childcare and Early Years Providers Survey, 2011*. London: DfE.

Department for Education (DfE) (2012c) *Statistical First Release: Early Years Foundation Stage profile results in England*. London: DfE.

Einarsdottir, J. and Wagner, J. (eds.) (2006) *Nordic Childhoods and Early Education*. Greenwich, CT: Information Age Publishing.

Evangelou, M., Sylva, K. and Kyriakou, M. (2009) *Early Years Learning and Development: Literature Review*. London: DCSF.

Feinstein, L. (2003) Inequality in the cognitive development of children in the 1970 birth cohort, *Economica*, 70: 73–97. Available at: http://www.rlab.lse.ac.uk/opening/papers/feinstein.pdf (accessed 2 February 2013).

Garrick, R., Bath, C., Dunn, K., Maconochie, H., Willis, B. *et al.* (2010) *Children's Experiences of the Early Years Foundation Stage*. London: DfE.

Gutman, L. and Feinstein, L. (2007) *Parenting Behaviours and Children's Development from Infancy to Early Childhood*. London: Centre for Research on the Wider Benefits of Learning.

Harms, T. and Clifford, R. (1998) *Early Childhood Environment Rating Scale – Revised*. New York: Teachers College Press.

Hart, B. and Risley, T. (1995) *The Early Catastrophe – The 30 Million Word Gap by Age 3: Meaningful differences in the everyday experience of young American children*. Baltimore, MD: Brookes.

HM Treasury/DfES/Department of Work and Pensions/Department of Trade and Industry (2004) *Choice for Parents, the Best Start for Children: A ten-year strategy for childcare*. London: HMSO.

Melhuish, E., Belsky, J., Leyland, A., McLeod, A., Saul, J. and Ashton, A. (2005) *National Evaluation of Sure Start*. London: Institute for the Study of Children, Families and Social Issues, Birkbeck, University of London. Available at: www.ness.bbk.ac.uk (accessed 3 February 2013).

Melhuish, E., Belsky, J., MacPherson, K. and Cullis, A (2010) *National Evaluation of Sure Start: Quality of childcare centres used by 3–4 year old children in Sure Start areas and the relationship with child outcomes*. London: Birkbeck, University of London.

Moss, P. and Pence, A. (eds.) (1994) *Valuing Quality in Early Childhood Services.* London: Paul Chapman.

Nutbrown, C. (2012) *Foundations for Quality: The Independent Review of Early Education and Childcare Qualifications: Final Report.* London: DfE. Available at: www.education.gov.uk/publications/standard/EarlyYearseducationandchildcare (accessed 25 March 2013).

Office for Standards in Education (OfSTED) (2011) *The Impact of the Early Years Foundation Stage.* London: OfSTED.

Pascal, C. and Bertram, T. (1997) *Effective Early Learning.* London: Sage.

Pugh, G. (2005) The policy agenda for early childhood services, in G. Pugh and B. Duffy (eds.) *Contemporary Issues in the Early Years.* London: Sage.

Qualifications and Curriculum Authority (QCA) (2000) *Curriculum Guidance for the Foundation Stage.* London: QCA.

Rumbold, A. (1990) *Starting with Quality.* London: HMSO.

Siraj-Blatchford, I., Muttock, S., Sylva, K., Gilden, R. and Bell, D. (2002) *Researching Effective Pedagogy in the Early Years.* London: Institute of Education/DfES.

Siraj-Blatchford, I., Siraj-Blatchford, J., Taggart, B., Sylva, K., Melhuish, E. *et al.* (2007) Qualitative Case Studies: How low SES families support children's learning in the home, in *Effective Pre-school and Primary Education 3-11: Promoting equality in the early years – Report to The Equalities Review.* Available at: http://www.ioe.ac.uk/EPPE_-_Promoting_Equality_in_the_Early_Years.pdf (accessed 17 June 2013).

Springate, I., Atkinson, M., Straw, S., Lamont, E. and Grayson, H. (2008) *Narrowing the Gap in Outcomes: Early years (0–5 years).* Slough: NFER.

Sure Start Unit (2003) *Sure Start: Making life better for children, parents and communities by bringing together early education, childcare, health and family support.* London: DfES Publications.

Sylva, K., Melhuish, E.C., Sammons, P., Siraj-Blatchford, I. and Taggart, B. (2001) *The Effective Provision of Preschool Education EPPE) Project: Findings from pre-school to Key Stage 1.* London: DfES/Institute of Education.

Sylva, K., Melhuish, E.C., Sammons, P., Siraj-Blatchford, I. and Taggart, B. (2004) *The Effective Provision of Pre-School Education (EPPE) Project. Technical Paper 12: The Final Report: Effective pre-school education.* London: DfES/Institute of Education.

Tickell, C. (2011a) *The Early Years: Foundations for life, health and learning.* London: DfE.

Tickell, C. (2011b) *The Early Years Foundation Stage (EYFS) Review.* London: DfE.

United Nations Convention on the Rights of the Child (UNCRC) (2006) *General Comment No. 7 (2005): Implementing child rights in early childhood.* Geneva: United Nations. Available at: www.uncrc.org (accessed 3 February 2013).

United Nations Convention on the Rights of the Child (UNCRC) (2013) *General Comment on Children's Right to Play.* Geneva: United Nations.

Uprichard, E. (2008) Children as beings and becomings: Children, childhood and temporality, *Children and Society***, 22(4): 303–13.**

PART 1
Quality and consistency

2 Playing, learning and developing

Linda Pound

Abstract

In this chapter, the positive aspects of the revised Early Years Foundation Stage are highlighted. The failure to differentiate between effective teaching and learning is explored and the paucity of references to the essential child-like qualities of childhood. These include playfulness, fun and above all joyfulness.

Introduction

The education of young children is vulnerable to the strongly held, loudly proclaimed and often conflicting views about what is best for parents or employers, for the state and the economy, or sometimes even for children. Disconnected elements of practice from other countries are seized upon as offering the panacea to resolve all the perceived issues. Less favourable staffing ratios, for example, will be less costly, but improved qualifications will lead to improved pay structures and thus cost more. Rigorous, extensive and, it must be added, expensive government-funded research (see, for example, Sylva *et al.*, 2004) is carefully trawled. The aim, all too often, is to seize on findings that will allow claims of creating evidence-based policy, while conveniently ignoring inconvenient evidence.

Practice within early childhood care and education in Great Britain has been very diverse. High/Scope practitioners, for example, run their sessions differently from Steiner practitioners and when asked to highlight key aims and beliefs are likely to headline different aspects of practice. But, since the time of Comenius – who, it is claimed, was 'the first to develop a special system of education for very young children' (Peltzman, 1991: 79) – there has been a clear thread of ideas about the nature of young children's thinking and learning running through the centuries. The subsequent thinking of eighteenth-century figures Rousseau and Pestalozzi was passed down in the nineteenth century to Owen and Froebel. Although their aims, approaches and main social focus differed, they in turn passed on many shared elements of philosophy to twentieth-century figures such as Margaret McMillan, Rudolf Steiner, Maria Montessori and Susan Isaacs. What all of these advocates for children had in common was an understanding of the nature of learning and development in early childhood. Their insights were based on astute and reflective observation.

One common and vital feature of all these different traditions is *play*. Historically, Montessori practice has been seen as undervaluing, or perhaps underplaying, play. However, the Montessori Schools Association emphasizes the relationship between work and play – a connection famously underlined by Froebel's description of play as the child's work. For Montessori practitioners, the connections are 'freedom of choice, the exercise of will and deep engagement, which leads to concentration' (Montessori Schools Association/DCSF, 2008: 21). This is a description of play that practitioners of most philosophical persuasions would accept.

Stewart (2012: 22) describes play in very similar words to those chosen by Montessorians, as an activity that is 'freely chosen', 'intrinsically motivated' and which 'actively engages the player'. She adds, however, that it 'is open-ended [and] involves exploration and imagination'. Conversations with children about what play is reveal that, for them above all else, play is something you choose to do (Gura, 1996). Once an activity chosen by children becomes teacher-directed, it ceases to be play and, regardless of the nature of the task, becomes work.

Much has been written about play. Although Guha (1987, citing Burghardt, 1984) suggests that to write about play is as difficult as looking for pots of gold at the end of rainbows, this has not deterred most early childhood specialists. Of course play can be interpreted in many ways but its power as a vital learning tool is increasingly well understood. In play children learn to learn; they learn to make sense of both the physical and social worlds. There is no better vehicle through which to explore – allowing children to explore while managing the risks. It supports creative and imaginative thinking – thinking beyond the day-to-day boundaries – and enables abstract thought. No wonder neuroscientist Greenfield (1996: 21) declares that 'play is fun with serious consequences'. Its function as a means of rehearsing skills or of promoting concentration is, however, underplayed in the revised Early Years Foundation Stage (EYFS) (DfE, 2012).

Positive change

The publication of the revised EYFS has been widely welcomed (see chapter 1). The reasons for this are many and varied. The most popular elements among practitioners are probably the reduction of paperwork and the inclusion of fewer elements in the Early Years Foundation Stage Profile (EYFSP) (Standards and Testing Agency, 2013). Two further positive features are highlighted here.

Prime areas of learning

The acknowledgement of prime areas of learning and development is an important improvement. The three prime areas are communication, personal and social emotional development (PSED), and physical development. They are described in the non-statutory guidance (Early Education, 2012) as both fundamental and as supporting development in all other areas. Moylett and Stewart (2012) characterize them as:

- having an element of time-sensitivity – that is, if they are not well developed in early childhood, they are more difficult to acquire at a later stage;
- being found in all cultures;
- not requiring understanding or knowledge of the specific areas of learning and development.

The fundamental importance of language and communication to future learning and development has been recognized for many decades and has been highlighted in government policy documents and related funded initiatives such as 'Every Child a Talker' (DCSF, 2008a).

The impact of children's emotional and social well-being was very much the focus of pioneers such as Susan Isaacs, a trained psychoanalyst, and remains so – at least on paper (DCSF, 2008b). Goleman's (1996) work has been very successful in highlighting the importance of emotions in learning, or emotional intelligence. Less well known among practitioners is the academic and arguably more rigorous work of researchers such as LeDoux (1998) and Siegel (1999) who also highlight, albeit in different ways, the role of PSED in learning. What has probably had the greatest impact on practitioners in this area of the curriculum is Laevers and colleagues' (2005) work on well-being and involvement. Its inclusion in the Effective Early Learning (EEL) project (Pascal and Bertram, 1997) has done much to popularize it but it has also paved the way for more extensive analysis of the 'soft' elements of effective practice (see, for example, Mashburn et al., 2008).

It is particularly pleasing that physical development is acknowledged to be vital to overall development. Despite the belief of many that the physical well-being of young children is an essential foundation to overall development, in the latter half of the twentieth century it was given much less importance. A report by Her Majesty's Inspectorate in 1989 (cited by Tovey, 2007) highlighted the fact that the value of outdoor play was not well understood. Of course, physical development is not confined to the outdoors (Greenland, 2000) but given concerns about the overall reduction in opportunities to play outside (Tovey, 2007), outdoor space and activity remains an essential plank in children's general health and well-being (see, for example, Little and Wyver, 2008). However, widespread concerns about obesity and inactivity have led to a greater recognition of the relationship between physical activity and children's overall development, including cognitive development (Goddard-Blyth, 2005; Evangelou et al., 2009).

The interrelatedness of the prime areas

The prime, foundational areas of development and learning work together to support all aspects of development. A wide range of research indicates their importance to all future learning, since intimacy and attachment help babies to communicate and to think (Goldschmied and Selleck, 1996). This in turn involves physical acts of exploration, imitation and symbolization – a link that remains true throughout life (Bresler, 2004). Namy (2005: vii) argues that 'symbol use...is fundamental to everyday cognitive functioning'. Rochat and Callaghan (2005: 44) conclude that 'infants become symbol minded primarily to find intimacy, make meaning and create values that can be shared with other, more advanced symbol minded individuals'.

The sustained shared thinking that goes on in extended conversations between children and adults (Sylva *et al.*, 2004) is identified as a characteristic of high-quality early education. Similarly, sustained interaction with adults in early years settings has been shown to have particular benefits for children deemed to be at risk of failure (Hamre and Pianta, 2005; Mashburn *et al.*, 2008).

Effective learning

Another positive feature of the revised EYFS (DfE, 2012) is the inclusion of require-ments about how children's learning should be supported. For the first time in Eng-land, there is now a statutory requirement to ensure that providers address not simply *what* is learnt (the content) but *how* children learn (the process of learn-ing). This is an important change, since learning processes as a determinant of quality is highlighted in a number of research studies. Hirsh-Pasek *et al.* (2009: 59), for example, in their set of seven evidence-based principles, include the impor-tance of learning processes claiming that such skills 'prepare confident, eager, engaged, and lifelong learners'.

On the face of it, the learning processes identified as effective in the revised EYFS (DfE, 2012: 7) can't be argued against:

- **playing and exploring** – children investigate and experience things, and 'have a go';
- **active learning** – children concentrate and keep on trying if they encoun-ter difficulties, and enjoy achievements; and
- **creating and thinking critically** – children have and develop their own ideas, make links between ideas, and develop strategies for doing things.

Concentration, perseverance, critical thinking and stimulating experiences are what all parents and practitioners would want for their children.

So what's the problem?

The revised EYFS states that 'it is expected that the balance will shift towards a more equal focus on all areas of learning as children grow in confidence and ability within the three prime areas' (DfE, 2012: 1.7) – herein lies the danger. The widespread emphasis placed by politicians and media on the increasingly early introduction of what Paley (2004) terms 'academics' is likely to mean that this will be misinterpreted. The potential for such misinterpretation is reinforced, in the same paragraph, by the stated link towards greater emphasis on the specific areas of learning and development. Meanwhile, for those with special educational need or disability, the prime areas are to remain the focus.

The four specific areas of learning and development (literacy, mathematics, understanding the world, and expressive arts and design) are acknowledged not to be time sensitive, but to require competence in the prime areas of learning.

This throws up interesting debates in the area of literacy and numeracy – the areas of greatest political interest. Many practitioners are optimistic that in separating literacy from communication, the communicative and expressive elements from the skill-based, it will be easier to focus on the expressive and communicative aspects of language. However, some see this as a retrograde step (see, for example, Cremin *et al.*, 2013), highlighting the risk that the benefits of enjoying and creating narrative, and of playing with language will be forced to give way to the skills of literacy such as phonic knowledge. In an area of the curriculum acknowledged not to be time sensitive, there is also growing and compelling evidence that an early start does not always lead to higher achievement (OECD, 2004; Suggate, 2011).

Many practitioners have welcomed the change of title for mathematics from problem solving, reasoning and numeracy – which many believe over-emphasized numerical aspects of mathematics at the expense of the many other facets of the subject. Others regret losing the focus on the processes of problem solving and reasoning, which, although included within the strategies for effective teaching, some fear will diminish mathematical content.

Effective teaching?

The description of effective learning is also said to represent the characteristics of effective teaching. The very fact that they are described as characteristics of both indicates a fundamental error. Teaching does not equal learning. Every practitioner knows that by no means everything that the one intends to teach is learnt. Conversely, many things that are not taught are all too readily learnt. Effective teaching includes (among other things) demonstrating and modelling, describing and recalling, encouraging and suggesting (MacNaughton and Williams, 2004).

While playing and exploring, active learning and creative, critical thinking can very easily be thought of as elements of successful teaching, they are far from the whole story. Moreover, in a climate that, despite the rhetoric, values achievement in particular directions above the processes of learning, they are the elements most likely to be suppressed. It takes an act of extreme faith and bravery on the part of a practitioner to go against directives that state that phonics must be taught in this way, or that by a certain stage children are expected to know particular things. Having a go, taking risks and exploring do not sit comfortably within this political climate and the associated demands of parents and media. It is also the case that for children and adults some vital aspects of teaching and learning have been ignored.

Playfulness and joyfulness

The main trouble with the revised EYFS (DfE, 2012) is that as worthy and unarguable many of its features are, all joy is gone from its mention of enjoyment, which is reduced to the quiet satisfaction of something achieved. The description of play included in the revised EYFS (DfE, 2012: 1.10), in which 'children investigate and experience things' and 'have a go', conveys nothing of the playfulness of play that is essentially what makes it such an invaluable learning tool. The wonder of play is that it enables success and failure – it takes much more than exhortation to have a go to learn to get to the top of a tree. You've only failed if someone else set the goal – your own goal leads you to try and try again.

In their commentary on the EYFS (DfE, 2102), Moylett and Stewart (2012) extend the notion of play by writing of pretence, representation, assuming a role and acting out experiences. Exploration is described as involving curiosity and the senses. 'Having a go' is linked to challenge, taking the initiative and risk-taking. It also involves, they suggest, a 'can do' attitude. No one could possibly object to these characteristics in learners, young or old. But what is sad is that the fun of play and exploration is not mentioned, even once. Play allows manageable risk – you can pretend to be swimming without drowning; you can pretend to step into a fire without getting burnt; and you can wrestle with monsters without being exterminated – and it's fun!

In popular thinking, active learning is often seen to be about movement, and although vital to learning and thinking (Greenfield, 1997), it involves much more. It is certainly about motivation. Moylett and Stewart (2012) emphasize persistence, concentration, awareness that success will be achieved through greater effort – this is all true (see, for example, Dweck, 2000), but it is also so much more. At its heart must be the natural and unstoppable activity of young children – mental and physical. Enjoyment is mentioned but in the context of 'meeting challenges', being proud of and 'showing satisfaction' in achievement. This is a very long way from the joy of childhood, the sheer exuberance that drives young children in their sense of being and becoming and of meeting their world.

Creating and critical thinking are contained and constrained within tight, pseudo-scientific boundaries; the essence of creativity is somehow missing from the description (see Chapter 12). The fun, the play, the rule-breaking and risk-taking of creative action and thinking is heavily masked by measured and cautious activities such as predicting, testing, grouping, linking, monitoring and reviewing. The child-like qualities referred to in, for example, Picasso's oft-quoted words 'it took me four years to paint like Raphael but a lifetime to paint like a child', have been identified in a wide range of creative, innovative and disparate individuals such as physicist Richard Feynman (Minsky, 1996) and Charles Darwin (Huxley, 1965) but are not to be found in the government document.

Missing from it is the exuberance; the imperatives that are the essence of young children's learning. The identified components of effective learning do not provide the whole picture of what young children's learning actually is – the sum is very much more than the parts. Nowhere in the statutory guidance can be found a trace of the joyfulness, characteristic of young children from infancy. Yet this is the enchantment of early childhood, the motivation that drives them to new learning. There is no evidence of the 'shrieks and gurgles and jumpings for joy' described by one visitor to Susan Isaacs' Malting House School; or the children's 'thirst for understanding' commented on by Isaacs herself (cited in Pound, 2011: 51). There is no mention of the exuberance described by Egan (1991: 86) in his memorable phrase describing young children's 'ecstatic responses'. There is no whisper of Paley's (1981: 4) 'magical thinking', described by her as characteristic of learning in the early years. Awe and wonder do not figure here, nor do Claxton's (1997: 3) 'slow ways of knowing' with his exhortation to recognize the importance of taking time, ruminating, pondering.

In a study looking at babies and music (Mazokopaki and Kugiumutzakis, 2008), the authors differentiate between babies' expressions of pleasure, joy and excitement. Trevarthen refers in much of his work to young children's humour, clowning and excitement (see, for example, Trevarthen, 2011). Both sets of research indicate that these are all important aspects of 'the developing sense of self' (Mazokopaki and Kugiumutzakis, 2008: 203) and that we cannot separate out the various elements that make up our humanity. The importance of the interrelatedness of the prime areas of learning and development begins to appear even more vital when seen in this light.

Neuroscience also highlights the function of excitement in learning. Eliot (1999) draws attention to the cognitive and motor benefits of rocking, swinging and hanging upside down in which all children engage – or as she terms it, 'vestibular stimulation'. Eliot also highlights the way in which excitement makes learning memorable. Willis (2012) highlights the importance of pleasure in learning, stating that children's brains need to acquire memory associations that link pleasure with learning.

Wolk (2008) argues for joyful learning, suggesting that when learning is pleasurable, learners are better able to cope with difficulties or failure and are therefore more open to taking vital risks in learning. For Wolk, joyful learning also includes choice, creative opportunities, story, increased physical activity, outdoor play and fun.

Whitehead (2010: 91) highlights the difference between fun and play. She writes:

> Fun is usually a light-hearted and superficial response or activity, but it can certainly make dull routines, repetition and drudgery manageable. In contrast, play can be 'deep' and challenging…as it pushes at boundaries and flows in unpredictable directions.

While joy encompasses fun, it is much more than that. Joy may be quiet satisfaction but it may also be exuberant excitement. Children may be playful when not playing – or may play without being playful. Perhaps fun can be seen as the playful link that bridges the gap between child-initiated play and adult-led activity. But for both children and adults, joyful learning is essential.

The challenge of joyful, playful, enabling learning

As Gardner (2006) points out, working with creative thinkers is not always comfortable. Thinking outside the box, non-conforming and unconventional behaviour, and challenging assumptions do not always make for easy interaction – and for these and other similar reasons may not always be valued by schools and early years settings. Gone is the image of the creative individual, lonely, in a garret, begging for food or enough money to buy the next sheet of manuscript paper or tube of white paint. Instead, we now know that creativity relies on social activity (Csikszentmihalyi, 1997; Gardner, 2006) and that therefore social and emotional development must be given a high priority.

Picture the scene described by Edmund de Waal (Desert Island Discs, BBC, 2012), a renowned potter and author. He revels in the mess associated with creative learning, stating that:

> I would say that it is a huge, huge mistake not to allow kids to make a mess... Mess is where it starts, it's in the flour on the floor... or the clay in your hair. That's when you get this extraordinary, extraordinary excitement about making something that you've never made before. That's really, really important.

This highlights perhaps the most immediate challenge to practitioners considering a joyful, playful, creative and genuinely enabling learning environment. Cleaners may complain about that flour on the floor, parents about clay in the hair and colleagues about the noise and bustle presented by excitement and exuberance.

In the world outside the classroom or setting, there are even bigger barriers. The politicization of early childhood care and education, alluded to in the introduction to this chapter, has meant that the interests of young children have not always come first. Early childhood care and education has been described as 'a public good' (Pound and Miller, 2011: 166) – supporting health issues, the needs or rights of women and the economy (Eisenstadt, 2011).

Other authors have focused on the dangers of both the 'schoolification' (Woodhead and Moss, 2007) and the linked disembodiment (Tobin, 2004) of early care and education. A premature, over-emphasis on academic and formal aspects of the curriculum is seen to squeeze out the benefits of play, which Paley (2004: 8) describes as 'the glue that binds together all other pursuits'. To extend her analogy one might suggest that the glue is one that needs time to dry before it can work.

Tobin (2004) argues that in the process of schoolification (or commodification as it is sometimes described, alluding to the perception of children as no more than goods on an assembly line), the brain is erroneously seen as of greater importance than the body and skills as more valuable than thought or emotion. Policy, he suggests, has tended to assume that all but the brain can be left behind – leaving educators to teach disembodied children.

Early childhood practitioners know better. They have known for centuries that young children are active, playful, creative and joyful creatures whose nature demands a holistic education if it is to be really effective. This view is increasingly supported by research. It is now for those who have observed and understood young children's imperatives to act as their advocates.

Points for reflection and discussion

1. Is money spent on rigorous research wasted if governments fail to act on the findings?
2. Do the prime areas of learning support learning in specific areas? Are they consistent with children's development?
3. What are the likely views on the curriculum of the parents of the children with whom you work? Is this what they want for their children?
4. What would you describe as the characteristics of effective teaching?

References and further reading

Bresler, L. (2004) *Knowing Bodies, Moving Minds: Towards embodied teaching and learning*. London: Kluwer Academic.

Claxton, G. (1997) *Hare Brain, Tortoise Mind: Why intelligence increases when you think less*. London: Fourth Estate.

Cremin, T., Swann, J., Flewitt, R., Faulkner, D. and Kucirkova, N. (2013) *Evaluation/Report of Make Believe Arts Helicopter Technique of Storytelling and Story Acting*. Maidenhead: Open University Press.

Csikszentmihalyi, M. (1997) *Creativity: Flow and the psychology of discovery and invention*. New York: HarperPerennial.

Department for Children, Schools and Families (DCSF) (2008a) *Every Child a Talker: Guidance for early language lead practitioners*. Available at: http://webarchive.nationalarchives.gov.uk/20110202093118/http:/nationalstrategies.standards.dcsf.gov.uk/node/153355 (accessed 18 December 2012).

Department for Children, Schools and Families (DCSF) (2008b) *Social and Emotional Aspects of Development*. Nottingham: DCSF Publications.

Department for Education (DfE) (2012) *Statutory Framework for the Early Years Foundation Stage: Setting the standards for learning, development and care for children from birth to five*. Available at: http://www.foundationyears.org.uk/wp-content/uploads/2012/07/EYFS-Statutory-Framework-2012.pdf.

De Waal, E. (2012) *Desert Island Discs*. BBC Radio 4 programme, 30 November.

Dweck, C. (2000) *Self-theories: Their role in motivation, personality and development*. Hove: Psychology Press.

Early Education (2012) *Development Matters in the Early Years Foundation Stage*. London: BAECE.

Egan, K. (1991) *Primary Understanding*. London: Routledge.

Eisenstadt, N. (2011) *Providing a Sure Start: How government discovered early childhood*. Bristol: Policy Press.

Eliot, L. (1999) *Early Intelligence*. London: Penguin Books.

Evangelou, M., Sylva, K., Kyriacou, M., Wild, M. and Glenny, G. (2009) *Early Years Learning and Development Literature Review*. DCSF Research Report RR176. Oxford: DCSF.

Gardner, H. (2006) *Five Minds for the Future*. Boston, MA: Harvard Business School Press.

Goddard-Blyth, S. (2005) *The Well Balanced Child*. Stroud: Hawthorn Press.

Goldschmied, E. and Selleck, D. (1996) *Communication between Babies in Their First Year* (video). London: National Children's Bureau.

Goleman, D. (1996) *Emotional Intelligence*. London: Bloomsbury Publishing.

Greenfield, S. (1996) *The Human Mind Explained*. London: Cassell.

Greenfield, S. (1997) *The Human Brain: A guided tour*. London: Weidenfeld & Nicolson.

Greenland, P. (2000) *Hopping Home Backwards: Body intelligence and movement play*. Leeds: Jabadao.

Guha, M. (1987) Play in school, in G. Blenkin and A.V. Kelly (eds.) *Early Childhood Education: A developmental curriculum*. London: Paul Chapman.

Gura, P. (1996) *Resources for Early Learning: Children, adults and stuff (zero to eight)*. London: Sage.

Hamre, B. and Pianta, R. (2005) Can instructional and emotional support in the first-grade classroom make a difference for children at risk of school failure?, *Child Development*, 76(5): 949–67.

Hirsh-Pasek, K., Golinkoff, R., Berk, L. and Singer, D. (2009) *A Mandate for Playful Learning in School*. Oxford: Oxford University Press.

Huxley, J. (1965) *Charles Darwin and His World*. New York: Viking Press.

Laevers, F., Debruyckere, G., Silkens, K. and Snoeck, G. (2005) *Observation of Well-being and Involvement in Babies and Toddlers: A video-training pack with manual*. Leuven: Research Centre for Experiential Education.

LeDoux, J. (1998) *The Emotional Brain*. London: Weidenfeld & Nicolson.

Little, H. and Wyver, S. (2008) Outdoor play: Does avoiding the risks reduce the benefits?, *Australian Journal of Early Childhood*, 33(2): 33–40.

MacNaughton, G. and Williams, G. (2004) *Teaching Young Children*. Maidenhead: Open University Press.

Manning-Morton, J. (2011) Not just the tip of the iceberg: Psychoanalytic ideas and early years practice, in L. Miller and L. Pound (eds.) *Theories and Approaches to Learning in the Early Years*. London: Sage.

Mashburn, A., Pianta, R., Hamre, B., Downer, J., Barbarin, O. *et al*. (2008) Measures of classroom quality in prekindergarten and children's development of academic, language, and social skills. *Child Development*, 79(3): 732–49.

Mazokopaki, K. and Kugiumutzakis, G. (2008) Infant rhythms: Expressions of musical companionship, in S. Malloch and C. Trevarthen (eds.) *Communicative Musicality: Exploring the basis of human companionship*. Oxford: Oxford University Press.

Minsky, M. (1996) Crazy ideas: Tiny writing and huge computers, in C. Sykes (ed.) *No Ordinary Genius*. New York: Norton.

Montessori Schools Association/Department for Children, Schools and Families (DCSF) (2008) *Guide to the Early Years Foundation Stage in Montessori Settings*. London: Montessori St. Nicholas/DCSF.

Moylett, H. and Stewart, N. (2012) *Understanding the Revised Early Years Foundation Stage*. London: Early Education.

Namy, L. (ed.) (2005) Preface, in *Symbol Use and Symbolic Representation*. Mahwah, NJ: Lawrence Erlbaum Associates.

OECD (2004) *Starting Strong: Curricula and pedagogies in early childhood education and care – Five curriculum outlines*. Paris: OECD Directorate for Education.

Paley, V.G. (1981) *Wally's Stories*. Cambridge, MA: Harvard University Press.

Paley, V.G. (2004) *A Child's Work: The importance of fantasy play*. London: University of Chicago Press.

Pascal, C. and Bertram, T. (1997) *Effective Early Learning: Case studies in improvement*. London: Hodder.

Peltzman, B. (1991) Origins of early childhood education, in P. Persky and L. Golubchick (eds.) *Early Childhood Education*, 2nd edn. Lanham, MD: University Press of America.

Pound, L. (2011) *Influencing Early Childhood Education*. Maidenhead: Open University Press.

Pound, L. and Miller, L. (2011) Critical issues, in L. Miller and L. Pound (eds.) *Theories and Approaches to Learning in the Early Years*. London: Sage.

Rochat, P. and Callaghan, T. (2005) What drives symbolic development? The case of pictorial comprehension and production, in L. Namy (ed.) *Symbol Use and Symbolic Representation*. Mahwah, NJ: Lawrence Erlbaum Associates.

Siegel, D. (1999) *The Developing Mind*. New York: Guilford Press.

Standards and Testing Agency (2013) *Early Years Foundation Stage Profile Handbook*. Available at: www.education.gov.uk/eyfsp (accessed 29 January 2013).

Stewart, N. (2012) *How Children Learn: The characteristics of effective early learning*. London: Early Education.

Suggate, S. (2011) Viewing the long-term effects of early reading with an open eye, in R. House (ed.) *Too Much, Too Soon? Early learning and the erosion of childhood*. Stroud: Hawthorn Press.

Sylva, K., Melhuish, E.C., Sammons, P., Siraj-Blatchford, I. and Taggart, B. (2004) *The Effective Provision of Pre-School Education (EPPE) Project. Technical Paper 12: The Final Report: Effective pre-school education.* London: DfES/Institute of Education.

Tobin, J. (2004) The disappearance of the body in early childhood education, in L. Bresler (ed.) *Knowing Bodies, Moving Minds: Towards embodied teaching and learning.* London: Kluwer Academic.

Tovey, H. (2007) *Playing Outdoors.* Maidenhead: Open University Press.

Trevarthen, C. (2011) What is it like to be a person who knows nothing? Defining the active intersubjective mind of a newborn human being, *Infant and Child Development,* 20(1): 119–35.

Whitehead, M. (2010) Playing or having fun? Dilemmas in early childhood, in J. Moyles (ed.) *The Excellence of Play,* 3rd edn. Maidenhead: Open University Press.

Willis, J. (2012) Executive function, arts integration and joyful learning, *Edutopia.* Available at: http://www.edutopia.org/blog/arts-inegration-joyful-learning-judy-willis-md (accessed 15 January 2013).

Wolk, S. (2008) Joy in school, *Educational Leadership,* 66(1): 8–15.

Woodhead, M. and Moss, P. (2007) *Early Childhood and Primary Education: Transitions in the lives of young children.* Available at: http://issuu.com/bernardvanleerfoundation/docs/enhancing_a_sense_of_belonging_in_the_early_years (accessed 23 March 2013).

3 Necessary paperwork: observation and assessment in the Early Years Foundation Stage

Paulette Luff

Abstract

This chapter considers the challenge of basing learning experiences for young children on observations of their interests while also aiming to reduce paperwork and spend time in meaningful interactions. The origins of the practice of observation in the early years is considered, before looking at the paperwork involved in documentation and considering strategies for recording observations and mindful ways of working with children. Ways to strengthen parental partnerships through participation in processes of documentation are explored, together with comment upon statutory assessments, including progress checks for two-year-olds. The focus throughout is on optimal ways of using observation as a basis for effective early education.

Introduction

Careful and thoughtful observation offers early years educators a vital means of getting to know children and then providing for their learning. Since the introduction of the Early Years Foundation Stage (EYFS) (DCSF, 2008), regular written observations have become integral to practice in every early years setting in England. These are used to identify children's interests, plan activities and educational experiences, and record achievements. One key reform of the EYFS framework, following the Tickell Review (2011), is reduction of paperwork and elimination of unnecessary bureaucracy. The EYFS Statutory Framework states that: 'Assessment should not entail prolonged breaks from interaction with children, nor require excessive paperwork. Paperwork should be limited to that which is absolutely necessary to promote children's successful learning and development' (DfE, 2012: 10). This presents a challenge for early years educators who have to reflect upon their current practices and decide what paperwork is 'absolutely necessary' when documenting children's learning.

Observation has been described as the 'foundation of education in the early years' (Hurst, 1991: 70). In the UK, we follow a rich tradition of observing children and using written accounts of observations to understand children's play and learning. Early childhood education pioneers, including Friedrich Froebel and Maria Montessori, emphasized the importance of observing children to ascertain their abilities and interests; and they encouraged the use of insights gained from observations as a basis for planning future learning. Susan Isaacs' (1930, 1933) observations of children at the Malting House School clearly demonstrated how accounts of children's chosen activities can provide illuminating information for the adults who work with them. Her ideas about the importance of basing education upon child observations were also evident in the design of Infant Admission Record cards and her recommendations for their use in Wiltshire schools (Isaacs *et al.*, 1936).

In contemporary practice, too, observations are used as a tool to discover what children already know in order to provide experiences that build upon and extend their existing abilities and ideas. The Possible Lines of Direction (PLOD) charts, developed at the Pen Green Centre (Whalley *et al.*, 2007), provide an effective method of carrying out observations from which plans are made to correspond with children's dominant interests. With increasing access to technological tools such as digital cameras, camcorders, dictaphones and scanners, we are now able to provide visual evidence to support and document these observations of children (Collins *et al.*, 2010).

Current use of observation to promote children's learning is influenced by inspirational practice in international contexts. Carr (2001; Carr and Lee, 2012) describes how the tradition in many early childhood settings of parents and practitioners exchanging informal observations about children at the beginning and end of the day, has developed into the 'learning story' approach to documenting learning in New Zealand. These learning stories, collated in a portfolio, record, reflect and promote positive learning outcomes in accordance with the strands of the Te Whāriki curriculum: well-being, belonging, communication, contribution and exploration (New Zealand Ministry of Education, 1996). This approach has been adapted by practitioners in England, who often record children's 'learning journeys' (Podmore and Luff, 2012).

It is from Reggio Emilia, in Italy, that we have adopted another means of making young children's learning visible: pedagogical documentation (Edwards *et al.*, 2012). In contrast to a typical British understanding of the word 'documentation', with its suggestion of dusty historical papers or excessive bureaucracy, the Italian term implies something much more lively. In the municipal early childhood centres of Reggio Emilia, documentation takes the form of photographs, written observations, children's drawings and paintings, and transcripts of audio-recorded conversations. This on-going record-keeping aims to capture the *progettazione* (open-ended project work), enabling teachers to see and hear the children's meaning-making, to understand the children's current thoughts, questions and strategies, and to form hypotheses about possible directions for future learning (Rinaldi, 2006, 2012). Documentation goes beyond the unidirectional activity of practitioners recording and analysing child observations to become a dynamic collaborative enterprise in which the child is an active participant and parents and others may become engaged.

There is a key difference between the practice of documentation in Reggio Emilia and the use of pedagogical documentation within the EYFS. Theirs is a collective society and those values are reflected in the approach to documentation. In Reggio Emilia, the sole focus is upon the project work in progress and the ideas of the group of children working on that project. There is no requirement to assess the progress of each individual child and so the production and analysis of documentation concentrates solely upon the children's thinking, and possible directions in which to take their learning. English early years practitioners face a more challenging dual task, as they aim to implement and evaluate group learning activities while also basing planning on individual interests and abilities and recording each child's development.

Processes of planning for learning using documentation are, therefore, highly complex. The EYFS requires practitioners to work in two potentially contradictory ways. On the one hand, as in Te Whāriki and the Reggio Emilia approach, open-ended learning opportunities are to be planned in response to children's actions and interests; yet, on the other hand, staff and children are expected to work towards specific, pre-set learning outcomes (Luff, 2012). As skilled early years practitioners we must, therefore, gain confidence in demonstrating how specified criteria can be met through flexible, holistic ways of working. We also need to find the most satisfactory means of using structured guidelines, such as 'Development Matters' (Early Education, 2012) and the EYFS Statutory Framework (DfE, 2012), to provide a basis for observation and documentation.

The main areas of revision and reform that were highlighted in the Tickell Review (2011), and are now being implemented through the EYFS Framework (DfE, 2012), in addition to reduction of paperwork, are: strengthening partnerships between parents and professionals; a focus on three 'prime' areas of learning; the detailing of an additional four 'specific' areas of learning; the introduction of a progress check for two-year-olds; and simplification of the statutory assessment at the end of the Reception Year. All of these changes have implications for the observation and assessment of children in early years settings, and I will now move to address challenges relating to paperwork, parental participation and profiling progress.

Paperwork

The previous version of this chapter highlighted early years practitioners' protests against a proliferation of paperwork and presented arguments for and against written documentation (Luff, 2007). This debate is now revisited, in the light of a requirement to reduce paperwork to that which is necessary in order to offer effective care and education to children. Educators who began their careers in the 1970s or 1980s, when there were few requirements to write observations and the majority of time could be spent engaging with children, might doubt whether there was ever a need to keep detailed records. In recent years, however, documenting observations and reflecting upon children's learning has undoubtedly enriched early years practice and has enabled settings to offer evidence of some inspirational work.

If time in a busy early years workplace is to be spent on observation and documentation, we have to be certain of its value to young children, promoting the quality of the care and education they receive, and to ourselves as professionals in enhancing our understanding of our work. For documentation to be worthwhile, it must support and enrich the learning of children and the practitioners who work with them. If the documentation completed in an early years setting is literally a paper exercise, a duty completed to ensure the required records are in place when an external inspector calls, it is probably of little value. If observation is reduced to checklists of pre-identified learning goals, it will provide very limited insights into the richness of children's learning. This paperwork can be discarded without loss. Here I reconsider four arguments made in favour of constructive, thoughtful observation and discuss the need for paperwork that serves to make children's learning visible.

First, observing and documenting learning can be an important way of valuing and listening to children. Elfer (2005) suggests that empathetic, respectful close observation can be an effective way of hearing young children's powerful communications and taking account of their perspectives, as required by The Children Act (HMSO, 1989) and the United Nations Convention on the Rights of the Child (UNCRC, 1989). In Reggio Emilia, too, documentation is seen as a way of building relationships with children and discovering the messages they convey about themselves through their actions (Rinaldi, 2000, 2012). In an English early years setting, three-year-old Tyler and four-year-old Skye were observed sitting at a table, paper in front of them and pens in hand, role-playing a staff meeting. Their talk as they played, about whether the children liked the garden, showed their awareness of the decision-making process at their day nursery and their potential to contribute to discussions about their learning. Nutbrown (1996) describes young children, such as Tyler and Skye, as wide-eyed and open-minded with an awesome capacity to observe and learn from those around them and to master all the complexities of early learning. This corresponds with Malaguzzi's (2012: 53) image of children as rich in potential with 'surprising and extraordinary strengths and capabilities linked with an inexhaustible need for expression and realisation'. The production of pedagogical documentation requires young children to be seen and respected, setting their own priorities for learning, with an ability to handle, develop and make sense of complex ideas.

Second, work on observation and documentation can be an important source of learning for practitioners as we seek to understand the language of children and appreciate their thinking. Drummond (2003) suggests that inquiring into children's learning is potentially fascinating, inspiring and likely to challenge teachers' practice. In the infant and toddler centres and pre-schools of Reggio Emilia, analysis of the meanings to be found in documentation is considered an essential aspect of every teacher's continuing professional development. Written observations and other forms of documentation allow for information to be presented and scrutinized and there is always something to be discovered and learned. A single observation, a photograph, a video clip, or a more extensive collection of documentation may provide the basis for reflection, linking with knowledge about theories of child development and areas of the curriculum. Where documentation is maintained over time, each individual child's unique progress can be noted and, across groups of children, common patterns of development may be seen to emerge. Analysis of documentation can also be used to assess the effectiveness of teaching strategies and as a basis for planning new teaching methods and approaches. This process of evaluation is not always easy, as observing closely and documenting what children are actually doing, rather than what we think they are doing, may challenge assumptions and lead to a need to reassess professional judgements.

Third, documentation provides a strong basis for collaborative work. Vygotsky's (1981) theory, that knowledge is co-constructed in relationship with other people and the environment, sees learning and teaching activities as processes of enquiry in which children and adults can be jointly involved. Capturing the learning that takes place in early years settings, through displaying documentation, also promotes communication with children's families. Discussion based upon observations, photographs and children's drawings are likely to be enjoyed by both parents and practitioners. These conversations provide ideal opportunities to talk confidently about what the children are learning and to gain important insights from parents about children's actions and reactions when at home. This collaboration is not always simple, as there is rarely one single possible interpretation of documentary evidence. When discussing observations and documentation with one another, and with children and parents, practitioners must be ready to offer suggestions, consider multiple possible explanations and be prepared to change their views.

Fourth, observation that occurs during the learning process, and is seen as integral to it, may raise the quality of educational experiences for all children. Observing what children can do and considering what this may lead on to makes teaching exciting and thought-provoking. Where learning activities are based upon children's abilities, ideas and interests, and then extended by attentive adults, they are likely to be stimulating for those children and sufficiently challenging. The excellence of the ideas and artwork presented in the 'Hundred Languages of Children' touring exhibition (of the work taking place in Reggio Emilia) bears testimony to this. In addition, observing different areas of provision and the ways in which the children use the facilities on offer in the nursery environment can help us to appreciate the value and potential of resources and learning areas. A group of nursery school staff reviewed a video of children enjoying socio-dramatic play with an ice cream stall. They saw not only the children's effective use of the props provided (ice creams made from balls of coloured tissue paper and cones and lollies cut from card) and considerable skills in taking the roles of both buyers and sellers of ice cream, but also observed the way in which the children improvised additional props, such as seat cushions for surf boards. This provided a stimulus for discussion of ways to develop this imaginative seaside play.

Following these arguments, discarding all the paperwork that serves to make children's learning visible would be a significant loss. There is, however, scope to scrutinize our record-keeping and to emphasize quality above quantity. In facing the dilemma of whether to create written records or to spend time interacting with children, one innovative approach is to spend time creating learning journey records with the children as an activity. As a practitioner who works with three- and four-year-olds explains: 'it's not something we sit and do, they do it with us so we put things in there and we talk about what they've done'. This shared approach to selecting photographs or drawings to go into a child's record, and deciding together upon simple captions, goes some way to address criticism that written 'learning journey' records may have limited significance for children who cannot yet read (Bath, 2012).

To what extent, though, is it possible to go further and to be tuned in to children and recognize their viewpoints without any written record? Gerber (2005: 49) contrasts the actions of 'caregivers', adults who always take the initiative, with those of 'educarers', who are genuinely attentive and responsive to cues from children. She exhorts those who care for babies and young children to 'Observe more, do less' (Gerber, 2005: 63). Writing from the same perspective, Money (2005) stresses the importance of sensitive observation for building respectful relationships and fostering the authenticity of a child. Being understood promotes the child's confidence and trust whereas being ignored or misunderstood can lead to insecurity and self-doubt (Memel and Fernandez, 2005).

In many nurseries, practitioners do not complete written observations but are highly sensitive to cues from children and consistently react in thoughtful ways to encourage their learning. K, for example, working with babies, sees fifteen-month-old S stretching up to put a toy car in a garage, which is on top of a storage unit. K goes across to her and S turns to K and says, 'car'. K says, 'S is playing with the car?' and lifts the garage down onto the floor. S smiles at K with a cheeky, pleased expression on her face and kneels to play with the garage. Nothing is documented but K works observantly with S, and the other babies in her care, using what she sees to respond well and enhance their experiences throughout the day. This type of observant behaviour, being prepared and able to see and follow the child, does not necessarily involve written recording but it requires a high level of awareness of oneself and the child and an ability to be flexible and respond in practical ways.

Parental participation

Whichever formats for paperwork are selected, it is very important that observations of children are shared with parents as a basis for dialogues about their child. A feature of the enabling environment for learning and development, within the EYFS, is strong partnership working between parents and practitioners. In most settings, this is mediated through the 'key person' role. A key person takes responsibility for a number of children, forms positive relationships with each child and their family and, according to the EYFS guidelines: 'must help ensure that every child's learning and care is tailored to meet their individual needs. The key person must seek to engage and support parents and/or carers in guiding their child's development at home' (DfE, 2012: 7). This presents a challenge to practitioners, who have to do their best to share their professional understandings of child development and communicate the value of play experiences while also taking into account parents' perspectives. In doing the former, it is easy to forget that practitioners in a nursery setting only have a partial view of the child and should not disregard the vital information that parents can supply about their child's abilities. This is reflected in one mother's response to being shown her four-year-old son's nursery records:

We've been able to look at all the things that he should be doing, every-thing he's attained and then the things that they haven't ticked, so the things that we think, this is what he should be achieving. He's completely on track for his age, he's ahead, he's done some other stuff. Some of the stuff wasn't ticked that we know he can do, but he hasn't necessarily exhibited it here.

It is clearly stated in Development Matters (Early Education, 2012) that the document should be used as guidance and not as a checklist but, as the view of the mother cited above suggests, children's progress is often mapped against the development statements for each age band in each area of learning. A discussion with a parent that is based upon a record of development might not be the most effective means of stimulating a genuine and informative dialogue about the child and there are several other strategies for sharing observations. Parents usually love to see photographs and videos of their child participating in activities (for examples, see Collins *et al.*, 2010), and talking about these with parents may spark ideas for future activities and projects. Children's portfolios containing written observations, the child's drawings and photographs of the child involved in activi-ties can be used in open and inclusive ways and offer an invaluable means of building relationships with the child and their family (Driscoll and Rudge, 2005), as can specially designed published tools (e.g. Fisher, 2011). As another parent's description of practice at her child's nursery shows, parents are keen to cooperate with settings to foster their children's learning:

They have exercise books, that it's written in there what they've done that day, it might only be, you know, they played in the water, or we went to the allotment, but parents are encouraged to also write in the books as well and perhaps I go a bit overboard when I write in [laughs] I write eve-rything they do! Well, not everything, but...it gives the carers and the staff at pre-school an idea of what they get up to outside of school...that we do try to back up what they're learning within pre-school as well.

Progress checks and profiling

There is an obligation, within the EYFS, for practitioners to discuss children's progress with their parents. There are also two points at which statutory sum-mative assessments must be made. First, for every child aged between two and three years, practitioners must provide parents with a written summary of the child's development in three prime areas of learning (communication and lan-guage, physical development, and personal, social and emotional development). This progress check at age two 'must identify the child's strengths, and any areas where the child's progress is less than expected' (DfE, 2012:10). If a child's progress gives cause for concern, practitioners are expected to discuss this with the child's parents and agree how to support the child. Second, in the final term of the Reception Year, the Early Years Foundation Stage Profile (EYFSP) is com-pleted for every child. For each of seventeen early learning goals, across seven areas of learning (the three prime areas and the 'specific areas' of literacy, mathematics, knowledge of the world, and expressive arts), practitioners must identify whether children are meeting, exceeding or not yet reaching expected levels of development. The EYFSP is shared with parents and passed on to the Year 1 teacher. The profile is expected to provide 'a well-rounded picture of a child's knowledge, understanding and abilities, their progress against expected levels, and their readiness for Year 1' (DfE, 2012: 11). EYFSP results are used as a benchmark of pupil attainment at the end of the first year in school. The school also has a duty to report all EYFSP results to the local authority.

This requirement to complete summative assessments raises further questions and challenges. Once again, there appears to be a contradiction within the EYFS. In the overarching principles, there is explicit recognition of the 'Unique Child' and the fact that 'children develop and learn in different ways and at different rates' (DfE, 2012: 3); and yet, there is measurement of whole cohorts of children at two points in their early childhood education, based upon achievement of developmental norms. The 'Kei tua o tepae' assessment for learning materials, linked with the Te Whāriki curriculum (New Zealand Ministry of Education, 2004, Book 1: 3), state: 'Assessments don't just foster learning, they also construct and foster it.' In the case of learning stories, narratives about the child's achievements are likely to promote his or her positive identity as a learner. There is a risk in the EYFS that while children's learning journeys might, similarly, highlight the successes of each unique child, for some children the outcomes of statutory assessments could undermine this.

Bradbury (2011) considers the relationship between outcomes of the EYFSP and educational attainment and suggests that, at this early stage in the education process, inequalities are created that reflect and perpetuate wider social inequalities. Results on the EYFSP since its introduction show, for example, that significant numbers of boys, children on free schools meals and those from minority communities are designated as failing to reach expected levels of development (Bradbury, 2011). EYFSP scores are used as a benchmark to set expectations and to judge the progress of pupils in later school assessments. With the introduction of a progress check at two years of age, early labelling and the consequent lowering of expectations of some children could begin even earlier. There is a danger that, where paperwork has been reduced and there is less written evidence to support decisions, important assessments of children may be based upon quite subjective and even biased judgements on the part of a practitioner.

Conclusion

In this chapter, I have highlighted some of the challenges relating to observation, documentation of children's learning and assessment for those working within the EYFS in England. While a move away from excessive paperwork is to be welcomed, practitioners need to think very carefully about the importance of observation, documentation and communication as a part of the early learning process. Even if little is written down, the skill of carefully observing and understanding each child must not be lost.

Points for reflection and discussion

1. What paperwork do you consider to be essential to the delivery of high-quality early years care and education? What 'paper-free' strategies are effective for knowing children and understanding their learning?
2. What are the best methods of engaging parents with observations and assessments of young children? How can parents' perspectives on their children's progress be taken into account more fully?
3. How can fair and objective assessments of children be made, at the age of two years and at the end of the Foundation Stage? How can we ensure that such assessments are used positively, to foster progress, avoiding early labelling of young children?
4. How can we achieve a satisfactory balance between documenting observations and spending time interacting with children?
5. Who is documentation for and who contributes to it? Are parents' views and assessments taken into consideration?
6. What is the relationship between assessments such as the EYFS Profile and educational inequality?

References and further reading

Bath, C. (2012) 'I can't read it; I don't know': Young children's participation in the pedagogical documentation of English early childhood education and care settings, *International Journal of Early Years Education*, 20(2): 190–201.

Bradbury, A. (2011) Rethinking assessment and inequality: The production of disparities in attainment in early years education, *Journal of Education Policy*, 26(5): 655–76.

Carr, M. (2001) *Assessment in Early Childhood Settings: Learning stories*. London: Paul Chapman.

Carr, M. and Lee, W. (2012) *Learning Stories: Constructing learner identities in early education*. London: Sage.

Collins, S., Gibbs, J., Luff, P., Thomas, L. and Sprawling, M. (2010) Thinking through the uses of observation and documentation, in J. Moyles (ed.) *Thinking About Play: Developing a reflective approach*. Maidenhead: Open University Press.

Department for Children, Schools and Families (DCSF) (2008) *Early Years Foundation Stage: Everything you need to know*. London: DCSF.

Department for Education (DfE) (2012) *Statutory Framework for the Early Years Foundation Stage: Setting the standards for learning, development and care for children from birth to five*. Available at: http://www.foundationyears.org.uk/wp-content/uploads/2012/07/EYFS-Statutory-Framework-2012.pdf.

Driscoll, V. and Rudge, C. (2005) Channels for listening to young children and parents, in A. Clark, A.T. Kjørholt and P. Moss (eds.) *Beyond Listening*. Bristol: Polity Press.

Drummond, M.J. (2003) *Assessing Children's Learning*, 2nd edn. London: David Fulton.

Early Education (2012) *Development Matters in the Early Years Foundation Stage*. Available at: http://www.education.gov.uk/childrenandyoungpeople/earlylearningandchildcare/delivery/education/a0068102/early-years-foundation-stage-EYFS (accessed 4 April 2013).

Edwards, C., Gandini, L. and Forman, G. (2012) *The Hundred Languages of Children: The Reggio Emilia experience in transformation*, 3rd edn. Santa Barbara, CA: Praeger.

Elfer, P. (2005) Observation matters, in L. Abbott and A. Langston (eds.) *Birth to Three Matters*. Maidenhead: Open University Press.

Fisher, K. (2011) *Early Years Daily Diary*. Bloomington, IN: AuthorHouse Publishing.

Gerber, M. (2005) RIE principles and practices, in S. Petrie and S. Owen (eds.) *Authentic Relationships in Group Care for Infants and Toddlers – Resources for infant educators: Principles into practice*. London: Jessica Kingsley.

Her Majesty's Stationery Office (HMSO) (1989) *The Children Act 1989*. London: HMSO.

Hurst, V. (1991) *Planning for Early Learning*. London: Paul Chapman.

Isaacs, S. (1930) *Intellectual Growth in Young Children*. London: Routledge & Kegan Paul.

Isaacs, S. (1933) *Social Development in Young Children*. London: Routledge & Kegan Paul.

Isaacs, S., Oliver, R.A.C. and Field, H.E. (1936) *The Educational Guidance of the School Child: Suggestions on child study and guidance embodying a scheme of pupils' records*. London: Evans Bros.

Luff, P. (2007) Written observations or walks in the park? Documenting children's experiences, in J. Moyles (ed.) *Early Years Foundations: Meeting the challenge*. Maidenhead: Open University Press.

Luff, P. (2012) Challenging assessment, in T. Papatheodorou and J. Moyles (eds.) *Cross-cultural Perspectives on Early Childhood*. London: Sage.

Malaguzzi, L. (2012) History, ideas and basic philosophy, in C. Edwards, L. Gandini and G. Forman (eds.) *The Hundred Languages of Children: The Reggio Emilia experience in transformation*, 3rd edn. Santa Barbara, CA: Praeger.

Memel, E. and Fernandez, L. (2005) RIE parent–infant guidance classes, in S. Petrie and S. Owen (eds.) *Authentic Relationships in Group Care for Infants and Toddlers – Resources for infant educators: Principles into practice*. London: Jessica Kingsley.

Money, R. (2005) The RIE early years curriculum, in S. Petrie and S. Owen (eds.) *Authentic Relationships in Group Care for Infants and Toddlers – Resources for infant educators: Principles into practice*. London: Jessica Kingsley.

New Zealand Ministry of Education (1996) *Te Whāriki. He Whāriki Mātaurangamō-ngā-Mokopuna o Aotearoa: Early childhood curriculum*. Wellington: Learning Media.

New Zealand Ministry of Education (2004) *Kei Tua o te Pae: Assessment for learning, Book One*. Available at: http://www.educate.ece.govt.nz/learning/curriculumAndLearning/Assessmentforlearning/KeiTuaotePae.aspx (accessed 13 January 2013).

Nutbrown, C. (1996) Wide eyes and open minds – observing, assessing and respecting children's early achievements, in C. Nutbrown (ed.) *Respectful Educators – Capable Learners: Children's rights and early education*. London: Paul Chapman.

Podmore, V. and Luff, P. (2012) *Observation: Origins and approaches in early childhood*. Maidenhead: Open University Press.

Rinaldi, C. (2006) *In Dialogue with Reggio Emilia*. London: Routledge.

Rinaldi, C. (2012) The pedagogy of listening: The listening perspective from Reggio Emilia, in C. Edwards, L. Gandini and G. Forman (eds.) *The Hundred Languages of Children: The Reggio Emilia experience in transformation*, 3rd edn. Santa Barbara, CA: Praeger.

Tickell, C. (2011) *The Early Years: Foundations for life, health and learning*. Available at: http://www.education.gov.uk/tickellreview (accessed 1 February 2013).

United Nations (1989) *Convention on the Rights of the Child*. Available at: http://www.crin.org/docs/resources/treaties/uncrc.asp (accessed 1 February 2013).

Vygotsky, L.S. (1981) The genesis of higher mental functions, in J.V. Wertsch (ed.) *The Concept of Activity in Soviet Psychology*. Armonk, NY: M.E. Sharpe.

Whalley, M. and the Pen Green Centre Team (2007) *Involving Parents in Their Children's Learning*, 2nd edn. London: Paul Chapman.

4   Enabling pedagogy: meanings and practices

Sue Rogers

Abstract

Adults clearly have a vital part to play in how and in what ways children acquire the tools of their culture and become motivated and effective learners. It is the nature and quality of interaction between adults and children in the pursuit of learning that lies at the heart of the definition of an enabling pedagogy. Obvious though it may be in theory, research has consistently shown that the dominant approach to pedagogy in many early years settings and especially in reception classes reflects a model of pedagogy reminiscent of the primary school rather than one of nursery or early years practice, with a focus on closed questions, the transmission of knowledge and the management of behaviour and risk. It is also the case that a pedagogy that enables children to engage in authentic and critical dialogue with more expert others can go some way towards addressing the pernicious issue of social and educational disadvantage (and is less likely to exclude children who struggle to make sense of the adult's pedagogic practice). One of the key challenges in the early years is that pedagogy is seen to be adult-led rather than co-constructed and participatory, both indoors and outdoors.

Introduction

The current climate of increased government interest, investment and intervention in early years education has brought about a number of policy initiatives, all of which have significant implications for the development of pedagogy which can support the complex learning needs and characteristics of young children in the twenty-first century (see chapter 1). This challenging policy context is further complicated by the relative lack of understanding of the term 'pedagogy' when applied to work with young children (Papatheodorou and Moyles, 2009; Stephen, 2010) and especially to their play (Rogers, 2010). This is often attributable to a peculiarly British resistance to and lack of tradition in pedagogy compared with international contexts. Many readers will be familiar with the Reggio Emilia preschools approach to pedagogy and the New Zealand Curriculum, Te Whāriki. Pedagogical approaches from such contexts, while persuasive are not easily transported into other cultural settings even when lessons can be learned from dialogue with colleagues in other countries; early years education is in many senses a global village. This chapter considers what is meant by an 'enabling pedagogy', in theory and in practice, with a focus on provision in England in light of the recent revision to the Early Years Foundation Stage (EYFS). It emphasizes interactive reciprocal and responsive pedagogic relationships in improving outcomes for children, an area that has international agreement and currency stemming as it does from social constructivist and socio-cultural perspectives on education.

The chapter is also shaped in response to the notable shift that has taken place in the revised EYFS to *how* children learn rather than *what* they learn, providing further justification for thinking more deeply about how and in what ways adults interact with children to enable them to become confident and effective learners. This is most evident in the introduction of three 'characteristics of effective learning', which provide the context for learning in the EYFS. These are (DfE, 2012: 7):

- **playing and exploring** – children investigate and experience things, and 'have a go';
- **active learning** – children concentrate and keep on trying if they encounter difficulties, and enjoy achievements; and
- **creating and thinking critically** – children have and develop their own ideas, make links between ideas, and develop strategies for doing things.

Such ideas will be familiar to early years practitioners, but the focus on *how* children learn is now mandatory as is the requirement for practitioners to provide a summative assessment on how each child demonstrates the characteristics of effective learning (Moylett, 2013) (see chapter 3). Furthermore, the EYFS does not explicitly include the term 'pedagogy'. It does, however, refer to 'enabling environments' where practitioners provide for children's learning in the context of positive relationships. Important though this shift in emphasis is, it is equally if not more important to consider also how we teach rather than simply what we teach and make explicit the complexity of working with young children and the many factors that contribute to – and ultimately shape – the pedagogic relationship.

Understanding pedagogy in the early years: work in progress?

Pedagogy is a complex and contested concept, difficult to explain and to enact; and, as Alexander (2008) contends, there is no complete, once and for all universal definition that is applicable to all educational settings. Yet reflecting on its meaning and practices can help us to uncover and understand better what it is that happens in early years settings and classrooms, between teachers and learners, between adults and children. In this chapter, I draw on a number of sources to fashion a broad definition of pedagogy that includes the interaction of teacher, child, culture and environment. By culture I mean the cultural norms, rules and rituals embedded in classrooms which influence what is possible and what is valued, as well acknowledging that children bring their own culture to the pedagogic relationship, which may in turn conflict with that of peers and adults in the early years setting. Sociologist Basil Bernstein viewed pedagogy as 'cultural relay' (Alexander, 2008), as a mechanism for the reproduction of particular kinds of (mainly middle-class) values. His often quoted statement that 'If the culture of the teacher is to become part of the consciousness of the child, then the culture of the child must first be in the consciousness of the teacher' (Bernstein, 1970) draws attention to the gap that often exists between children's culture and the dominant culture of school, between the everyday knowledge that children bring to the classroom and the types of school knowledge they are required to learn by the State and society more generally.

Culture in this sense is central to the pedagogic relationship formed between learners and educators, between children and adults in early years and school settings. But it is still necessary in any discussion of pedagogy to ascertain in more concrete terms how this is to take place. What is it that early years practitioners actually need to do or for that matter *not* do? What is the nature of the pedagogic relationship that best enables young children to become effective and ultimately independent learners? These are challenging questions to ask in a policy climate that requires greater accountability on the part of early years practitioners to deliver results and prepare children for school, and where there is little time to reflect upon why we do things in a particular way.

Hildebrand (1999) comments on the high level of consistency in the pedagogical practices used by teachers, which creates a sense of what is 'normal' and what is 'other' in classrooms. She identifies *hegemonic pedagogy* as the set of teaching practices that have become dominant over time, but suggests also that such strong allegiance to particular ways of doing things also 'perpetuates power/knowledge inequities and sustains the current regimes of truth in society' (Hildebrand, 1999: 2), where practices become so established that they are beyond reflection and the possibility of change. Children also participate in this process of hegemonic pedagogy because they too come to expect that nursery and school provide certain experiences and routines. Hildebrand (1999: 2) describes this as the 'pre-existing pedagogic contract that has been generated by the collective approaches used by teachers in the past: and the particular set of pedagogical practices that has become so established that they form hegemonic pedagogy'.

From a critical and socio-cultural approach to pedagogy, recognition of children's agency is central in pedagogic relations between adults and children. 'Agency' is understood here as a person's way of being, seeing and responding in the world, as taking control of one's own mental activity within particular socio-cultural contexts (Edwards, 2001). We can observe babies' agency as they actively signal a wide range of feelings such as contentment, discomfort or distress through their bodily movement, non-verbal communication and by modifying their behaviour in response to others, such as turning away from the gaze of an adult. As children develop and become more independent, so they also learn how to resist and challenge adult requests and rules and express their desires, as in the case of Mia, aged four, who, when attempting to climb a tree that is off limits in the playground says to Lisa, 'It doesn't matter... She's [the teacher] not even out here.'

The development of human agency is closely tied to young children's development of self-regulation and metacognitive strategies. A further important consideration for pedagogy, therefore, is that agency is not only inherent in the individual child but mediated by the interactions between children as well as with adults, particularly in peer group play. Indeed, play offers the potential for children to negotiate and contain their desire to act impulsively with other children, and thus to self-regulate behaviours and feelings. The child at play is bound by the rules of the game, so she is positioned between her desire to act spontaneously on the one hand and by the need to subordinate those desires to the rules of the game on the other. If children do not 'play the game' within the boundaries of the imaginative frame and rules, the play will not be sustained. This is why Vygotsky (1978: 99) contends that 'the child's greatest control occurs in play'. We have all observed examples where play breaks down between children because they are unable to negotiate a joint solution to disagreements. This is all part of children's emergent sense of their place in the world and of their growing recognition that to stay in the play, it is necessary to curb impulses and to compromise.

Research suggests that one of the real benefits of play is that it enables young children to demonstrate and internalize self-control and self-regulated behaviours (Whitebread, 2013). The rule-bound nature of play and the self-control children require for play to be sustained emphasize the importance of play *between* children. It enables children to confirm or challenge their own perspective on phenomena. An enabling pedagogy recognizes and supports children's agency and the self-regulatory behaviour that stems from it, which is essential to social learning. This may mean reflecting upon the rules and routines of the early years setting, which if imposed too rigidly might limit what is possible and come to dominate the child's experiences. In turn, this may require early years practitioners to reconsider their established ways of working and the traditional hierarchical relationship between adults and children, and to consider co-constructive ways of interacting with children.

It is also possible that if we assume too much for children's agency we fail to see the times when they need adult guidance, instruction and help in setting social and physical boundaries. Bernstein's work is again of interest here and in particular his articulation of two dominant approaches to pedagogy or what he calls 'pedagogic modes'. The first of these is the 'performance mode', which focuses on what the child does not know (or absences). Control on the part of the adult/teacher is made explicit. An example of performance mode might be a phonics lesson where children are listening to the teacher and required to provide correct answers to the adult questions. By contrast, in the competence pedagogic mode, it is what children know that is evaluated and adult/teacher control is implicit or 'hidden'. These ideas stem from Bernstein's earlier work on visible and invisible pedagogies. He proposed that even in the most child-centred practices, the adult holds an authority that may be masked yet is ever-present and where children's activity, particularly their free play, may be under surveillance and hence also available to regulation and evaluation (Bernstein, 1975). In relation to children's agency, these ideas are important because they remind us that even in free play contexts, there is an implicit pedagogy that shapes what children can do and what is valued. To genuinely understand pedagogy, we need to acknowledge what is 'hidden' and work with it.

In empirical research with colleagues, I observed the hidden pedagogy of free play environments both indoors and outdoors, where children resisted adults' pedagogic approaches and where taken-for-granted practices such as giving choice and extended free play episodes (what we might call a surface competence/ child-centred approach) were in fact subject to strongly performance-orientated approaches of interaction. Adult interventions in play, where they happened at all, could be described as directive and strongly orientated towards a specific learning objective or for the purposes of managing behaviour and perceived risk, particularly in outdoor play. What was revealed through observation was a more complex model of pedagogy that did not reflect a clear distinction between Bernstein's performance and competence modes (previously visible and invisible) or to use more familiar terms, play and formal teaching. The exclusive or overuse of either mode is counterproductive; overuse of a performance mode may bewilder children since they may not have the socio-cultural tools to make sense of the teacher's discourse in classroom interactions. Hence the potential for shared meaning and understanding breaks down.

Similarly, over-emphasis on a competence pedagogic mode may exclude those children who need more explicit signposting in order to access knowledge and information about how things are done in the classroom, or access or withdraw from groups where peer group culture dominates, particularly in free play environments (Ivinson and Duveen, 2006). To illustrate, Max is playing alone outdoors in a foundation stage reception class. It is free play with little adult intervention. A group of children are playing near him and start chanting 'Gaylord, Gaylord'. He is clearly upset but does not appear to have the strategies to deal with this situation, nor does he elicit adult help. He stops playing and runs indoors. Although this episode was recorded by a researcher, it was missed by the adults who were supervising the play at a distance. It raises some important questions about how we capture these important 'teachable' moments without 'policing' children's play (Waite *et al.*, 2013).

Moving from enabling environments to enabling pedagogy

The way in which the environment is resourced and used is indicative of teacher-educators' pedagogic approaches but does not explicitly deal with the nature of adult–child interactions in the pedagogic relationship. One useful framework for thinking about the implications of the way in which the environment is organized and which might move us closer to a consideration of an enabling pedagogy is suggested by Claxton and Carr (2004). They distinguish between four types of environment that adults can create for young children:

- a prohibiting environment;
- an affording environment;
- an inviting environment;
- a potentiating environment.

A *prohibiting* environment is one which is tightly managed and controlled by adults and provides an activity schedule where there is little time for children to be engaged over any length of time and where adults may inadvertently discourage children's positive dispositions. An example of a prohibiting environment might be where a 'carousel' of play activities is laid out by adults and the children are allowed a fixed period of time at each activity before moving on to the next (Rose and Rogers, 2012). Such an approach does not enable children to have a deep experience of play with materials and with peers.

In an *affording* environment, a very different approach is taken. Children are offered an array of activities and opportunities, but with little adult involvement, co-construction or episodes of sustained shared thinking.

An *inviting* environment is one that not only affords the opportunity for learning but is one in which adults draw attention to its value and interest. An example of this might be a nursery where adults and children co-construct the activities and the adults engage in meaningful conversations with children about what they are thinking and feeling.

Finally, Claxton and Carr (2004) identify *potentiating* environments, which recognize children's emerging dispositions but also actively 'stretch' and develop them. Potentiating environments, they argue, involve frequent participation in shared activity and proactively 'share the power between teachers and learners' (Claxton and Carr, 2004: 92). Claxton and Carr suggest that adults need to balance two main processes in creating and sustaining a potentiating learning environment. The first of these is 'reification', which means to make experiences concrete in some way. An example in the early years context might be to document and make visible to others children's learning, perhaps through annotated drawings and photographs (see chapter 3). The second process is 'participation', which places relationships at the heart of the learning process and the development of shared understanding between adults and children and between children (see also Rogers and Evans, 2008; Bath, 2009). An example might be to consult with children over play provision and resources, about the timing and pacing of certain activities. How often do we ask children how they have experienced the learning process and what they would like to change? The model proposed by Claxton and Carr (2004) points towards more recent conceptualizations of relational pedagogy (Papatheodorou and Moyles, 2009), and links also to a move towards co-constructed approaches to play pedagogy.

Interactive pedagogies stemming from the socio-constructivist theory of Vygotsky (1978) and followers (e.g. Rogoff, 1990) are contingent and reciprocal, and foster shared meaning in the wider social and cultural contexts of teaching and learning. The research literature that considers this approach in the context of classrooms and early years settings has been roundly critical of the limited styles of adult–child or teacher–pupil talk available in classrooms and the prevalence of the so-called 'Initiation, Response, Feedback or Evaluation' (IRF or IRE) style, which invariably follows the sequence of the teacher's 'initiation' of an idea or question, followed by pupil 'response'. The sequence is then completed by the teacher's feedback or evaluation (Mercer and Littleton, 2007). This approach is further characterized by a prevalence of closed questions (Siraj-Blatchford and Manni, 2008), the transmission of knowledge and facts resulting in few opportunities for children to question, expand or reflect on what they have learned. It may lead children to engage in 'guess what's in the teacher's head' routines.

In early childhood settings specifically, sustained shared thinking that builds on dialogic pedagogy and work on 'scaffolding' has been identified as an effective pedagogic interaction, where two or more individuals 'work together' in an intellectual way to solve a problem, clarify a concept, evaluate activities or extend a narrative alongside open-ended questions (Siraj-Blatchford and Manni, 2008). A somewhat different approach to interaction is suggested in the findings of the Oxford Preschool Project (led by Jerome Bruner in the late 1970s). The project endorsed the use of scaffolding and open-ended questions as the most productive forms of interaction. However, the research also showed that a range of different adult utterances produced significant effects on children's use and extension of language. Among the many speech types employed by early years educators, the most likely to prompt children's extended language use were those the authors described as 'phatic' or 'contributions': briefly, phatic utterances are short insertions that keep the conversation going ('Really?'; 'Did he?'; 'OK') while contributions are the adult's own offerings ('I really love that colour. My house is blue'; 'I don't like this cold weather. I like the sunshine'; 'You're eating an apple. That's my favourite fruit'). Both types of utterance were found to encourage children to go on talking for longer to a far greater extent than being asked questions of any kind that had the potential to intimidate children and close down opportunities for talk. The importance of this conversational type of interaction is hinted at by Papatheodorou and Moyles (2009: 11), who argue that we need a pedagogical model that invests in our connectivity and interconnectivity as human beings. Similarly, research conducted by Payler (2009) is important, since it highlights differences between the more familiar pedagogic tool of scaffolding with co-construction where conversational styles of interaction are more likely to take place. Payler argues that in co-construction the adult role involves 'ascertaining, suggesting or jointly creating a role with the child' (Payler, 2009: 121). Co-construction assumes a more flexible, responsive and participatory approach than scaffolding where there may be a clearer intention or learning objective in mind. The study found that co-construction was more common in pre-school settings, whereas scaffolding was the preferred approach in the reception classes. Co-construction is distinguished from scaffolding, which aims to extend the child's understanding of a particular concept or skill.

Shifting the focus in this chapter from enabling environments to a more explicit focus on enabling pedagogy in which interaction is central might help to overcome some of the traditional dichotomies that persist between free play and structured play, between adult-led and child-led activity, and between traditional and child-centred approaches. I have written elsewhere that play pedagogy can be conceptualized as 'a conflict of interests', since it challenges us to balance children's desires and motivations with our own desire to participate in ways that enhance rather than inhibit the course of the play. In the next section, I consider how an enabling pedagogy has play at its heart and how early years practitioners might rethink their role in it.

An enabling pedagogy of play

There is a consensus from research in the field that play appears to be the principal way in which young children come to know their material and physical environment and relationships with others. Early years practitioners can create provision that gives children real choices about where, with whom, what and how they play and create spaces both indoors and outdoors that allow for uninterrupted time to play, to revisit, rebuild and recreate ideas (Rogers and Evans, 2008). Through co-constructive pedagogy, practitioners can negotiate pedagogy with children and through careful observation, verbal and non-verbal feedback, adults act as knowledgeable observers, assessors, carers, communicators and facilitators, which may provoke them to initiate activities with the children or simply help to create provision that empowers all children to self-initiate in an enabling environment (Rose and Rogers, 2012). It is important to recognize the ways in which play changes as children progress through the EYFS, from the earliest playful interactions with primary caregivers to the highly sophisticated social pretend play of four-year-olds. Understanding play development is vital, but the fundamental principles of enabling pedagogy remain the same throughout. For example, secure attachment is achieved through adults being empathetically responsive (Underdown, 2007), by looking closely for verbal and non-verbal signals from the child that reflect how the child is feeling and what their needs and interests might be (Rose and Rogers, 2012). This 'attunement' between baby and caregiver creates a powerful context for reciprocal connectedness that influences the synaptic make-up of the brain and provides the foundation for learning and well-being. According to Arredondo and Edwards (2000), attunement depends on the following key elements:

- emotional availability of the adult;
- high degree of flexibility from the adult;
- display of a range of affect (emotion);
- capacity for genuine playfulness;
- initiation of affectionate interactions;
- sense of humour;
- patience.

Drawing on research on interactions between parents and babies, Parker-Rees argues for all practitioners in early years settings to engage in playful interactions with babies and toddlers, suggesting that 'reciprocal imitation with familiar partners reminds us that our delight in the company of other people lies at the very heart of the uniquely human process of intentional pedagogy' (Parker-Rees, 2007: 14). These pleasurable and playful reciprocal interactions give babies the feedback they need to affirm their individual place in the world and to motivate them to communicate. However, playing and exploring with children does not come as easily to some adults as to others, and indeed it may be particularly challenging to be playful in the face of pressure to meet the demands of the external regulatory context or, for that matter, the pressures of life experienced by many parents/adults in contemporary society.

In relation to older children, Bernstein's insight that, even when adults adopt a mainly non-interventionist strategy in a free play pedagogy, the adult's authority and control of what is going on and what is valued is always present. He argued also that play, far from being a neutral, innocent activity of the child, can also be read as the 'means by which the child exteriorizes himself [*sic*] to the teacher' (Bernstein, 1975: 10). Thus he explains that 'Play does not merely describe an activity: it also contains an evaluation of that activity. Thus, there is productive play and less productive play, obsessional and free-ranging play, solitary and social play' (ibid.). In previous research projects, I noted that certain pedagogical practices observed in early years settings appropriate the meanings that children bring to their play. These may take the form of, for example:

- achieve prescribed learning objectives through play;
- assign children to particular play groups (see also Trawick-Smith, 1998);
- subject classroom play to frequent interruptions (Rogers and Evans, 2008).

There has been considerable debate about the right balance between adult-initiated and child-initiated experiences in the EYFS and this is left largely to the judgement of practitioners who know best the needs and interests of the children in their settings. One of the difficulties in marrying what we know about adult–child interactions that support and extend children's thinking and what we know about children's play, is that each seems to suggest a very different role for adults and children. Adults' reluctance to participate in play may stem from a number of different sources. First, there may be an ideological commitment to children's free play as the 'child's world', a view that is often linked to the ideas of the early pioneer educators and the theories of learning of Piaget. Alternatively, practitioners may adopt a more pragmatic approach to play. From this perspective, play is viewed as something that children can do and benefit from either alone or with peers, which in turn releases the practitioner to attend to other tasks such as teaching small groups specific knowledge and skills. Drawing on two research studies, I asked the question 'what kind of pedagogy is a pedagogy of play'? (Rogers, 2010). How and in what ways do pedagogical practices shape the play experiences of young children across diverse social, educational and cultural settings? One of the difficulties in the coupling of *play* with *pedagogy* is that play simply becomes a vehicle through which to meet the demands of the prescribed curriculum rather than as an activity that is genuinely child-led. One possible way to rethink the relationship between play and pedagogy is to view play pedagogy 'as a negotiated and relational "space" both physical and conceptual' (Rogers, 2010: 15), which would include adults and children co-constructing. Adults would need also to relinquish some of the power and control they hold in managing the play material environment and curricular agenda. Pedagogical strategies that would enable adults and children to enter the play frame together would include adopting a playful stance and entering into role without leading the direction of the play. Young children in early years and early school settings demand adults that recognize the important relationship between children's everyday experiences and knowledge, and the concepts and knowledge they require to be active participants in society.

Conclusion

In developing an enabling pedagogy, creating a stimulating and appropriately challenging environment is central, but the environment is only as good as the pedagogic relationships established between adults and children and the interactions that take place in the context of play and learning. In some cases, providing an enabling pedagogy might require us to rethink the traditional hierarchical relationship between adults and children, and ensure that we allow the culture of the child to enter into our consciousness.

Points for reflection and discussion

1. What kind of 'pedagogic contract' have you established in your setting? For example, are children expected mainly to talk or to listen? Are children expected to find solutions rather than bring problems?
2. Is the climate you have established one where knowledge is produced or reproduced?
3. How often is negotiation part of the pedagogic contract on offer in your setting?

References and further reading

Alexander, R. (2008) *Essays on Pedagogy*. London: Routledge.

Arredondo, D.E. and Edwards, L.P. (2000) Attachment, bonding and reciprocal connectedness: Limitations of attachment theory in the juvenile and family court, *Journal of the Center for Families, Children and the Courts*, 2: 109–27.

Bath, C. (2009) *Learning to Belong: Exploring young children's participation at the start of school.* **London: Routledge.**

Bernstein, B. (1970) Education cannot compensate for society, *New Society*, 26 February, pp. 344–47.

Bernstein, B. (1975) *Class Pedagogies: Visible and invisible*. Washington, DC: OECD.

Claxton, G. and Carr, M. (2004) A framework for teaching learning: The dynamics of disposition, *Early Years*, 24(1): 87–97.

Department for Education (DfE) (2012) *Statutory Framework for the Early Years Foundation Stage: Setting the standards for learning, development and care for children from birth to five*. Available at: http://www.foundationyears.org.uk/wp-content/uploads/2012/07/EYFS-Statutory-Framework-2012.pdf.

Edwards, A. (2001) Researching pedagogy: A sociocultural agenda, *Pedagogy, Culture and Society*, 9(2): 161–86.

Hildebrand, G.M. (1999) *Con/testing Learning Models*. Available at: http://publications.aare.edu.au/99pap/hil99582.htm (accessed 20 March 2013).

Ivinson, G. and Duveen, G. (2006) Children's recontextualisations of pedagogy, in R. Moore, M. Arnot, J. Beck and H. Daniels (eds.) *Knowledge, Power and Educational Reform: Applying the sociology of Basil Bernstein*. London: Routledge.

Mercer, N. and Littleton, K. (2007) *Dialogue and the Development of Children's Thinking: A sociocultural approach*. London: Routledge.

Moylett, H. (2013) How young children learn: Introduction and overview, in H. Moylett (ed.) *The Characteristics of Effective Learning: Helping young children become learners for life*. Maidenhead: Open University Press.

Papatheodorou, T. and Moyles, J. (eds.) (2009) *Learning Together in the Early Years: Exploring relational pedagogy*. London: Routledge.

Parker-Rees, R. (2007) Liking to be liked: Imitation, familiarity and pedagogy in the first years of life, *Early Years*, 27(1): 3–17.

Payler, J. (2009) Co-construction and scaffolding: guidance strategies and children's meaning-making, in T. Papatheodorou and J. Moyles (eds.) *Learning Together in the Early Years: Exploring relational pedagogy*. London: Routledge.

Rogers, S. (2010) Powerful pedagogies and playful resistance: researching children's perspectives, in E. Brooker and S. Edwards (eds.) *Engaging Play*. Maidenhead: Open University Press.

Rogers, S. and Evans, J. (2008) *Inside Role-Play in Early Education*. London: Routledge.

Rogoff, B. (1990) *Apprenticeships in Thinking*. New York: Oxford University Press.

Rose, J. and Rogers, S. (2012) *Adult Roles in the Early Years*. Maidenhead: Open University Press.

Siraj-Blatchford, I. and Manni, L. (2008) 'Would you like to tidy up now?': An analysis of adult questioning in the English Foundation Stage, *Early Years: An International Journal of Research and Development*, 28(1): 5–22.

Stephen, C. (2010) Pedagogy: The silent partner in early years learning, *Early Years: An International Journal of Research and Development*, 30(1): 15–28.

Trawick-Smith, J. (1998) Why play training works: An integrated model for play intervention, *Journal for Research in Childhood Education*, 12: 117–29.

Underdown, A. (2007) *Young Children's Health and Well-being*. Maidenhead: Open University Press.

Vygtosky, L. (1978) *Mind in Society: The development of higher psychological processes*. Cambridge. MA: Harvard University Press.

Waite, S., Rogers, S. and Evans, J. (2013) Freedom, flow and fairness: Exploring how children develop socially at school through outdoor play, *Journal of Adventure Education and Outdoor Learning*, 13(3): 255–76.

Whitebread, D. (2013) The importance of self-regulation for learning from birth, in H. Moylett (ed.) *The Characteristics of Effective Learning: Helping young children become learners for life*. Maidenhead: Open University Press.

5 Qualifications and quality in the Early Years Foundation Stage

Jane Payler and Jan Georgeson

Abstract

The training, education and qualifications of staff are considered among the most important factors that contribute to the quality of early childhood education and care. Minimum acceptable qualification requirements are identified in the Early Years Foundation Stage (EYFS) (DfE 2012), mirroring those from the earlier version of EYFS (DCSF, 2008). Yet in the intervening years, investment in early years training and education in England led to distinctive gains in qualification levels. A drive towards both graduate leadership for all early years settings and a minimum requirement of vocational training (Level 3) for *all* staff resulted in more individuals gaining degrees and a proliferation of vocational qualifications, though not without controversy and discomfiture. So if qualifications and training are so important to high-quality provision, why were these aspirations – and the progress already made towards them – not reflected in the 2012 statutory framework? This chapter aims to locate qualifications and staffing of early years settings in their socio-cultural-historical context and raise issues for critical reflection.

Introduction

A story about Marni and Allie

Marni came into early years having become involved in a pre-school playgroup where her children attended, helping on the committee, filling in for staff on odd days, eventually becoming a member of staff. She had a small number of O and A levels, but had not considered going to university. After several years of working at preschool and attending short early years courses, she was asked to do the Diploma in Preschool Practice with a view to taking over as the Deputy Supervisor. She enjoyed the course, took on the deputy role and then found herself being asked to become supervisor. As Foundation Degrees (FD) were introduced, she took up the opportunity to study part-time and achieved the qualification in three years. Although enjoyable, it was difficult to juggle family commitments, work and study. Nonetheless, through her studies, by talking to people on the course in other good settings, reading and working with the team to make the best provision that they could for the local children, the setting achieved a 'Good' rating from Ofsted. During the third year of her FD, just as she felt the end was in sight, Early Years Professional Status was introduced, requiring GCSE maths, which she didn't yet have. Two years later, after considerable hard work, placement in a baby room of a nursery and now as an experienced early years practitioner and leader, Marni achieved Early Years Professional Status. Then 'More Great Childcare' announced EYPS would be replaced by Early Years Teacher...

Allie started her studying as a young undergraduate in psychology. She loved learning about learning and so went on to do a PGCE in primary education, completing when she was around 22. She enjoyed working with the younger end of the age group and spent several years after her NQT year working in Key Stage 1, including Year 2 with its SATS testing and Reception, where she used the Literacy and Numeracy Hours to structure her teaching for young children. After five years, she applied to be a teacher at the new Children's Centre nearby and was delighted to get the job as it was part-time and would fit in with her family commitments now that she had a little girl. She worked across the Centre, advising staff on educational programmes for the young children, toddlers and babies in the attached nursery. In an attempt to plug the gap in her knowledge about baby and toddler development, she attended several short courses run by the local authority.

Marni and Allie's stories capture different routes into working in early years – a vocational route where working and training take place at the same time and an academic route in which academic study, for the most part, precedes practice. Although there are now many variations in the timing and content of study and practice, these two routes represent different trajectories that are still evident in the early years workforce today. During discussions at a recent professional development day, practitioners were able to identify advantages in each route; they agreed that having the time and 'head space' to devote to academic study unencumbered by the demands of a job can make it easier to digest abstract theories and challenging ideas but, on the other hand, it can be much easier to understand these ideas when you can relate them directly to what is happening in your own workplace, particularly if you have grappled with such issues for some time. Furthermore, practitioners on the academic route remembered leaving university with a degree and postgraduate certificate in education after successfully completing teaching practice, but not knowing how to recreate the established systems and routines they had inherited while on teaching practice. Practitioners on a vocational route, on the other hand, recalled feeling unsettled by new policies or a child's unusual behaviour patterns but not knowing how to articulate this unease. All, however, agreed on the importance of having time to talk through difficult issues and view them through different theoretical lenses, and that this was important because it helped them to explain to other people (and they mentioned OfSTED here) why they did things in particular ways.

This chapter looks at systems of qualifications that ensure that practitioners acquire both the theoretical and practical knowledge needed to work effectively in early years. Historically, the vocational apprenticeship route into early years practice has predominated and we have found it helpful to use Lave and Wenger's concept of legitimate peripheral participation in communities of practice to understand how a new practitioner learns how to do the job simply by participating in the work (Lave and Wenger, 1991; Georgeson, 2009: 119; Payler and Locke, 2013). Early years settings are communities of practice, that is, groups of practitioners – and often parents – who learn through their mutual engagement in a shared practice. The new entrant starts on the periphery, watching those with more experience carrying out the work, gradually taking on simple and then more complicated tasks. As they move towards the centre of the community of practice, not only do they become more skilled, they can also change the practice through the personal resources that they bring with them to the enterprise in which the community is engaged. In the last few years, the range of people entering the early years sector in the UK has been expanding and practitioners enter settings with a wider variety of different kinds of knowledge and experience. This includes what Eraut defines as 'codified' or formal knowledge acquired through study and then internalized so that practitioners can draw on it as part of their personal resources, as well as 'everyday knowledge of people and situations, know-how in the form of skills and practices, memories of cases and episodic events' (Eraut, 2007: 405, 406). Much of this personal knowledge can remain tacit unless practitioners have opportunities to engage in discussions to help them to find the words to express what can otherwise seem intuitive. Being able to make their tacit knowledge explicit by connecting their intuitions to theoretical frameworks makes practitioners feel stronger and more able to resist the 'terror of performativity' (Ball, 2003: 216); that is, they are less likely to be doing something in order to be seen to be doing the right thing, and more confident to operate according to acknowledged principles. This points to an inherent tension that has accompanied the professionalization of the early years workforce; being professional combines expertise and commitment to a set of principles; in the early years this includes understandings about how children learn and these do not lend themselves easily to the assessment of expertise needed for qualifications.

How have early years qualifications proliferated and changed in recent years and to what effect?

The professionalization of the early years workforce has been a contentious issue for many years. Some feel that routes into early years should continue to be open to those with fewer academic qualifications but who are vocationally oriented with practical skills and qualities for working with young children. Others feel that given the importance of the earliest stage of learning and development, only highly qualified staff should lead practice (Owen and Haynes, 2008: 13).

Historically, the maintained nursery education sector was staffed by early years teachers, originally with certificate level qualifications, supported by nursery nurses usually with a two-year level vocational diploma in nursery nursing from the Nursery Nurse Examination Board (NNEB). Certified teachers were eventually replaced by graduate teachers with qualified teacher status (QTS). Meanwhile, in the private, voluntary and independent (PVI) sector including day nurseries and preschool play-groups, NNEB or equivalent vocational qualifications were considered adequate to lead and manage settings, while many other staff had no early years qualifications at all. It is important to note that the PVI early years sector at this time was (and mostly remains) made up of part-time female employees with low pay and poor working conditions (McGillivray, 2008; Miller, 2008; Georgeson, 2009).

Since 2001, a practitioner-based route into and through higher education developed – Foundation Degrees in Early Childhood (DfES, 2004). This was a new way for early years staff, most of whom had not previously aspired to higher education, to achieve Level 5 qualifications while working and earning. The lure of the part-time, funded 'sector-endorsed'[1] qualification was to gain Senior Practitioner Status and many early years staff eagerly took up the challenge.

In 2006, however, the government of the day introduced a new push towards raising the level of qualifications in early years. Taking its lead from (although not accurately reflecting) research findings of the study on Effective Provision of Pre-school Education (EPPE; see section below on 'What is the evidence showing that qualifications matter in early years?'), the Children's Workforce Development Council (CWDC) set out requirements for a new graduate level early years status, Early Years Professional Status (EYPS). Government targets were introduced for all Children's Centres to employ an EYP by 2010, full day care settings by 2015, and all settings to move towards National Vocational Qualification Level 3 (equivalent to A levels) as the minimum qualification of staff to be counted in ratios in the PVI sector.

Graduate level status

Early Years Professional Status caused consternation across the sector, not least because it paved the way for graduate entrants new to early years to achieve leadership level status – a status, it was emphasized by CWDC, not a qualification – within one year of full-time study. It challenged the historic practice of early years largely involving an apprenticeship model of learning and leading outlined above. In spite of vociferous opposition across several quarters (see, for example, Payler and Locke, 2013), EYPS gained momentum. With financial support from local authorities[2] for settings to employ and train an EYP, a route to EYPS for practitioners from the foundation degree route was embraced by the sector, with staff achieving an Ordinary degree[3] along the way (Mathers *et al.*, 2012). The requirement for a grade C at GCSE for mathematics and English before the status could be achieved caused an unanticipated difficulty for would-be entrants, as few staff in the sector had maths at that level. However, the sector once again rose to the challenge and this predominantly female mature workforce with the support of local authorities undertook further education to gain the required qualifications.

There were several features of EYPS that were particularly positive (see, for example, Greenfield, 2011; Whalley, 2011: 21). The status required evidence of knowledge and practice with regard to the full age range from birth to five years, whereas teaching qualifications with an early years specialism generally covered three to seven years, missing out the vital birth to three period. It involved being assessed for multi-agency working, leadership, and combined care and education to support the holistic development of babies and young children. Findings from Hadfield *et al.* (2010, 2012) show that EYPs improved the quality of pedagogical processes in their settings, and progress had been made in the proportion nationally of day care staff qualified to at least Level 6, rising from 5 per cent in 2007 to 8 per cent in 2010 (DfE, 2010: 20). Less positive, however, was the fact that EYPS was not widely recognized outside the early years sector, even by parents, and that aside from the support of local authority supplements, the status did not allow staff to command commensurate increases in pay.

Qualifications at Level 3

The Labour government's 2006 call for Level 3 to become the minimum qualification for early years staff by 2015 led to a proliferation of courses, although not all were viewed as being of high quality (Nutbrown, 2012). A framework of 'full and relevant' qualifications to meet the legal requirements of the Statutory Framework for the EYFS (DCSF, 2008; DfE, 2012) was set up by CWDC, aimed at rationalizing qualifications and ensuring sufficient quality. By 2010, significant progress had been made; nationally, 74 per cent of staff had qualifications of at least Level 3 (up from 65 per cent in 2007), with over 90 per cent of day care staff at Level 3 in some local authorities (DfE, 2010: 20).

Were rising qualification levels reflected in the 2012 EYFS?

Surprisingly, given the increasing proportion of qualified staff and the subsequent acceptance by the sector of the qualification targets, the progress made was not reflected in the staffing requirements of the 2012 EYFS. The Coalition government of 2010 had removed the targets and the 2012 Statutory Framework carried identical qualification requirements to that of 2008, allowing half of staff to be unqualified and Level 3 to be an acceptable level for leadership (DfE, 2012). The opportunity to instate the aspiration of a better qualified workforce in statute was missed.

In June, 2012, the final report of the Independent Review of Early Education and Childcare Qualifications in England was published (Nutbrown, 2012). Among its nineteen recommendations, the report suggested replacing Early Years Professional Status with a new early years specialist route to Qualified Teacher Status, specializing in the years from birth to seven. It also recommended reinstating the requirement for Level 3 as a minimum qualification, but suggested delaying it until 2022.

Let us now examine the research evidence on which qualifications matter in early years and why.

What is the evidence showing that qualifications matter in early years?

The evidence most often cited to support increasing the qualifications of early years practitioners is the Effective Provision of Pre-school Education (EPPE) project, the first major European longitudinal study of a national sample of young children's development (Sylva *et al.*, 2004). The EPPE team collected a wide range of information on more than 3000 children, their parents, their home environments and the wide range of pre-school settings they attended, in order to investigate, using multilevel modelling, the effects of pre-school education for three- and four-year-olds. As well as teasing out the association between different patterns of attendance, different home environments and different settings, the study also collected information about staff qualifications. The final report included the finding that '[s]ettings that have staff with higher qualifications have higher quality scores and their children make more progress' (Sylva et al., 2004: v). The report provides more detail about the associations found through statistical analyses between high levels of qualification, good environmental ratings and good child outcomes when various background factors were held constant. The team acknowledged the limitations of educational effectiveness studies such as EPPE (Sylva et al., 2011: 120), and the study was supplemented by findings from twelve case studies of selected settings where children made most progress. As the findings have become more widely known, a certain amount of 'dissemination creep' has set in and unfortunately the study is now frequently cited as demonstrating that high staff qualifications, and teaching qualifications in particular, lead to improvements in child outcomes (Georgeson, 2009: 122). The EPPE data can, however, only demonstrate an *association* between high environmental ratings, level of staff qualification and good child outcomes; it could of course be the case that there is something else – such as a favourable financial environment – that is resulting in both staff with high qualifications and high environmental ratings, and the fact that staff qualifications were not independent of type of provision has been noted by the EPPE team (Sylva, 2001: 11).

The EPPE report asserts, nonetheless, that the most important finding is the fact that the divide between graduate and all other levels of qualification is always much greater than the gap between Levels 3/4 and those below, and concludes that this supports recent initiatives to ensure that those who manage and lead early childhood settings should be trained teachers. However, the EPPE data are grounded in 1997, when the early years landscape was very different and *before* the recent expansion in levels of qualification outlined above, thus we should be cautious about extrapolating the findings to the situation today. There is a tendency to refer the comparisons forward, to assume that it is today's practitioners who are less effective than teachers. Most Level 4 qualifications at that time were not about early childhood and child development, but were management related. Only the introduction of Foundation Degrees saw the start of increased study in these areas at a higher level for PVI staff.

It is also worth noting that EPPE did not include any staff with graduate qualifications other than teaching in the statistical models used in their analysis, possibly because at the time it appeared unlikely that there would be graduates from other backgrounds.[4] In the last fifteen years, however, there has been a huge expansion in degrees such as in Early Childhood Studies, and graduates from these courses are naturally finding their way into the workplace.

A recent study of provision in Scotland reports that:

> …highly effective centres show common characteristics which make for
> very good practice. These were most often, but not always, where teachers

were deployed. Evidence from inspections showed that children's experiences were often of a higher standard in centres where, traditionally, teachers were deployed, or staff had undertaken higher level qualifications and training. However, in centres where staff demonstrated effective practice, and there was no teacher deployed, the report found that staff had often undertaken additional higher level qualifications and training. This, alongside tailored, continuing professional development (CPD) and high quality support from the local authority, led to a positive impact on practice.

(Education Scotland, 2013: 4)

This brings into question the special status accorded to teacher professional qualifications both in the EPPE findings and more recently in the Nutbrown Review, especially as EPPE does not include data on outcomes for children cared for and educated by practitioners with degree level qualifications other than teaching.

What are the links between qualifications, adult–child ratios and costs?

Governments need to be sure that they are making the most effective use of resources to deliver the outcomes they seek. Since the 2012 EYFS came into being, the Coalition government responded to the Nutbrown Review of early years qualifications (Nutbrown, 2012) in 'More Great Childcare' (DfE, 2013). More Great Childcare claimed that childcare in England was too expensive compared with other countries. It claimed that this could be addressed by changing the qualification specifications for early years staff (although there was no associated change in the requirements for early years settings to *employ* staff with those qualifications), thus raising quality. Having more 'highly' qualified staff, it suggested, would allow the numbers of babies and children aged under three years each adult could look after to be increased without any loss of quality. These qualification changes and proposed increases in child to adult ratios[5] were to solve a number of problems: they would lead to care and education that was cheaper, of better quality, in more plentiful supply and that offered staff a higher status – an attractively magical solution.

The claims in More Great Childcare, however, were widely criticized for not paying careful attention to research evidence (e.g. Eisenstadt *et al.*, 2013) and were overwhelmingly opposed by the sector. Research on the relationships between ratios, qualifications and quality shows variation in effect according to different age groups. For children aged three years and over, ratios and qualifications were associated with different aspects of quality – qualifications were associated with language and learning; ratios were associated with care and individualized provision. Thus, raising qualifications while at the same time raising ratios of children to adults would leave quality at the same point, but with a different profile (Mathers and Sylva, 2007; Mathers *et al.*, 2007, 2011; Eisenstadt *et al.*, 2013: 1). Eisenstadt and colleagues made the point that qualifications make most difference only where the adult is working directly with children. In fact, More Great Childcare did not suggest raising ratios for children aged over three years, but rather making use of those allowed in the EYFS Statutory Framework of 1:13 where the adult has EYPS or QTS. Its associated recommendation for changing EYPS to Early Years Teacher without QTS might be argued not to raise qualifications at all.

> The introduction of a new qualification – the 'Early Years Teacher' – to replace existing Early Years Professionals (EYPs) will not necessarily enhance the status of those working with young children because they will not have comparable training, or Qualified Teacher Status (QTS), and will not be eligible for teacher pay and conditions. They will simply be second class 'teachers'.
>
> (Eisenstadt *et al.*, 2013: 2)

The research evidence for babies and young children aged under three years, however, was very different. Here, ratios were far more important than qualifications to quality. Therefore, the planned ratio rise of babies and toddlers to adults would have reduced quality, regardless of the qualifications of staff (Mathers *et al.*, 2011): 'Being well qualified does not necessarily help staff to cope with the demands for feeding, changing and caring for very young children' (Eisenstadt *et al.*, 2013: 2). Fortunately, in June 2013, the planned ratio rises for children aged under three years were dropped. The sector currently awaits further announcements from the government as to how it plans to ameliorate the costs of childcare and early education.

To conclude, we look now at issues of inclusion and social mobility in the early years workforce.

How well are adults from diverse backgrounds or with disabilities represented in early years settings?

Professionalization of the early years workforce forms part of successive government agendas to improve the quality of early years provision in order to improve child outcomes, with a view to taking children out of poverty by increasing their eventual employability. There is, however, another aspect of professionalization that could impact on raising households out of poverty, and that concerns entry into the workforce itself. Analyses of the early years workforce reveal that it is not evenly constituted with respect to age, gender and background. The average age of employees in the early years sector is forty and workers are predominately female; the proportion of female childcare workers has increased in the last twenty years compared with female workers in other related professions. This suggests that childcare is becoming an even more gendered occupation, although the proportion of new entrants who are male is increasing (Machin *et al.*, 2010: 10). And while qualifications have risen since 2002, with wages for most highly qualified workers and lowest paid workers increasing markedly, wages for those in the middle range have changed little (Machin *et al.*, 2010: 11). Different groups within the workforce have different average levels of pay; although the sector is predominantly female, it is men who get the best paid jobs. Immigrant workers, on the other hand, are the least well paid and work the longest hours (Machin *et al.*, 2010: 18). There is an under-representation of employees from black minority ethnic backgrounds in most types of early years provision and anecdotal evidence that fewer are likely to be qualified at Level 3 and above (Nutbrown, 2012: 48). The proportion of employees with disabilities (1 per cent) is still low compared with an all industry average of 5.18 per cent of the total workforce (National Careers Service, 2010: online). It could therefore be argued that expansion and upskilling of the early years workforce has yet to result in an even spread of opportunities for advancement.

Initiatives to encourage social mobility through opportunities for lifelong learning have often failed to reach poorer families and, while the playgroup model provided a template for this in the past, the current emphasis on Level 3 and above may be making it more difficult for workers from disadvantaged backgrounds to move into the early years workforce (Lochrie, 2009: 17). Nutbrown (2012: 48) recognized that we need more research to tease out the connections between qualifications and employees' backgrounds so that viable progression routes are available to all. Recruitment of early years staff from minority and marginalized groups enhances the workforce by increasing diversity and providing all children with role models, because it demonstrates that people from backgrounds similar to their own can follow a rewarding, responsible and important career like working in the early years sector.

Continuing challenges

We end with an acknowledgement that many challenges remain in the drive to increase professionalism and improve qualifications in the early years sector, and to do so in a manner that really impacts on the quality of provision. Given the current tightening of government purse strings, it is ever more important to (re) consider the evidence carefully on the links between qualifications and quality, as well as wider issues of social mobility, inclusion and diversity and how these play out in the early years sector. Early years care and education provision continues to grow as an employer. The challenge is to ensure that it does so in such a way that young children, families and society receive maximum benefit.

Points for reflection and discussion

1. How might we best combine academic study and practical experience in designing qualifications for working in the early years sector?
2. How useful do you think it is to compare patterns of qualifications, ratios, costs and provision between countries? What other issues does this raise?
3. Where are the men? And why are the men who are in early years treated as 'celebrities'?

Notes

1. The Children's Workforce Development Council endorsed specific early childhood foundation degrees and, through local authorities, provided financial support for practitioners to complete them.
2. The Transformation Fund was introduced in 2006, and replaced by the Graduate Leader Fund in 2007.
3. Ordinary degrees are pass degrees with 300 credits without Honours.
4. We are grateful to Christine Stephen for bringing this to our attention.
5. Up from three babies to four babies aged under two years to each adult, and up from four children to six children aged two to three years to each adult. No change to the ratio of 13 three- to five-year-olds to adults with specified graduate qualification was suggested.

References and further reading

Ball, S. (2003) The teacher's soul and the terror of performativity, *Journal of Educational Policy*, 18(2): 215–28.

Department for Children, Schools and Families (DCSF) (2008) *Early Years Foundation Stage: Everything you need to know*. London: DCSF.

Department for Education (DfE) (2010) *Childcare and Early Years Providers Survey: Research brief*. Available at: https://www.gov.uk/government/publications/childcare-and-early-years-providers-survey-2010 (accessed 16 May 2013).

Department for Education (DfE) (2012) *Statutory Framework for the Early Years Foundation Stage: Setting the standards for learning, development and care for children from birth to five*. Available at: http://www.foundationyears.org.uk/wp-content/uploads/2012/07/EYFS-Statutory-Framework-2012.pdf.

Department for Education (DfE) (2013) *More Great Childcare*. Available at: http://www.education.gov.uk/childrenandyoungpeople/earlylearningandchildcare/a00220847/more-great-childcare (accessed 16 May 2013).

Department for Education and Skills (DfES) (2004) *Foundation Degree Task Force Report to Ministers*. Nottingham: DfES. Available at: http://webarchive.nationalarchives.gov.uk/20130401151715/https://www.education.gov.uk/publications/eOrderingDownload/FDTF%201.pdf.pdf (accessed 16 May 2013).

Education Scotland (2013) *Making the Difference: The impact of staff qualifications on children's learning in early years*. Available at: http://www.educationscotland.gov.uk/inspectionandreview/Images/Making%20the%20Difference_tcm4-735922.pdf (accessed 12 June 2013).

Eisenstadt, N., Sylva, K., Mathers, S. and Taggart, B. (2013) *More Great Childcare: Research evidence*. Available at: http://www.ecersuk.org/resources/More+Great+Childcare+Research+Evidence+March+2013.pdf (accessed 16 May 2013).

Eraut, M. (2007) Learning from other people in the workplace, *Oxford Review of Education: Special Issue on Professional Learning*, 33(4): 403–22.

Evangelou, M., Sylva, K., Kyriacou, M., Wild, M. and Glenny, G. (2009) *Early Years Learning and Development Literature Review*. DCSF Research Report RR176. Oxford: DCSF.

Georgeson, J. (2009) The professionalisation of the early years workforce, in S. Edwards and J. Nuttall (eds.) *Professional Learning in Early Childhood Settings*. Rotterdam: Sense Publishers.

Greenfield, S. (2011) Working in multidisciplinary teams, in L. Miller and C. Cable (eds.) *Professionalization, Leadership and Management in the Early Years*. London: Sage.

Hadfield, M., Jopling, M., Royle, K. and Waller, T. (2010) *First National Survey of Practitioners with EYPS*. Leeds: Children's Workforce Development Council.

Hadfield, M., Jopling, M., Needham, N., Waller, T., Coleyshaw, L. *et al.* (2012) *Longitudinal Study of Early Years Professional Status: An exploration of progress, leadership and impact*. Final Report for the DfE. Wolverhampton: CeDARE, University of Wolverhampton.

Lave, J. and Wenger, E. (1991) *Situated Learning: Legitimate peripheral participation*. Cambridge: University of Cambridge Press.

Lochrie, M. (2009) *Lifelong Learning and the Early Years*. IFLL Sector Paper 3. Leicester: National Institute of Adult Continuing Education.

Lumsden, E. (2012) *The Early Years Professional: A new professional or a missed opportunity? Research overview*. Northampton: University of Northampton.

Machin, S., McNally, S. and Ou, D. (2010) *The Children's Workforce: A data scoping study*. London: Centre for Economics in Education.

Mathers, S. and Sylva, K. (2007) *National Evaluation of the Neighbourhood Nurseries Initiative: The relationship between quality and children's behavioural development*. DfES Research Report SSU/2007/FR/022. Available at: https://www.education.gov.uk/publications/eOrderingDownload/SSU-2007-FR-022.pdf (accessed 16 June 2013).

Mathers, S., Sylva, K. and Joshi, H. (2007) *Quality of Childcare Settings in the Millennium Cohort Study*. DfES Research Report SSU/2007/FR/025. Available at: https://www.education.gov.uk/publications/eOrderingDownload/SSU2007FR025.pdf (accessed 16 May 2013).

Mathers, S., Ranns, H., Karemaker, A., Moody, A., Sylva, K. *et al.* (2011) *Evaluation of the Graduate Leader Fund Final Report*. Research Report 144. Available at: https://www.education.gov.uk/publications/eOrderingDownload/DFE-RR144.pdf (accessed 16 June 2013).

Mathers, S., Singler, R. and Karemaker, A. (2012) *Improving Quality in the Early Years: A comparison of perspectives and measures*. London: Nuffield Foundation. Available at: http://www.education.ox.ac.uk/wordpress/wp-content/uploads/2012/03/Early-Years-QualityMathers-et-al-Final-Report-2012.pdf (accessed 17 June 2013).

McGillivray, G. (2008) Nannies, nursery nurses and early years professionals: Constructions of professional identity in the early years workforce in England, *European Early Childhood Education Research Journal*, 16(2): 242–54.

Miller, L. (2008) Developing professionalism within a regulatory framework in England: Challenges and possibilities, *European Early Childhood Education Research Journal*, 16(2): 255–68.

National Careers Service (2010) Available at: https://nationalcareersservice.direct.gov.uk/Pages/Home.aspx.

Nutbrown, C. (2012) *Foundations for Quality: The independent review of early education and childcare qualifications. Final Report*. Available at: www.education.gov.uk.publications (accessed 17 May 2013).

Owen, S. and Haynes, G. (2008) Developing professionalism in the early years: From policy to practice, in L. Miller and C. Cable (eds.) *Professionalism in the Early Years*. Abingdon: Hodder Education.

Payler, J. and Locke, R. (2013) Disrupting communities of practice? How 'reluctant' practitioners view early years workforce reform in England, *European Early Childhood Education Research Journal*, 21(1): 125–37.

Sylva, K. (2001) *An introduction to EPPE and its methodology.* Paper presented at the BERA EPPE Symposium at BERA 2003. Available at: http://eppe.ioe.ac.uk/eppe/eppepdfs/berapaper2001.pdf (accessed 16 June 2013).

Sylva, K., Melhuish, E., Sammons, P., Siraj-Blatchford, I. and Taggart, B. (2004) *The Effective Provision of Pre-School Education (EPPE) Project: Technical Paper 12 – The Final Report.* London: DfES/Institute of Education.

Sylva, K., Melhuish, E., Sammons, P., Siraj-Blatchford, I. and Taggart, B. (2011) Pre-school quality and educational outcomes at age 11: Low quality has little benefit, *Journal of Early Childhood Research,* 9(2): 109–24.

Whalley, M. (2011) Leading and managing in the early years, in L. Miller and C. Cable (eds.) *Professionalization, Leadership and Management in the Early Years.* London: Sage.

PART 2
A secure foundation

6 Having real conversations: engaging children in talk to extend their language and learning

Michael Jones and Judith Twani

Abstract

Children learn to talk through interaction with adults and other children. The process begins at home, in infancy, as part of parent–child interaction and later through conversations as part of daily life. Conversations at home differ from those in early years settings and can be markedly different from those in school. In this chapter, we argue that parents' interactions with their children and the pedagogy adopted by practitioners and teachers will strongly influence the types of conversations that children will be involved in. This in turn has a significant influence on opportunities for developing language, and on learning in general.

Introduction

Photographs used to illustrate literature about young children's language and learning at home invariably include images of children in conversation while playing or reading with a parent. Photos for language in early years settings show children talking and playing with an adult, or two children talking together. Images in books and articles about primary education are, however, more likely to show a teacher addressing a large group of children, who are sitting on the floor with their hands up. This variation reflects differences in prevailing approaches to communication; young children in early years settings learn through child-initiated activities with supportive adults, while older children in school take part in adult-led, structured activities where the adult exerts control over much that children do, including how they talk and what they talk about.

This change in approach is dictated, to a large extent, by differences in the legal adult-to-child ratios in early years settings and primary schools. There is also a shift in curriculum (in England from Early Years Foundation Stage to National Curriculum), guiding *what* children will be taught and how adults decide to operate within their given framework for organizing and assessing learning. *How* children will be taught is, however, shaped by the accepted group pedagogy – that is, the shared understanding of how children learn and the approaches that are needed to best facilitate learning.

This was reiterated by Tickell in her review of the Early Years Foundation Stage (EYFS) (DfE, 2011) and has been adopted in the revised EYFS (DfE, 2012). The revised EYFS clearly states that the characteristics of effective teaching and learning are (DfE, 2012: 10):

- **playing and exploring** – children investigate and experience things, and 'have a go';
- **active learning** – children concentrate and keep on trying if they encounter difficulties, and enjoy achievements; and
- **creating and thinking critically** – children have and develop their own ideas, make links between ideas, and develop strategies for doing things.

These characteristics provide the foundation for learning, and all depend on the quality of adult interactions with children within the environment (DCSF, 2009a; Sylva *et al.*, 2010; Stewart, 2011). Adults' judgements about when and how to be involved in interactions with children remain central to the EYFS:

> Practitioners must respond to each child's emerging needs and interests, guiding their development through warm, positive interaction.

> Each area of learning and development must be implemented through planned, purposeful play and through a mix of adult-led and child-initiated activity.

> (DfE, 2012: 6)

What constitutes 'planned purposeful play'? Most definitions of 'play' describe it as being chosen and directed by the child. In the National Strategies Publication, *Learning, Playing and Interacting*, it states:

> Play is freely chosen by the child, and is under the control of the child. The child decides how to play, how long to sustain the play, what the play is about, and who to play with... Play is usually highly creative, open-ended and imaginative. It requires active engagement of the players, and can be deeply satisfying.

> (DCSF, 2009a: 10)

It could be argued that all play is purposeful to the child and the adult's role is to discern what that purpose is. By doing so we gain a glimpse into a child's thinking processes and stage of development. Adults' listening and observations provide a platform for sensitive interactions.

Bearing this in mind, how adults and children interact will be influenced by whether the activity in question is 'child-initiated' or 'adult-led'. In child-initiated activities, children decide how an activity will develop and adults extend the children's learning by responding to them through conversation (DCSF, 2009a). Children involved in child-initiated activities in a well-resourced and stimulating environment are likely to talk spontaneously with each other and with adults. This contrasts with adult-led activities, which typically take place in groups and where adults have planned for a possible learning outcome. Where topics are unfamiliar, adults are more likely to lead the conversation and questioning may become closed. The challenge for teachers is how to participate in children's play without taking over: allowing them to lead the conversations and yet also model new vocabulary and develop sustained shared thinking (Siraj-Blatchford *et al.*, 2002). When planning adult-led activities, teachers often identify key vocabulary and some open-ended questions that will support the conversations that they expect to have. One effective strategy that taps into children's natural curiosity is the use of the words "I wonder...", where the adult becomes a learning partner with the children, pondering possibilities aloud.

Detailed case study evidence has shown that effective pedagogy in high-quality settings offers a balance between adult-initiated and child-led activities (Sylva *et al.*, 2010). This balance is best achieved as a natural ebb and flow during the day where experiences and activities are almost seamless. One might contrast this with the situation where a child is deeply engaged in his play with the train set when the practitioner calls him over to 'do an activity'. Immediately the boy's body language changes from being animated and involved to almost dragging himself across the room, to participate in an activity that for him has no meaning or purpose. He simply has to obey a set of instructions that will indicate whether or not he can identify numerals. The sooner he can do this the sooner he can return to what really interests him. It would be much more effective for the practitioner to sit alongside the boy in his play and engage with him in meaningful explorations of ideas and concepts.

This dichotomy particularly needs to be addressed in relation to children with additional speech and language needs, those with relatively limited life experiences, shy children and those who are learning English as an additional language. These children in particular benefit from activities that promote conversation without the teacher leading that conversation.

Language learning begins and continues with relationships

Research into communication in infancy has contributed to a widely held view that we are born with an innate ability to interact with other people. Babies are active in attempting to build relationships, learn new skills and to find out about the world around them (Stern, 1977; Gopnik *et al.*, 1999; Trevarthen, 2003; Gopnik, 2009). Recent research into the process of attachment makes a direct link between babies' experiences of healthy relationships and social interaction with adults in early life and the influences these have on the infant's brain development (Gerhardt, 2008). Gerhardt argues that the key attribute of the baby's parent/carer is that they should be 'tuned in and emotionally available to the child'. Gerhardt's work has had a significant impact on the advice and support given to practitioners, impacting on the way that very young children are cared for within day care settings (Evangelou and Sylva, 2003; Lawrence and Stevenson, 2009; Jones, 2012a). In day care settings, the adult-to-child ratio needs to be maintained at an appropriate number in order to facilitate this close relationship.

Once children begin to talk, interaction changes significantly and includes 'conversation', where language is used to explore ideas through a series of turns. There is evidence that much of children's learning comes from involvement in everyday activities at home with parents, siblings and members of the extended family. The influential Bristol Study (Wells, 2009) analysed interactions between mothers and children at home, and acknowledged the value of children being included in routine daily activities. It was noted that parents engaged children in lengthy and detailed conversation if it was part of what the adults were doing, though only a minority took time to play with their children. Children nonetheless asked complex questions and received satisfactory answers that stimulated their language, learning and understanding of the world and about their place within their family culture and relationships. The study concluded that children have a natural desire to find out about adult activities, and that talking about routine chores is one of the ways they can develop language and learning.

There is recognition that there is a wide variation in parenting styles and children's home experiences, which can have a significant impact on language development and learning (Roulstone *et al.*, 2011). The impact of a positive home learning environment, which includes involvement in everyday conversation, has been shown to have a long-lasting influence on children's learning in early years and later in school (Sylva *et al.*, 2010). Experience of positive sessions with parents, including singing songs, learning nursery rhymes and the basics of number and letter–sound correspondence, had the strongest influence on children's *self-regulation*; that is, where children are actively engaged and thinking about their learning because they are highly motivated (Stewart, 2011). Sylva and colleagues conclude that self-regulation is the aspect of children's development that most influences academic achievement.

The England-wide Every Child a Talker (ECaT) Project was set up in response to major reports that many children in the UK were growing up with language impoverishment, caused largely by lack of experience and limited conversation at home (DfES, 2005; I CAN, 2006; DCSF, 2008b). ECaT has produced many innovative projects and resources to develop parent–child interaction and to improve children's language and communication experiences in early years settings (DCSF, 2008a, 2009b). Central to most ECaT projects was a belief that positive interactions with children at home and in settings are crucially important for well-being, language development and learning. While the impact of the ECaT Project has yet to be officially evaluated, there is anecdotal evidence of major improvements in children's language and social development, due to practitioner training, and improved links between settings and families, including raising parents' awareness of the importance of talk (DCSF, 2009b; Jones, 2009).

Language away from home and the influence of pedagogy

Comparisons between conversations at home and those in nursery schools have found major differences in length of conversations and the complexity of their subject matter. Conversations at home between four-year-old girls and their mothers were generally lengthy, rich in content and satisfying for child and parent. This was in sharp contrast to the generally much shorter and superficial conversations between the same children and staff in their nursery schools (Tizard and Hughes, 2008). Differences between the length and quality of conversations at home and in settings are probably inevitable, primarily due to higher adult-to-child ratios.

Findings of the Researching Effective Pedagogy in the Early Years (REPEY) study and the Effective Provision of Pre-school Education (EPPE) have influenced what is regarded as best practice in conversations between children and adults. REPEY explored the pedagogy within settings identified as 'effective' to find out what it was about their learning environments that might be making them successful (Siraj-Blatchford *et al.*, 2002). One notable feature of their practice was staff's ability to involve children in deep levels of conversation, or sustained shared thinking. This was defined as 'a way of interacting with children that supports and challenges their thinking through conversations'. This level of involvement occurs when 'the interest of both parties' is engaged (Sylva *et al.*, 2010: 3). In other words, just as in the Bristol Study (Wells, 2009), the adult and child need to have something genuinely interesting to talk about and be interested in what each other has to say.

It is therefore essential that priority is given to training staff about the importance of quality conversations with children and engaging babies in stimulating interactions. The Brighton and Hove Quality Improvement in Learning and Teaching (QuILT) Scheme, which is widely used to assess quality in early years settings, contains nine modules, the first of which is 'Relationships and Interactions'. This module must be achieved at the highest level before moving on to other modules, thus acknowledging the central place that quality relationships and interactions should have in any setting.

The potential and challenge of conversation with children

Judith Twani observes: 'I remember sitting down at the end of one particularly long and tiring day in my Reception class and reflecting on my day. I realised that I had not had a conversation with any child during the day. I had taught phonics, asked lots of questions, given instructions, and reminded children how to behave. But I had not engaged in any meaningful conversations all day. I had not had time to listen and respond, and that saddened me. I was left with a feeling of frustration and dissatisfaction and I vowed that things would change.'

If we accept that meaningful conversations in settings and schools are vital for learning, and build on the foundations of language created at home, then we need to explore how to create appropriate opportunities for children to talk. All practitioners need to consider:

- How do my interactions with the children I work with motivate and engage them?
- Do my questions challenge them to think and find out?
- Do I encourage them to speculate and have a go?
- Do I model good spoken English and introduce them to rich vocabulary?
- Do I show that I value their ideas?
- Do I ponder possibilities aloud?

As children get older and adult-to-child ratios change, we need to acknowledge the particular challenges faced by teachers. Opportunities for conversation are significantly restricted and children in large groups are more likely to be competing for adult attention. The EYFS has drawn attention to the importance of a key person approach and in schools this can work most effectively when smaller groups are formed and led by consistent adults. Children are able to grow in confidence and find their voices in smaller groups. Riley (2006) suggests that children and adults need to be involved in real and meaningful conversation about what children are doing. Drawing on the work of Clay (1998), she emphasizes that teachers in classrooms need to maximize the conversational approach of the EYFS by encouraging children to talk with each other and with adults about matters that are important and of shared interest, and particularly capturing children's interests by commenting on and talking about what the children are doing.

To conclude this chapter, we share some examples from our practical experiences of meeting the challenge of having real conversations with children, including those in school, maximizing the 'conversational approach' of the EYFS.

Role play that encourages imagination, children talking together and learning

Role play, in which a child is able to 'become' someone or something else, encourages children to see how it feels to have another point of view and learn that the world looks different to other people (Community Playthings, 2012). Children can act out and make sense of what they have experienced at home, in the local community and in the wider world. Role-play areas, often based on a particular theme, offer rich opportunities for conversation, where children can rehearse roles and the language that goes with them. Role play also helps children to learn how to play and talk with each other, and can give adults a deeper insight into each child's personal world. For example, in a particularly well-resourced home corner with a lounge, bedroom and kitchen, one four-year-old boy sat down on the couch, picked up a magazine and called to the little girl playing with him, 'Make me a cuppa tea, love.'

Language can be enhanced when adults make time to be involved: modelling appropriate use of the space and resources and supporting children to talk together (DCSF, 2009a; Johnson and Jones, 2012). Judith Twani recalls the day she visited a day nursery and became involved in their role-play hospital. Following some in-depth conversations with the children about her symptoms, she found herself wrapped from head to foot in toilet roll (bandages).

However, role play can occur wherever children take part in imaginative play, for example, when adults regard ride-on toys as role-play resources and not simply for physical development; this then influences how staff set up and resource the outdoor play area, which in turn creates more opportunities for conversations and learning. Adults at Quarry Hill Primary School in Thurrock introduced the idea of children passing a 'driving test' before they could go on the ride-on toys. Children had checklists on clipboards which they used as they tested the skills of the 'drivers'. Other children created licences for those children who had passed the test. This project involved adult-led elements and discussions where the teacher helped to introduce the concept of the test and supported children in making the resources. This led to child-initiated activities where the children were able to play and talk together.

Using block play to stimulate all areas of learning

Play with wooden blocks is traditionally associated with construction and often confined to a particular 'construction area'. Used in this way, it has great potential as a tool for learning (Jenner, 2010). However, when block play is used outside the construction area and linked to small world play and writing, the potential for learning and conversations is greatly increased (Community Playthings, 2012).

Staff at Gateway Primary School in Westminster worked with a small group of children with a set of wooden blocks and natural materials including pine cones, twigs, shells, pebbles and pieces of fleece. The children in the school are predominantly from homes where English is the second language. The project began with an adult-led group session where children were supported to create a group story using only the wooden blocks. Children then developed their own stories in smaller groups with sensitive adult support. This type of activity is now part of child-initiated play where children are choosing to involve themselves in the activity. Children are using a high level of abstract thinking, which has had an impact on their use of language and vocabulary development (Jones, 2012b).

Chapel Street Nursery School in Luton took this approach a stage further by combining block play and natural materials with mark making, to stimulate children's language development, and particularly their narrative skills. A group of up to five children and an adult were based around a table covered with white paper. Using small wooden blocks and natural materials and marker pens, they were able to create detailed narratives. The children showed high levels of involvement and cooperation, leading to detailed conversations with each other and with the supporting adult. The adults' ability to remain with the activity and interact sensitively were the most important factors in enabling children initially to join in and remain constructively involved throughout the activity. The adult encouraged the children to talk with each other, show each other what they had been doing, and helped them to share, swap and take turns with resources. Taking a similar approach that includes small world resources is a natural extension of role play and often involves children in highly sophisticated play sequences and use of imaginative language.

Talking about 'Me'

Children will talk about what interests them and nothing interests them more than themselves! Many baby and toddler rooms now incorporate photos of the children's families and themselves, displayed at the children's eye level. This supports their well-being and sense of identity. One baby crawled over to a photo of her mother and kissed it.

As children get older they still enjoy talking about their own experiences and families, such as the three-year-old who told Judith Twani recently that she had 'three cats, two dogs and a brother'. Again, photos of the children can be displayed in different areas of the room that show children involved with each other in activities or demonstrating adult expectations. One preschool created a Golden Rules display using photos of the children to illustrate each of their rules. It was not uncommon to hear the children refer to 'Freddy's Rule' or 'Dami's Rule'.

As part of ECaT in Thurrock, 'All About Me Boxes' have been used successfully to encourage conversations. Children decorate a shoe box and then, at home, with the help of their parents, fill it with things that are special to them. They then have the opportunity to share their box with other children during a small group time (Jones and Belsten, 2011). At Quarry Hill Primary School, one Reception teacher developed this further by creating a corner where the children's boxes were kept. Children could sit on the special chair and share their box freely with their friends without any adult involvement. Most children used this area regularly, and the teacher was able to listen in to their conversations, which supported her assessments.

Talk partners

The creation of 'talk partners', where children are paired up to support each other in talking in large groups, has an impact on the participation of children who may not otherwise be confident enough to join in verbally. The quiet child can find his or her voice when a teacher asks a question by simply turning and talking to the child sitting next to them. This can be used just as effectively in small groups, where children are encouraged to think out loud, problem solve and share their own ideas. At Crays Hill Primary School in Thurrock, for example, the Reception teacher uses talk partners throughout the day. On one occasion, the children had been making a roof for the climbing frame using bamboo sticks. At the end of the session she took the group outside and the initiator of the activity shared what he had done. The children then chatted with their partner about how they could continue this and make the roof even better.

Sharing books

Sharing books with children has great potential for 'real conversations' between children and adults, given that there is something of interest for both to talk about and explore. However, the experience will be greatly enhanced if the child is able to choose a book that is relevant to their interests and prior knowledge. This may be a non-fiction book that has a particular interest and allows the child to talk in detail about the photographs on any page, as opposed to a story book that has to be read and talked about in sequence to make any sense. This observation is reinforced by research investigating the causes of low achievement in reading (Nicolls, 2004). In this study, regular sessions where children were allowed to talk about a non-fiction book of their choice increased children's reading ability and comprehension of vocabulary. As part of the process, children were able to have genuinely interesting and stimulating conversations with the teacher about a subject that the child had knowledge of – that is, a 'real conversation'. This indicates the value of using pedagogy perhaps more associated with younger children to support the learning of older children, and the power of conversation to support learning.

Interesting places and spaces

This chapter would be incomplete without some reference to how a well-planned environment can enable conversation. Quarry Hill, a three-form entry primary school in Thurrock, decided to create different zones in the three Reception class-rooms to provide three different experiences for children during 'free-flow'. One room was specifically designed to promote communication and language, so included a well-resourced role-play area, numerous small world resources, a Chat-terbox area and investigative resources.

The outdoor area can provide a vast storehouse of possibilities for rich con-versations, particularly where there is access to the natural world. Judith Twani describes her first experience of an afternoon in the forest with Mr. Noah's Nursery School in Iden Green, Kent: 'We were walking through the village to the woods and I followed two boys who were deep in conversation. I was intrigued and drew closer only to hear one boy say, "But my favourite sort of leaf is one that is pale green and shiny." They had engaged with one another and with the natural world, which resulted in a rich descriptive vocabulary and this level of conversation was heard throughout the afternoon.'

Conclusion

The frameworks that adults use to support children's learning, including the EYFS, will shape opportunities for language development through conversation. Chal-lenges exist when trying to engage children in conversation in group situations, particularly with older children in school. We have offered practical suggestions and a theoretical rational for the development of 'real conversations' between chil-dren and adults, and to encourage children to talk with each other.

Points for reflection and discussion

1. Sustained shared thinking takes time. How can we best deploy staff to be able to remain at an activity without being disturbed, so that child and adult can explore their ideas through sustained shared thinking? And how can we encourage deeper conversations between children?
2. The environment is a powerful 'third teacher'. Where do the best conver-sations take place? Do my displays prompt discussions? Have we created areas specifically to support conversations?
3. Sharing books with children from an early age is important and particularly for children requiring support with language development and reading. Are all staff involved with sharing books, and know how to do this effectively and appropriately?
4. Outline what training might be required so that all staff have a shared vision of how children can be engaged in play that promotes language development and learning.

References and further reading

Clay, M. (1998) *By Different Paths to Common Outcomes.* York: Stenhouse Publishers.

Community Playthings (2012) *Play and the Revised EYFS: How role play embraces all aspects of learning and social development.* Available at: www.communityplaythings. co.uk (accessed 10 May 2013).

Department for Children, Schools and Families (DCSF) (2008a) *Every Child a Talker: Guidance for early language lead practitioners.* Available at: www.education.gov.uk (accessed 10 May 2013).

Department for Children, Schools and Families (DCSF) (2008b) *The Bercow Report: A review of services for children and young people (0–19) with speech, language and communication needs.* Available at: http://dera.ioe.ac.uk/8405/1/7771-dcsf-bercow.pdf (accessed 12 May 2013).

Department for Children, Schools and Families (DCSF) (2009a) *Learning, Playing and Interacting: Good practice in the Early Years Foundation Stage.* London: DCSF.

Department for Children, Schools and Families (DCSF) (2009b) *Every Child a Talker: Guidance for consultants and early language lead practitioners. Third Instalment: Destination every child a talker.* Available at: http://webarchive.nationalarchives.gov. uk/20130401151715/https://www.education.gov.uk/publications/eOrderingDownload/ DCSF-00971-2009.pdf (accessed 15 May 2013).

Department for Education (DfE) (2011) *The Early Years; Foundations for life, health and learning (The Tickell Review).* Available at: www.education.gov.uk (accessed 15 May 2013).

Department for Education (DfE) (2012) *Statutory Framework for the Early Years Foundation Stage: Setting the standards for learning, development and care for children from birth to five.* Available at: http://www.foundationyears.org.uk/wp-content/ uploads/2012/07/EYFS-Statutory-Framework-2012.pdf.

Department for Education and Skills (DfES) (2005) *National Evaluation of Sure Start.* Available at: http://www.ness.bbk.ac.uk/implementation/documents/1185.pdf (accessed 20 May 2013).

Evangelou, M. and Sylva, K. (2003) *The Effects of the Peers Early Educational Partnership (PEEP) on Children's Developmental Progress.* DfES Research Report No. 489. Available at: www.education.gov.uk (accessed 10 May 2013).

Gerhardt, S. (2008) *Why Love Matters: How affection shapes a baby's brain.* London: Routledge.

Gopnik, A. (2009) *The Philosophical Baby.* London: Bodley Head.

Gopnik, A., Meltzoff, A. and Kuhl, P. (1999) *How Babies Think: The science of childhood.* London: Weidenfeld & Nicolson.

I CAN (2006) *The Cost to the Nation of Children's Poor Communication.* Available at: www. ican.org.uk (accessed 1 May 2013).

Jenner, F. (2010) *Block Play: A guide for Early Years Foundation Stage practitioners.* Suffolk: Suffolk County Council.

Johnson, M. and Jones, M. (2012) *Supporting Quiet Children.* Birmingham: Lawrence Educational.

Jones, M. (2009) Make every child a talker, *Early Years Educator,* 11(6): 64–6.

Jones, M. (2012a) Baby room brilliance, *Early Years Educator,* 13(10): 35–7.

Jones, M. (2012b) Building blocks to literacy, *Early Years Educator,* 14(5): 35–7.

Jones, M. and Belsten, J. (2011) *Let's Get Talking!* Birmingham: Lawrence Educational.

Lawrence, V. and Stevenson, C. (2009) *The Northamptonshire Baby Room Project: Facilitators' manual.* Available at: www.northamptonshirebabyroom.org (accessed 10 May 2013).

Nicolls, E. (2004) *The contribution of the shared reading of expository books to the development of language and literacy.* Unpublished PhD thesis, University of Oxford.

Office for Standards in Education (OfSTED) (2012) *Conducting Early Years Inspections.* Available at: http://www.ofsted.gov.uk/resources/conducting-early-years-inspections (accessed 10 June 2013).

Riley, J. (2006) *Language and Literacy 3–7*. London: Paul Chapman.

Roulstone, S., Law, J., Rush, R., Clegg, J. and Peters, T. (2011) *Investigating the Role of Language in Children's Early Educational Outcomes.* DfE Research Report No. 134. London: HMSO.

Siraj-Blatchford, I., Sylva, K., Muttock, S., Gilden, R. and Bell, D. (2002) *Researching Effective Pedagogy in the Early Years (REPEY)*. DfES Research Report No. 356. London: HMSO.

Stern, D. (1977) *The First Relationship: Infant and mother.* Cambridge, MA: Harvard University Press.

Stewart, N. (2011) *How Children Learn: The characteristics of effective early learning*. London: The British Association for Early Childhood Education.

Sylva, K., Melhuish, E., Sammons, P., Siraj-Blatchford, I. and Taggart, B. (2010) *Early Childhood Matters: Evidence from the Effective Pre-school and Primary Education Project (EPPE)*. London: Routledge.

Tizard, B. and Hughes, M. (2008) *Young Children Learning.* London: Blackwell.

Trevarthen, C. (2003) Video discussing infants' development of communication. Available at: http://www.educationscotland.gov.uk/earlyyears/prebirthtothree/nationalguidance/conversations/colwyntrevarthen.asp (accessed 11 May 2013).

Wells, G. (2009) *The Meaning Makers: Learning to talk and talking to learn*, 2nd edn. Bristol: Multilingual Matters.

7   Physical development and outdoor play

Jane Waters

Abstract

This chapter contextualizes and critically considers the opportunities for children's physical development and outdoor play in the early years. It includes an overview of contemporary and neurological research indicating the importance of movement for children's general development, highlights key aspects of high-quality provision and outlines critical issues, such as providing for exploratory and risky play. Effective outdoor play provision has the potential to support children's secure foundations; however, such outcomes are at risk within a content-driven and instrumental approach to early years provision. The chapter concludes with guidance for practitioners to overcome the obstacles inherent in such an approach by working in partnership with stakeholders.

Introduction: Movement and development

The development of neuroscience has brought with it the possibility that we can know 'what works' in early childhood in terms of healthy (or even accelerated) cognitive development. However, neuroscientists have consistently warned against educators making inferences based on neuroscientific research and assuming application to educational practice (e.g. Bruer, 2002, 2006; Blakemore and Frith, 2005). Despite this, preliminary and exploratory research in neuroscience has led to some simplistic and even mass-market responses. For example, the myths that surround accelerated learning and critical periods; the links between cross-lateral movements (gym for the brain) and cognitive development; and the cognitive benefits of exposing a baby to music by certain composers in the pre- and post-natal periods; are all based on preliminary research or studies that claim to have a 'brain-based' evidence base (Bruer, 2006).

Pellegrini and Smith (1998: 577) hypothesized that 'there may be cognitive benefits of exercise play'. There is now a growing evidence base in neurological research (e.g. Diamond, 2000; Munakata *et al.*, 2004) as well as psychological research (e.g. Hillman *et al.*, 2009; Roebers and Kauer, 2009; Davis *et al.*, 2011) that movement and cognitive development are associated. Davis *et al.* (2011) charted the interrelation between cognitive and motor skills in 248 typically developing children aged four to eleven years from one county in the UK in order to explore whether the underlying neural network serving cognitive and motor functioning is linked (as suggested by Diamond, 2000) or distinct (as suggested by Dyck *et al.*, 2009). The authors concluded that the 'neural structures recruited for cognitive and motor tasks are connected, even in early childhood, and mature at similar rates' (Davis *et al.*, 2011: 580). The implication of this significant finding is that:

> ... the child's dynamic interaction with the environment is important for learning...this interaction is supported by a close coupling of the primary sense, that is VP [visual processing], and a physical connection with the environment, that is fine motor control.
>
> (Davis *et al.*, 2011: 580)

The provision of environments for childcare and early education that are highly stimulating to all aspects of motor and cognitive skill are recommended so as to 'exploit this association and maximise learning potential' (Davis *et al.*, 2011: 581). Importantly, it is acknowledged that any causal direction or underlying reciprocity in the development of this relationship is yet to be determined.

Learning theory that relates movement to cognitive development is not new – see, for example, Wood's (1997: 21) consideration of Piagetian theory: 'thought is internalised action'; and Athey's work (2007) based on schema theory in which the child uses different movement forms to make sense of, explore and test the boundaries of the external world and their understanding of it. That developments in neuroscience and psychology appear empirically to support such theoretical links between movement and cognitive development encourages us as a community of educators and learners to attend closely to the movement opportunities we provide in the child's earliest years.

While physical development receives less attention in the literature than cognitive and social development (Lindon, 2005), healthy physical development is predicated upon having the opportunity to move frequently and vigorously in early childhood (see overview given by Bilton, 2010; Tovey, 2007). To refine and practise skills involving gross motor movements such as kicking, throwing, jumping, hopping and running requires ready and frequent access to spaces that actively encourage and support such activity, both physically (in terms of what is provided) and socially (in terms of what is allowed). Outdoor spaces tend to meet these requirements (see Maynard *et al.*, 2013). But as Bilton (2010: 31) clearly states, 'there is movement and there is physical development; the former is a mode through which children can learn and the latter is one aspect of child development'. In addition to building strong muscles and bones, being vigorously active in childhood may support a healthy disposition to movement and physical activity throughout childhood and in later life (see Ouvry, 2003; Tovey, 2007). Exercise also improves brain function (Blakemore and Frith, 2005). The development of increasingly refined motor coordination is also offered by playful activity in the outdoor environment; such opportunity is essential for successful engagement in activities that require good hand–eye coordination such as manipulation of tools, writing, drawing, sorting, dressing and feeding.

The potential of high-quality provision

Outdoor spaces have long been associated with gross physical development in the early years; this section briefly outlines the potential to support fine motor skill development, positive attitudes to risk, provision of challenge, problem solving and enquiry, as well as high-quality interactions with adults (see also Bilton, 2010).

White's (2008, 2013) work with babies and very young children playing and exploring the outdoor environment provides an excellent resource for the consideration of what is possible in terms of high-quality outdoor provision for very young children. The features of high-quality provision that recur throughout this body of work include physical features (e.g. variability, flexibility, high number of loose parts) as well as social/cultural features (e.g. having control, being allowed to lift, move, redesign, build, break, destroy, reconstruct, look, listen).

Effective outdoor provision in the early years has the potential to support children's secure foundations. The affordance of different spaces for children's motor skills development is well documented (see, for example, Fjørtoft, 2004; Tovey, 2007; Storli and Hagen, 2010); the inclusion of variation in the environment – slopes, mixed vegetation, natural obstacles – can support multiple, varied play themes (Fjørtoft and Sageie, 2000); and access to the changing seasons within the outdoor space offers opportunities for additional variation – a dry slope to roll down in the summer becomes a precarious challenge in the winter for superhero players. The appearance of seeds and nuts in autumn provides an opportunity for sorting, gathering and natural small world play. If such varied outdoor provision is not possible within the setting's site, then even infrequent visits to local natural spaces can offer benefits that are not available inside the school grounds (Waters and Maynard, 2010).

Sandseter (2009) outlines how children can develop positive and appropriate attitudes to risk in their physical play in outdoor spaces that support 'risky play'. While the potential association with a healthy approach to risk in later life remains theoretical (Sandseter and Kennair, 2011), Waller (2007) has identified how positive learning dispositions can be observed in children's playful engagement with the natural environment. The child–adult interactions afforded by young children's interest in the natural world offers the opportunity for sustained and shared thinking between teachers and children, which is directly related to children's enquiry-based interests (Waters, 2011; Waters and Bateman, 2013).

Tension in provision: risk, challenge and autonomy

There are inherent challenges for early years practitioners in providing an outdoor environment that fulfils the potential identified above. Curricular restrictions are considered below but possibly the most significant challenges lie in the cultural restrictions imposed by a risk-averse (e.g. Furedi, 2002, 2008) and increasingly litigious society (e.g. Davies, 2009). When practitioners are working within a culture that seeks to protect children from any harm, where bruising or a scratch from a bramble are cause for concern and there is a belief that a broken bone is likely to lead to litigation, then the safest route for the early years practitioner is to provide a carefully planned, safe and sterile outdoor space in which children engage with objects in a structured manner (albeit on a large scale) that are health-and-safety checked to ensure minimum risk of any harm.

Stephenson sums up the risk of this type of response clearly: if you make an environment risk-free it becomes challenge-free, and then 'children have less experience in making decisions on their own, less opportunity to assess their own personal frontiers and less opportunity to gain confidence and self esteem through coping independently' (Stephenson, 2003: 42).

However, resilience is increasingly considered as an important learning disposition (Claxton and Carr, 2004; Siraj-Blatchford, 2010). Resilient children (Werner and Smith, 1982) are those who are able to experience a setback and recover without retreating into a 'helpless' orientation (Dweck and Leggett, 1988) to the task. 'Mastery-oriented' children tend to focus strategies for success instead of worrying that they are incompetent. These dispositions to learn seem to be very powerful and are associated with the development of positive early personal and social identities (Dweck and Leggett, 1988; Carr and Lee, 2012). While these identities can be associated with the home learning environment (see, for example, Siraj-Blatchford, 2010), they have also been associated with exposure to self-directed risky play (e.g. Stephenson, 2003). Many children enjoy risk taking and seek out risky play (Stephenson, 2003; Sandseter, 2009; Sandseter and Kennair, 2011) and the provision of unchallenging play spaces threatens to forfeit children's meaningful engagement in outdoor play and exploration.

Prepared for school, prepared for life?

Within the early years national curricula of Scotland, Wales, Northern Ireland and England, different approaches are taken to the provision, use and value of outdoor play/learning spaces. Arguably, the English model is the most restrictive, indicating an instrumental view of children's play and outdoor provision, where the other curricula indicate that the outdoor space is seen as a route to conceptual, personal and instrumental aspects of learning and development.

In Scotland, the Curriculum for Excellence 3–18 aims to ensure that all children and young people in Scotland develop the attributes, knowledge and skills they will need to flourish in life, learning and work. As part of the Early Years Framework (Scottish Government, 2008a), ten elements of transformational change are identified, the eighth being 'Improving outcomes and children's quality of life through play' (p. 18). Within this element there is an explicit commitment to outdoor play provision including open and green space provision. The Scottish Government have explicitly sought to address concerns about risk to children when they play:

> While we must act to limit young children's exposure to risks they cannot control, giving children responsibility and allowing them to explore the world in a way that is appropriate to their age and development in a way that they can control is a key part of developing confidence. There is a feeling that, in recent times, there has been too much focus on eliminating all

risk to children rather than understanding risk. We must reverse this trend and equip children with the skills to manage risk and make positive choices based on assessing the situation facing them.

(Scottish Government, 2008b: 29)

Similarly, the Welsh Foundation Phase Framework for Children aged 3–7 Years (DCELLS, 2008) positions the outdoor space as a learning space, used to support concept development as well as physical, social and emotional development on an equal footing with the indoor space:

> Indoor and outdoor environments that are fun, exciting, stimulating and safe promote children's development and natural curiosity to explore and learn through first-hand experiences. The Foundation Phase environment should promote discovery and independence and a greater emphasis on using the outdoor environment as a resource for children's learning.

(DCELLS, 2008: 4)

The need for children to 'take risks' is explicitly acknowledged (e.g. DCELLS, 2008: 4, 16).

In Northern Ireland (CCEA, 2007), the Foundation Stage requires that children use the outdoor space for play in order to develop physical (fine and gross motor) skills, to explore and solve problems and for social/emotional development. In documentation recommended by CCEA, risk management is seen to be the role of the child as well as the adult (EYIP 2005: 138); risk taking is acknowledged as an essential part of children's play behaviour and the taking of 'safe risks' (EYIP 2005: 121) encouraged.

The recently revised English early years curriculum document, the 'Foundation Stage' (DfE, 2012), is aligned with a readiness agenda; in its opening statement it refers to the promotion of 'teaching and learning to ensure children's "school readiness"' (DfE, 2012: 2). The document positions the child as a *person-in-waiting* (e.g. Wyness, 2006; Dahlberg *et al.*, 2007), being prepared for school by the adults with whom he or she comes into contact. The references to the outdoor space are limited to the requirement to ensure access to an outdoor play space on a daily basis (DfE, 2012: 24). Other than that, references to physical development are highly instrumental: related to the development of coordination, and the understanding that physical activity is important for long-term health (e.g. DfE, 2012: 8). Risk is mentioned only in relation to the need for adults to assess risk; there is no reference to the conceptual learning opportunities inherent in rich outdoor experiences. This approach, if adhered to without question, risks losing the potential for deep learning in outdoor spaces, based on social constructivist principles of meaning making (e.g. Aasen *et al.*, 2009; Dahlberg and Moss, 2009; Waters and Bateman, 2013).

Overcoming the obstacles together

The foregoing indicates that there may be significant challenges for early years practitioners in resolving the issues inherent in providing valuable outdoor spaces for children's play and learning, especially in an English context. There are three specific aspects that may help early years setting managers and practitioners overcome the obstacles:

Partnership working

By being clear in policies, guidance and promotional material that the setting values children's outdoor activity, including the opportunities it offers for challenge and managed risk-taking, parents/carers are able to make an informed choice about the provision they choose for their children. Explaining why the setting adopts such an approach also allows stakeholders to understand and offer support in the event of minor bumps and bruises resulting from effective engagement in stimulating outdoor play. 'Write a safeness policy that can be passed on to the parents and carers' (EYIP, 2005: 138) in order to develop a shared understanding of the approach taken to risk and challenge.

Planning together for risky play

The approach promoted by the EYIP (2005: 138) in Northern Ireland involves the notion of 'safeness' as 'enabling things to happen, not shutting down opportunities'. Children are involved in regular discussion about safeness, risk and challenge, raising the children's awareness of the need to take risks 'safely'. By scaffolding children into pro-active risk consideration in this way, practitioners support them to share the responsibility of keeping safe when taking part in physically challenging play and exploration. Such an approach indicates respect for children's developing capabilities and an expectation of their independence; in addition, according to Stephenson (2003), it may also support children's development of positive dispositions to learning such as resilience and a willingness to 'have a go'.

Careful consideration of outdoor provision in terms of its affordances for children's development

Review the setting's outdoor provision regularly; consider the opportunities it offers for children's development in terms of engaging cognitive enquiry, exploration and sustained talk, as well as gross and fine motor skills development and the development of specific curriculum-related learning goals. There are three aspects to consider when thinking of the opportunities ('affordance') offered by an environment for specific individuals:

1. The *physical* aspect: this includes what and who is in the space with which/ whom to interact;
2. The *intrapersonal* aspect: this relates to the interests and motivation of particular children; and
3. The *cultural aspect*: this relates to the 'rules of the space'; what is encouraged, sanctioned and allowed to happen in the space (Waters, 2011).

By considering these three aspects when we evaluate what children do in the environments provided for them, we can review how we may need to alter aspects of the space to maximize its potential.

Conclusion

Planning and working together means that providers can maximize the potential of outdoor provision, despite the challenges of social and curricula restrictions, to ensure young children's life-long needs for physical activity, play, exploration and movement are, in part at least, catered for in their early years.

Points for reflection and discussion

1. How do I feel about allowing children to take risks in my outdoor space? What if a child sustained a minor injury?
2. Are the children in my care exposed to a rich environment outside that affords exploration, multiple interpretations as well as the development of gross and fine motor skills?
3. How do I interact with children outside? Does this support them in making meaning from their experiences?
4. With parents: how can we all work together to make sure our children get the most out of the opportunities provided by being outside?
5. With early years staff: what strategies and procedures do we need in place to allow children to take risks while ensuring they are not in danger?
6. Generally: what kind of learning does our current outdoor provision support – instrumental learning or conceptual learning?

References and further reading

Aasen, W., Grindheim, L.T. and Waters, J. (2009) The outdoor environment as a site for children's participation, meaning-making and democratic learning: Examples from Norwegian kindergartens, *Education 3–13*, 37(1): 5–13.

Athey, C. (2007) *Extending Thought in Young Children: A parent/teacher partnership*. London: Sage.

Bilton, H. (2010) *Outdoor Learning in the Early Years: Management and innovation*. London: Routledge.

Blakemore, S. and Frith, U. (2005) *The Learning Brain*. Oxford: Blackwell.

Bruer, T. (2002) Avoiding the paediatrician's error: How neuroscientists can help educators (and themselves), *Nature Neuroscience Supplement*, 5: 1031–3.

Bruer, T. (2006) *Brain-based Education*. PhiDeltaKappa International. Available at: http://www.dr-hatfield.com/educ538/docs/Bruer,%2B2006.pdf (accessed 20 January 2013).

Carr, M. and Lee, W. (2012) *Learning Stories: Constructing learner identity in early education*. London: Sage.

Claxton, G. and Carr, M. (2004) A framework for teaching learning: Learning dispositions, *Early Years: An International Journal of Research and Development*, 24(1): 87–97.

Council for Curriculum Examinations and Assessment (CCEA) (2007) *Northern Ireland Curriculum Primary*. Belfast: CCEA. Available at: http://www.nicurriculum.org.uk/docs/key_stages_1_and_2/northern_ireland_curriculum_primary.pdf (accessed 20 January 2013).

Dahlberg, G. and Moss, P. (2009) Foreword, in L.M. Olsson, *Movement and Experimentation in Young Children's Learning: Deleuze and Guattari in early childhood education*. London: Routledge.

Dahlberg, G., Moss, P. and Pence, A. (2007) *Beyond Quality in Early Childhood Education and Care*, 2nd edn. London: RoutledgeFalmer.

Davies, T.A. (2009) The worrisome state of legal literacy among teachers and administrators, *Canadian Journal for New Scholars in Education*, 2(1). Available at: http://www.cjnse-rcjce.ca/ojs2/index.php/cjnse/article/view/116 (accessed 24 May 2013).

Davis, E.E., Pitchford, N.J. and Limback, E. (2011) The interrelation between cognitive and motor development in typically developing children aged 4–11 years is underpinned by visual processing and fine manual control, *British Journal of Psychology*, 102: 569–84.

DCELLS (2008) *Framework for Children's Learning for 3-to-7 Year Olds in Wales*. Cardiff: Welsh Assembly Government. Available at: http://wales.gov.uk/dcells/publications/policy_strategy_and_planning/early-wales/whatisfoundation/foundationphase/2274085/frameworkforchildrene.pdf (accessed 20 January 2013).

Department for Education (DfE) (2012) *Statutory Framework for the Early Years Foundation Stage: Setting the standards for learning, development and care for children from birth to five*. Available at: http://www.foundationyears.org.uk/wp-content/uploads/2012/07/EYFS-Statutory-Framework-2012.pdf

Diamond, A. (2000) Close interrelation of motor development and cognitive development and of the cerebellum and prefrontal cortex, *Child Development*, 71: 44–56.

Dweck, C. and Leggett, E. (1988) A social-cognitive approach to motivation and personality, *Psychological Review*, 95(2): 256–73.

Dyck, M.J., Piek, J.P., Kane, R. and Patrick, J. (2009) How uniform is the structure of ability across childhood?, *European Journal of Developmental Psychology*, 6(4): 432–54.

Early Years Interpanel Board (2005) *Learning Outdoors in the Early Years*. Northern Ireland: EYIP.

Fjørtoft, I. (2001) The natural environment as a playground for children: The impact of outdoor play activities in pre-primary school children, *Early Education Journal*, 29(2): 111–17.

Fjørtoft, I. (2004) Landscape as playscape: The effects of natural environments on children's play and motor development, *Children, Youth and Environments*, 14(2): 21–44.

Fjørtoft, I. and Sageie, J. (2000) The natural environment as a playground for children: Landscape description and analyses of a natural playscape, *Landscape and Urban Planning*, 48(1/2): 83–97.

Furedi, F. (2002) *Culture of Fear*, 2nd edn. London: Continuum.

Furedi, F. (2008) *Paranoid Parenting*, 2nd edn. London: Continuum.

Hillman, C.H., Pontifex, M.B., Raine, L.B., Castelli, D.M., Hall, E.E. and Kramer, A.F. (2009) The effect of acute treadmill walking on cognitive control and academic achievement in preadolescent children, *Neuroscience*, 159(3): 1044–54.

Lindon, J. (2005) *Understanding Child Development: Linking theory and practice*. London: Hodder/Arnold.

Maynard, T. and Waters, J. (2007) Learning in the outdoor environment: A missed opportunity?, *Early Years: An International Journal of Research and Development*, 27(3): 255–65.

Maynard, T., Waters, J. and Clement, J. (2013) Child-initiated learning, the outdoor environment and the 'underachieving' child, *Early Years: An International Journal of Research and Development*, 33(3): 212–25.

Munakata, Y., Casey, B.J. and Diamond, A. (2004) Developmental cognitive neuroscience: Progress and potential, *Trends in Cognitive Sciences*, 8(3): 122–8.

Ouvry, M. (2003) *Exercising Muscles and Minds*. London: National Children's Bureau.

Pellegrini, A.D. and Smith, P.K. (1998) Physical activity play: The nature and function of a neglected aspect of play, *Child Development*, 69(3): 577–98.

Roebers, C.M. and Kauer, M. (2009) Motor and cognitive control in a normative sample of 7-year-olds, *Developmental Science*, 12(1): 175–81.

Sandseter, E.B.H. (2009) Children's expressions of exhilaration and fear in risky play, *Contemporary Issues in Early Childhood*, 10(2): 92–106.

Sandseter, E.B.H. and Kennair, L.E.O. (2011) Children's risky play from an evolutionary perspective: The anti-phobic effects of thrilling experiences, *Evolutionary Psychology*, 9(2): 257–84.

Scottish Government (2008a) *Early Years Framework (Part I)*. Edinburgh: Scottish Government. Available at: http://www.scotland.gov.uk/Resource/Doc/257007/0076309.pdf (accessed 20 January 2013).

Scottish Government (2008b) *Early Years Framework (Part II)*. Edinburgh: Scottish Government. Available at: http://www.scotland.gov.uk/Resource/Doc/257007/0076310.pdf (accessed 20 January 2013).

Siraj-Blatchford, I. (2010) Learning in the home and at school: How working class children 'succeed against the odds', *British Educational Research Journal*, 36(3): 463–82.

Stephenson, A. (2003) Physical risk taking: Dangerous or endangered?, *Early Years: An International Journal of Research and Development*, 23(1): 35–43.

Storli, R. and Hagen, T.L. (2010) Affordances in outdoor environments and children's physically active play in pre-school, *European Early Childhood Education Research Journal*, 18(4):445–56.

Tovey, H. (2007) *Playing Outdoors: Spaces and places, risks and challenges*. Maidenhead: McGraw-Hill.

Waller, T. (2007) The trampoline tree and the swamp monster with 18 heads: Outdoor play in the Foundation Stage and the Foundation Phase, *Education 3–13*, 35(4): 393–407.

Waller, T., Sandseter, E.B.H., Wyver, S., Ärlemalm-Hagsér, E. and Maynard, T. (2010) The dynamics of early childhood spaces: Opportunities for outdoor play?, *European Early Childhood Education Research Journal*, 18(4): 437–43.

Waters, J. (2011) *A sociocultural consideration of child-initiated interaction with teachers in indoor and outdoor spaces*. Unpublished PhD thesis, University of Swansea.

Waters, J. and Bateman, A. (2013) Revealing the interactional features of learning and teaching moments in outdoor activity, *European Early Childhood Education Research Journal*. Available at: http://www.tandfonline.com/doi/pdf/ 10.1080/1350293X.2013.798099 (accessed 24 May 2013).

Waters, J. and Maynard, T. (2010) What elements of the natural outdoor environment do children of 4–7 years attend to in their child-initiated interactions with teachers?, *European Early Childhood Education Research Journal*, 18(4): 473–83.

Werner, E.E. and Smith, R. (1982) *Vulnerable but Invincible: A longitudinal study of resilient children and youth*. New York: McGraw-Hill.

White, J. (2008) *Playing and Learning Outdoors: Making provision for high-quality experiences in the outdoor environment*. Abingdon: Routledge.

White, J. (2013) *Jan White Natural Play*. Available at: http://janwhitenaturalplay.wordpress.com (accessed 4 January 2013).

Wood, D. (1997) *How Children Think and Learn*, 2nd edn. Oxford: Blackwell.

Wyness, M. (2006) *Childhood and Society: An introduction to the sociology of childhood*. Basingstoke: Palgrave Macmillan.

Useful websites

http://janwhitenaturalplay.wordpress.com – 'Natural Play, Natural Growth, in the Early Years' resources, readings, practical ideas and inspiring images.

http://www.ncb.org.uk/cpis – The Children's Play Information Service (CPIS) is a national information service on children's play, part of NCB's Information Centre; includes an extensive reference library that holds considerable material pertaining to outdoor play.

http://www.educationscotland.gov.uk – Search 'outdoor play' and find over 80 articles related to practice-based solutions to issues related to outdoor play provision across the school age range.

8 Personal, social and emotional development

Anita Soni

Abstract

Personal, social and emotional development (PSED) has been identified as a prime area of learning and development within the Statutory Framework for the Early Years Foundation Stage (EYFS) (DfE, 2012). This chapter discusses the importance of PSED as a prime area, a foundation for all learning, and the relationship of the prime areas and the specific areas as children progress from birth to seven years. The way in which the Key Person approach is reflected in PSED and in the EYFS will be examined, followed by a review of continuity relating to PSED and the Key Person approach from birth, through the EYFS and into Key Stage 1.

Introduction: The importance of personal, social and emotional development as a prime area

Tickell (2011) recommended there should be three prime areas of learning and development in the revised Early Years Foundation Stage (EYFS). She identified these prime areas as foundations for healthy development, essential to promoting children's interest in learning both in the immediate term and for the future. Indeed, Tickell went as far as to say:

> Without secure development in these particular areas during this critical period, children will struggle to progress…It is when those foundations are not strong that we can see children struggle, finding it difficult to focus, to adapt to routines, and to cooperate with others.
>
> (Tickell, 2011: 21)

Personal, social and emotional development (PSED) is one of these prime areas, and was viewed by many practitioners (89 per cent) and parents (81 per cent) as one of the foundations for learning (Tickell, 2011). Tickell identified the importance of self-regulation in the early years for later success within the 'academic' subjects such as literacy and numeracy as one of the reasons for selecting PSED as a prime area. The ability to self-regulate is dependent on the early experiences a child has, including those in early years settings, and occurs universally across different cultures. Tickell defines self-regulation as the 'will' to learn and the 'skill' to be aware of one's own thinking, feelings and behaviour. Within PSED, self-regulation can be seen to relate to the ability to control and manage one's own behaviour and to understand and manage emotion.

Schaffer (1996) states that in their earliest years, babies rely on adults to support their emotional regulation, as babies require help with soothing and comfort. He suggests self-control occurs at about two years onwards and self-regulation at about three years onwards, as both are linked to cognitive prerequisites such as representational thinking and recall memory. Blair *et al.* (2004; cited in Evangelou *et al.*, 2009) identify that early years practitioners working and playing with young children should talk about and discuss different emotions using stories and scenarios to help children develop emotional awareness and self-regulation. Denham *et al.* (2003) suggest direct teaching about feelings is helpful for children aged four years and under and that children who are less emotionally regulated may benefit from learning constructive emotion regulating strategies such as active problem solving, cognitive restructuring and avoidance. Active problem solving occurs through discussions about different ways to resolve situations; cognitive restructuring involves reviewing alternative ways of thinking about the situation; and avoidance means helping the child identify situations that they find emotionally difficult.

Kochanska *et al.* (2001) researched children's self-regulation of behaviour through comparison of situational compliance: comparing children's *superficial compliance* with adult requests when the adult is there, with children's *committed compliance* with an adult's wishes regardless of the adult's presence. Children tend to move from situational compliance to committed compliance over the first three years, demonstrating voluntary, adaptive self-regulatory behaviour. However, Schaffer (1996) states that a degree of non-compliance should be anticipated at about two years, as children are learning to assert their own autonomy and independence. Kochanska and Aksan (2006) suggest that 'effortful control' such as the ability to wait for a turn emerges in the child's second year, and predicts self-regulation of behaviour in later years. This is related both to the internal temperament of the child and the socialization of the family in relation to the style of parental discipline and quality of the parent–child relationship. Furthermore, Laible *et al.* (2008) examined the link between conflict and attachment and found that the manner with which conflict was *negotiated* and *resolved* was significant in promoting a secure attachment rather than the level of conflict that occurred.

While this research on the self-regulation of behaviour is focused on parents, it can be applied to other caregivers such as those in early years settings. The Report, 'Conception to Age 2 – the Age of Opportunity' (DfE/Wave Trust, 2013), recommends that practitioners need to have a good understanding of social and emotional development in children, have age-appropriate expectations, understand early brain development and understand the cultural, social and emotional factors that can impact on behaviour. Practitioners need to understand how to promote emotional and behavioural self-regulation and have realistic age-related expectations in these aspects of development and therefore PSED.

The relationship between the prime areas of learning and development and the specific areas

The prime areas are regarded as fundamental to children's experiences in the specific areas of learning and development (Tickell, 2011). Children need their skills and knowledge in PSED, communication and language, and physical development, it is argued, to engage in activities that support their learning in the specific areas. Tickell (2011: 96) highlights three key differences between the prime and specific areas of learning and development:

- Prime areas are based on sensitive periods of development in the early years of life, in comparison to the specific areas of learning and development, which can be acquired at later stages of life.
- Prime areas are universal and occur in all socio-cultural contexts, whereas the specific areas are skills and knowledge that are highly valued and prioritized within some socio-cultural contexts.
- Prime areas are not dependent on learning in the specific areas, but the specific areas are dependent on learning in the prime areas.

Tickell (2011) does not view the prime areas of learning and development as needing initial achievement followed by subsequent sequential understanding of specific areas of learning and development but, instead, sees them as symbiotic. The prime areas and specific areas are interdependent as development is holistic. So, in the earliest years, development occurs predominantly within the prime areas, which underpin later development in the specific areas. In turn, children's experiences in the specific areas contribute to continued development in the prime areas.

Hall's (2005) distinction between 'experience expectant' learning and 'experience dependent' learning is used by Tickell to help explain the positioning of the prime and specific areas of learning and development. She places the prime areas as experience expectant and the specific areas as experience dependent:

> 'Experience expectant' learning has been conditioned by our evolutionary development and is where the brain expects certain kinds of input (e.g. visual, tactile or auditory stimulus) to which it will adapt itself. It is a response to our environment which allows the brain to fine-tune itself, and it may be subject to 'sensitive periods' when the brain is particularly ready to respond to these stimuli, which are ever-present in the environment... 'Experience dependent' learning does not have these constraints. It is the type of learning which will only occur if the need arises for it, and tends to be of the sort which features in culturally transmitted knowledge systems.
>
> (Hall, 2005: 16)

Tickell places the prime areas including PSED as 'experience expectant' and literacy and mathematics and the other specific areas of learning and development as 'experience dependent'. Gopnik *et al.* (1999) state that young babies are attuned to make contact with the people around them from birth and these interactions impact on the child's developing brain. Therefore, Tickell argues that PSED has a biological basis in terms of brain development and attachment with its impact on the child's emotional well-being, pro-social behaviour and self-regulation, and must therefore be placed as a prime area of learning and development. While particularly important from birth to three years, it continues to play a vital role in subsequent learning and development for children aged three upwards.

The Key Person approach in PSED and the EYFS

Emotional warmth and security are vital in supporting young children in PSED. A large body of research evidence shows children's need for high-quality, reliable relationships with all the people in their lives, including those in the early years setting (National Scientific Council on the Developing Child, 2004). Children's relationships and interactions affect almost all aspects of their development beyond PSED, including cognitive and physical development. In England, the development of consistent, nurturing interactions has been promoted through the appointment of secondary attachment relationships, the basis of the Key Person approach in settings (Elfer *et al.*, 2003). Within this approach, specific practitioners are linked to specific children. Elfer *et al.* describe the Key Person approach as:

> ...a way of working in nurseries in which the whole focus and organisation is aimed at enabling and supporting close attachments between individual children and individual staff. The Key Person approach is an involvement, an individual and reciprocal commitment between a member of staff and a family.
>
> (Elfer *et al.*, 2003: 18)

This became a statutory requirement within the EYFS (DCSF, 2008; DfE, 2012). Since this point, a child attending an early years setting has to have a named Key Person, who will seek to form a close, successful relationship with the child and his or her parents or carers. A Key Person is defined by the EYFS (DCSF, 2008) as a practitioner who has special responsibilities for working with a small number of children and building relationships with their parents.

Elfer's (2006) argument for the Key Person approach is based on attachment theory, as young children need a secondary attachment figure at the setting to promote positive self-esteem and reduce their anxiety, which in turn allows greater exploration. It is thought that the Key Person approach supports children to develop the three building blocks of being close: feeling secure; separating and exploring; seeking help and comfort (National Evaluation of Sure Start, 2003: 54). They will feel secure in the early years setting, enjoy their growing independence and be able to separate, explore and learn with confidence; yet will be aware that they can turn to their Key Person when upset and in need of help or comfort. Therefore, the Key Person must be able to form warm, settled, emotionally close relationships with the children allocated to them. The role of a secondary attachment figure is not an easy role and places high emotional demands on early years practitioners. As stated by DCSF (2008: 1), 'The key person approach is intense, involving hard work and a big professional and emotional commitment.' This needs to be considered when early years settings have a low ratio of adults to children, where the demands on the practitioner may be beyond what they can cope with physically and emotionally.

The Key Person approach is further justified by increased understanding of early brain development. The security of the relationships children have with their caregivers plays a critical role in regulating stress hormone production during the early years of life; children with secure relationships have a more controlled stress hormone reaction to challenging situations (National Scientific Council on the Developing Child, 2011). This means that children are able to explore and develop, while the presence of a sensitive Key Person can act as a buffer in stressful situations.

This growing body of knowledge has led to the DfE/Wave Trust (2013) suggesting that it is a priority for those working in childcare settings with birth-to-two-year-olds to understand attachment and its important role in good early years practice in relation to continuous and consistent care through the Key Person approach. In addition to the emotional competence of practitioners, the role and competence of managers in providing high-quality supervision has also been highlighted.

However, there are critics of the Key Person approach and it is not used in all countries. Dahlberg *et al.* (1999) suggest that the Key Person approach restricts children's opportunities to access a wider group of adults and peers and it unnecessarily seeks to replicate family relationships in early years settings. Penn (1997) argues that the Key Person overlooks the importance of the peer group and the relationships that a child may form. Indeed, Elfer's (2006) own detailed case studies of Graham and Harry, aged 12 and 16 months respectively, support some of these criticisms. Elfer found that although a nursery following a Key Person system facilitated Harry's independent learning through his strong feelings of security, it may have prevented his interaction with other adults and children and heightened frustration when his Key Person was attending to other children. In comparison, Graham attended a nursery with a reduced focus on attachment interactions and Elfer identified that while Graham may have had some strong feelings from his individual needs not always being met, he appeared more integrated and emotionally attached to his peer group.

Despite these criticisms, longitudinal research on vulnerability and resilience indicates the importance of close relationships within the family and beyond. Resilience has been identified as the ability to bounce back from negative life experiences or events. In the their literature review, David *et al.* (2003) concluded that a key factor to promote resilience was the presence of at least one highly nurturing relationship. Werner (1989, 1993; cited by Schaffer, 1996) noted that resilient children tend to seek and find emotional support outside the family, from relatives, teachers and friends, indicating the value of creating close relationships and the importance of additional caregivers beyond the parents throughout a child's life. Rutter (1999) goes further in suggesting that experiences of positive relationships can neutralize and compensate children who have experienced a higher level of risk factors for adversity, basing his research on the children adopted into the UK from Romanian orphanages.

Is the Key Person approach only needed for babies and toddlers?

Jamie, aged four years, is a very shy child who has not attended an early years setting before. Her setting is a large open plan Reception and nursery unit and it can be difficult for practitioners to support her needs. Jamie is very quiet and although she has been at nursery for six months, she tends to stay in the base room where her Mum drops her in the morning and where her group time takes place. The practitioners are based in different parts of the nursery for a week at a time. Jamie is benefiting from accessing the range of play experiences and activities in this room but rarely ventures to other parts of the nursery and is not forming relationships with other children.

How could Jamie best be supported and enabled to develop?

While the Key Person approach is a statutory requirement (DfE, 2012), its presence within 'Development Matters' (Early Education, 2012), the non-statutory guidance to the EYFS, is focused in the younger age bands (birth to 11 months, 8–20 months and 16–26 months). As would be anticipated, the Key Person approach features most frequently in 'Making relationships' and is referred to briefly in 'Self-confidence and self-awareness' and 'Managing feelings and behaviour'. However, there is no mention of the Key Person at all by the 40–60 month+ age band across PSED. The term Key Person is not used consistently within the guidance; other terms such as key practitioner, special person, familiar person and carer feature throughout the guidance for PSED. Within the enabling environment guidance, the need for time with the Key Person is included within the 'Making relationships' aspect in the age band 22–36 months and stability in Key Person relationships at 30–50 months, but most other references are to familiar adults. This suggests less of a need for the Key Person approach as children grow older and has implications for Key Stage 1.

How might Jamie in the case study above have been better supported in her PSED if there had been a continued emphasis on the Key Person approach?

It could be be that Jamie's Key Person, Samia, decides to help Jamie explore different parts of the Reception and nursery unit. She discusses this with other members of the Foundation Stage team, explaining that she needs some individual time with Jamie and an opportunity to show Jamie different parts of the setting. Together they decide that Jamie could have ten minutes a day with her Key Person while another member of staff covers Samia's room. In addition, Samia will try and support Jamie more actively in her room by talking to her and encouraging her to interact with another child, Suki, who Jamie knows outside the setting. Samia will take photographs of Jamie in the different areas of the setting to create a little book that can be re-read and re-visited with her Mum or during story time.

The continuity of PSED and the Key Person approach from birth into Key Stage 1

The intention outlined within the EYFS is that practitioners working with the youngest children should focus on the three prime areas, as they form the basis for successful learning in the remaining four specific areas of learning and development (DfE, 2012: 6). As the child grows older and becomes more confident within the three prime areas, it is anticipated that there will be a shift towards a balance of both the specific and prime areas of learning and development. This indicates a continuation of PSED alongside the other areas of learning and development. Indeed, Tickell (2011) recommended the English government to recognize that the early years provide the foundation for Key Stage 1 and beyond, and that the connections should be reinforced. This would indicate that PSED should continue to play a role into Reception, Key Stage 1 and beyond. However, the government's 2013 definition of the Good Level of Development measure for the end of the Reception Year, by the Standards and Testing Agency (2013), undermines this approach, stating that:

> From 2013, children will be defined as having reached a good level of development at the end of the *EYFS* if they achieve at least the expected level in:
>
> • the early learning goals in the prime areas of learning (personal, social and emotional development; physical development; and communication and language); and
> • the early learning goals in the specific areas of mathematics and literacy.

While this recognizes Tickell's position on the prime areas of learning, it adds: 'The government also believes that a good foundation in mathematics and literacy is crucial for later success, particularly in terms of children's readiness for school' (Standards and Testing Agency, 2013: 12).

The government has effectively moved literacy and mathematics to become equivalent to prime areas of learning as part of the focus on readiness for school. In practice, this causes difficulties because when working with children in Reception and Year 1, the focus shifts to literacy and mathematics as these are tracked through primary school assessment systems. The following case study illustrates the difficulties that relate to a rapid move away from a focus on the prime areas of learning and development.

> *Jay is a child in Year 1 who has difficulties in class. He has made some progress in literacy and numeracy and the teachers are working hard to support him. However, they are concerned that his progress is slow. He talks to the other children and is beginning to write some words and letters, but struggles to focus in large groups. A suggestion was to review his progress in other areas of the curriculum beyond literacy and numeracy. The review of progress of the prime areas of learning and development in the EYFS highlight that Jay had made limited progress with PSED and communication and language.*

How can progress be reviewed in the prime areas of learning?
How can this situation be prevented from re-occurring for
other children?

This recurring difficulty is not new and was noted by OfSTED in 2004, as pressure on Year 1 teachers from the subject-based approach of the National Curriculum, the constraints of timetabling and the need to ensure children make good progress towards the standards expected in literacy, numeracy and science can lead to 'abrupt transitions'. Indeed, the current proposals on the revised National Curriculum include no details on PSED beyond the following:

> All schools should make provision for personal, social, health and economic education (PSHE), drawing on good practice. Schools are also free to include other subjects or topics of their choice in planning and designing their own programme of education.
>
> (DfE, 2013: 5)

Conclusions

Personal, social and emotional development needs to be recognized as a prime area for learning and development throughout children's early years, starting at birth and continuing through Key Stage 1. The Key Person approach is a helpful way of supporting all children and has particular relevance for supporting children's PSED. It is therefore needed throughout children's early years and into Key Stage 1. It is important to continue to support and monitor children's PSED (and the remaining prime areas of learning and development) as they progress into Key Stage 1, as the specific areas of learning rely on firm foundations in the prime areas for optimum development. This type of approach to tracking development would have highlighted Jay's continuing need for opportunities in PSED, alongside literacy and numeracy in Year 1.

Points for reflection and discussion

1. How would you describe the relationship between the prime areas and specific areas of learning and development?
2. How can PSED be supported in a meaningful way in Reception classes and into Key Stage 1?
3. How can the Key Person approach continue to be implemented from birth into Key Stage 1?
4. What are the aspects of children's development and learning you believe should be tracked from birth to seven and why?

References and further reading

Dahlberg, G., Moss, P. and Pence, A. (1999) *Beyond Quality in Early Childhood Education and Care: Postmodern perspectives*. London: Falmer Press.

David, T., Goouch, K., Powell, S. and Abbott, L. (2003) *Birth to Three Matters: A review of the literature*. Nottingham: Department for Education and Skills.

Denham, S.A., Blair, K.A., DeMulder, E., Levitas, J., Sawyer, K. *et al.* (2003) Preschool emotional competence: Pathway to social competence?, *Child Development*, 74(1): 238–56.

Department for Children, Schools and Families (DCSF) (2008) *Effective Practice: Key person*. Available on EYFS CD-Rom. Nottingham: DCSF Publications.

Department for Education (DfE) (2012) *Statutory Framework for the Early Years Foundation Stage: Setting the standards for learning, development and care for children from birth to five*. Available at: http://www.foundationyears.org.uk/wp-content/uploads/2012/07/EYFS-Statutory-Framework-2012.pdf.

Department for Education (DfE) (2013) *The National Curriculum in England: Framework document for consultation*. Available at: http://www.education.gov.uk/schools/teachingandlearning/curriculum/nationalcurriculum2014/b00220600/consultation-national-curriculum-pos (accessed 24 May 2013).

Department for Education (DfE)/Wave Trust (2013) *Conception to Age 2: The age of opportunity*. Croydon: Wave Trust. Available at: http://www.wavetrust.org/key-publications/reports/conception-to-age-2 (accessed 24 May 2013).

Early Education (2012) *Development Matters in the Early Years Foundation Stage*. London: Early Education.

Elfer, P. (2006) Exploring children's expressions of attachment in nursery, *European Early Childhood Education Research Journal*, 14(2): 81–95.

Elfer, P., Goldschmied, E. and Selleck, D. (2003) *Key Persons in the Nursery: Building relationships for quality provision*. London: David Fulton.

Evangelou, M., Sylva, K. and Kyriakou, M. (2009) *Early Years Learning and Development: Literature Review*. London: DCSF.

Gopnik, A., Meltzoff, A. and Kuhl, P.K. (1999) *How Babies Think: The science of childhood*. London: Phoenix.

Hall, J. (2005) *Neuroscience and Education: A review of the contribution of brain science to teaching and learning*. Glasgow: The Scottish Council for Research in Education.

Kochanska, G. and Aksan, N. (2006) Children's conscience and self-regulation, *Journal of Personality*, 74(6): 1587–1618.

Kochanska, G., Coy, K.C. and Murray, K.T. (2001) The development of self-regulation in the first four years of life, *Child Development*, 72(4): 1091–1111.

Laible, D., Panfile, T. and Makariev, D. (2008) The quality and frequency of mother–toddler conflict: Links with attachment and temperament, *Child Development*, 79(2): 426–43.

National Evaluation of Sure Start (2003) *Cost Effectiveness in Sure Start Local Programmes: A synthesis of local evaluation findings*. London: Institute for the Study of Children, Families and Social Issues, Birkbeck, University of London.

National Scientific Council on the Developing Child (2004) *Young Children Develop in an Environment of Relationship*. Working Paper No. 1. Cambridge, MA: Harvard University Press.

National Scientific Council on the Developing Child (2011) *Building the Brain's Air Traffic Control System: How early experiences shape the development of executive function*. Working Paper No. 11. Cambridge, MA: Harvard University Press.

Office for Standards in Education (OfSTED) (2004) *Transition from Reception Year to Year 1*. Available at: http://www.ofsted.gov.uk/resources/transition-reception-year-year-1-evaluation-hmi (accessed 26 May 2013).

Penn, H. (1997) *Comparing Nurseries: Staff and children in Italy, Spain, and the UK*. London: Paul Chapman.

Rutter, M. (1999) Resilience concepts and findings: Implications for family therapy, *Journal of Family Therapy*, 2(2): 119–45.

Schaffer, H.R. (1996) *Social Development*. Chichester: Wiley Blackwell.

Standards and Testing Agency (2013) *FAQs on EYFS Profile Assessment and Moderation 2013*. Available at: http://www.education.gov.uk/schools/teachingandlearning/assessment/eyfs/a00213878/eyfs-2013 (accessed 24 May 2013).

Tickell, C. (2011) *The Early Years Foundation Stage (EYFS) Review: Report on the evidence*. Available at: https://www.gov.uk/government/publications/the-early-years-foundation-stage-review-report-on-the-evidence (accessed 24 May 2013).

9 Early literacy learning in the contemporary age

Rosie Flewitt

Abstract

In this chapter, I discuss some of the complex challenges facing young children as they learn to become literate in today's multi-media world. Definitions of literacy have changed over time, and for many years different understandings of what 'literacy' is and how it should be taught have fuelled contentious debates. Here, I review contemporary thinking about early literacy including the emphasis of the current curriculum on the teaching of phonics. I also discuss new terms that have emerged, such as the plural *literacies* to indicate the many different ways that children and adults engage with literacy in different contexts, and *multimodal literacies* to describe how young children become literate not just through language but through learning to use and understand different combinations of modes, such as gesture, gaze, body movement, sounds and spoken language in face-to-face communication, and images, layout, colours and written and spoken language in printed and digital texts. Finally, drawing on examples from recent research, I discuss how practitioners can adopt inclusive approaches to supporting early literacy development through playful activities with traditional and 'new' media, which respect the diversity of young children's lives and needs.

Introduction

Four-year-old Barney has just walked home from nursery with his mum and two younger brothers (Adam, aged 2½ years and Chris, aged 9 months). He and Adam play in the garden while mum prepares lunch. After eating, he stays at the table to look at one of his favourite books – an adult coffee-table tome on contemporary architecture from the popular TV programme 'Grand Designs', which features innovative building projects. Barney's father is a builder, and the family have just moved into a new, compact house that he built. Barney and his mum talk about the pictures in the book, and about their new home, while Adam flicks through the pages of a travel brochure, exclaiming in wonderment at the images he finds and baby Chris watches this activity from the security of his mother's embrace. After a while, Barney helps his mum write a shopping list on her mobile phone. They then play an online game based on a BBC television programme called 'Springwatch', which is about wildlife, and his mum helps him to navigate around the screen and to use his growing knowledge of birds, animals and the seasons to complete on-screen activities. Later, Barney and his brothers enjoy listening to a storybook their mum reads, before settling down to play with puzzles.

From my recent research into young children's early experiences of literacy at home and in nursery, this multi-media pattern of activities emerged as fairly typical in many households. Even in homes where young children do not have access to computers, digital media in the form of TVs, mobile phones and portable e-devices are ubiquitous in the communicative patterns of most families' lives (Flewitt, 2010, 2013; Plowman *et al.*, 2010). These digital devices are woven into the fabric of their everyday literacy practices, and, from an early age, young children endeavour to read meaning from different signs and symbols in printed and digital texts across diverse media.

These comparatively recent changes in literacy practices have begun to challenge conventional understandings of literacy as reading and writing language based texts, and have led to a questioning of what literacy is in the contemporary age. There is a strong and established body of research about how young children develop early literacy knowledge and skills as they go about their everyday lives, observing and imitating others who they meet in their families, schools and wider communities (see, for example, Roskos and Christie, 2001; Olson and Torrance, 2009; Larson and Marsh, 2012). Yet guidance for early years practitioners on how to support young children's literacy development is often ambiguous about new technologies, and fails to take full account of the complexity of the challenges young children face as they endeavour to become literate members of today's multi-media world. This is due partly to a lack of consensus among academics, policy makers and practitioners about what literacy is, and about whether it is appropriate for young children to use digital media. To understand these different viewpoints, and the knowledge claims that they have led to, it is helpful to consider briefly how definitions of literacy and understandings of how children become literate have changed over the course of time.

What is early literacy? A historical perspective

In the seventeenth, eighteenth and nineteenth centuries, reading and writing instruction was based on the belief that children could only understand complex entities if they were broken down into their component parts. Children were taught through the grading of words, beginning with words of one syllable, gradually increasing to two, then three or more syllables, ultimately culminating in the ability to read religious texts (Michael, 1984). As the science of psychology grew in influence from the late nineteenth century, understandings of literacy became firmly rooted in cognitive approaches, which viewed 'literacy' as the perceptual ability to master sound–symbol relationships, and the notion of readiness to read (Patrick, 1899). (According to the *Oxford English Dictionary*, the term 'literacy' was first found in print in 1883.) As early as 1908, Huey countered this approach by suggesting that effective literacy pedagogy for young children should root their experiences of early writing in play. However, the 'readiness' argument prevailed, and continues to this day to have a profound effect on literacy policy and pedagogy (see Gillen and Hall, 2013).

Psychological approaches continued to dominate literacy pedagogy throughout the twentieth century. From a cognitive psychology perspective, 'learning' was constructed as occurring within the mind of an individual, and 'becoming literate' involved being taught a narrowly defined set of transferable decoding and encoding skills, including letter–sound combinations and phonic knowledge. It was only after the Second World War that the notion of 'functional literacy' emerged, and researchers began to investigate what literacy was used for in everyday life. Previous definitions of literacy began to be questioned, first by Smith (1971) who drew together research from multiple disciplines and concluded that rather than being a simple decoding process, reading involved complex strategic and cognitive behaviour. He also proposed that meaning did not sit in a text waiting to be *decoded*, but that readers *interpreted* meanings according to their experiences.

By the 1980s, researchers had begun to observe that people experience different literacy practices depending on what they are doing and where they are: at school they do different literacy-related things than at work, and different again at home. Street (1984) coined the term 'autonomous model' to describe cognitive approaches that had constructed literacy as a 'thing-like' object, a set of decontexualized skills that could be acquired once and for all and then carried around. In place of this autonomous model, Street proposed an 'ideological model' to describe how literacy is grounded in social practice – that literacy is embedded and used in many different ways and for many different purposes in everyday life, and that learning how literacy is used in practice is central to becoming a literate member of society. Street's 'ideological' model led to literacy being viewed not as one 'thing' but as different kinds of activities, which had different purposes and which varied according to social and cultural practices. Hence the plural 'literacies' came to be used to describe the many different ways children and adults engage in different literacy-related practices. A rich body of research in this field began to emerge, including ethnographic studies of how different peoples in different communities and cultures engaged with literacy as part of their everyday lives. Research in this field, which views literacy as embedded in social practice, has shown that children may be gifted in the literacy practices they encounter at home, but these talents may not be recognized in 'schooled' literacy (Heath, 1983).

This social practices approach to literacy supported the notion of 'emergent literacy' (see Gillen and Hall, 2013) to describe how young children's literacy knowledge develops slowly over a long time as they experience purposeful literacy activity with more experienced readers and writers, such as writing a shopping list or talking about a favourite TV programme, as we saw in the example with Barney. Emergent literacy research has shown how young children encounter many different kinds of literacies (Hall, 1998), in diverse 'literacy eco-systems' (Kenner, 2005), gaining a wealth of knowledge about different literacy materials and practices as they go about their everyday lives within their families and communities (Gregory *et al.*, 2004). Research has also shown how children come to school with rich 'funds of knowledge' (Moll *et al.*, 1992), which provide rich and often untapped resources for literacy learning. Emergent literacy studies have found that homes that previously were assumed by educators to lack literacy opportunities were filled with many different practices that had not previously been acknowledged as effective or valuable. So, for example, Nieto (1999) reflects on how emergent literacy studies captured the richness of her own childhood experiences of literacy as she grew up in the USA:

> As a young child in a working-class family where no one had even graduated from high school, I do not remember any books or reading activities taking place in our apartment... but this does not mean that we had no experience with literacy. I remember sitting around our kitchen table listening to stories in Spanish... or tall tales of family exploits. I also recall my mother repeating the rhymes and riddles (in Spanish) that she herself had learned as a child and my aunt telling us scary stories (in English) in the dark.
>
> (Nieto, 1999: 7)

These definitions of literacy as embedded in complex social and cultural practices stand in contrast to the increasingly narrow definitions of literacy implied by the Revised Early Years Foundation Stage (EYFS) (DfE, 2012a, 2012b), which support a phonics and readiness-based approach and which are reminiscent of definitions of literacy from previous centuries. While there is no doubt that the systematic teaching of phonics has an important role to play in early reading as one aspect of a rich and varied curriculum (Ehri *et al.*, 2001), research evidence does not support the notion that *synthetic* phonics is the single or most important aspect of learning to read (see NELP, 2008; Wyse and Goswami, 2008; Dombey, 2010). Why, then, have policy makers in England continued to promote a primarily cognitive or 'autonomous' model of literacy, and why does synthetic phonics feature so prominently in the current drive for improved literacy standards?

Why phonics?

As mentioned, there is a strong body of research evidence suggesting that the systematic, direct and explicit teaching of phonics is an important part of an integrated approach to teaching reading (Wyse and Styles, 2007; Wyse and Goswami, 2008). However, in England, the government enquiry into the teaching of early reading (Rose, 2009) reached a narrower conclusion. Rather than allowing the space for practitioners to use their experience, professional judgement and observation of pupil progress to decide upon an approach to the systematic teaching of phonics that was appropriate for their setting, the report promoted the exclusive use of synthetic phonics. The Rose Report also recommended a 'simple view of reading' (Rose, 2009: para 3.23), a model that had been used in the 1980s as a way for teachers to differentiate between children's progress in word recognition and their progress in reading comprehension. While the Rose Review now officially 'should not be considered to reflect current policy or guidance' (DfE, 2013), its impact with regard to the teaching of synthetic phonics has not diminished.

There can be little doubt that a skills-based, autonomous model of literacy, which has been entrenched in literacy policy and teaching for so many years, lends itself to the interests of educational regimes that are driven by assessment and accountability, as it provides both the means and the justification for 'measuring' outcomes. It also offers a conveniently prescriptive approach to 'fixing' literacy, which in turn can be seen as justification for direct political intervention in the early years and primary literacy curriculum. However, the current phonics-driven approach to early literacy learning has several weaknesses: it fails to take into account the complexity of early literacy development and the complexity of the English language; it does not recognize the diversity of individual students' motivations for learning; and it does not recognize the many different ways that young children express their understandings, and how those ways are valued in different communities and cultures as part of everyday practice.

Literacy learning as a complex process

There is now considerable agreement among researchers and practitioners that literacy learning is a complex process of making sense of many different signs and symbols which gain meaning from the social and cultural contexts in which they are used. Far from being a 'simple' process, reading 'is one of the most complex achievements of the human brain' (Wyse and Goswami, 2008: 706). Research investigating literacy as social practice, as discussed earlier, has drawn attention to the socially embedded nature and diversity of literacy practices. It has also shown that children learn best when they are interested and engaged in what they are learning, particularly when these activities have a recognizable purpose with which they identify, and where there is a degree of choice and collaboration.

A further complexity with learning to read and write in English is that for all its richness and beauty, the English language is highly irregular in the relationship between phonemes (a speech sound) and graphemes (such as a letter of the alphabet or a punctuation mark). In English, a single speech sound can be spelt in many different ways, such as the phoneme /e/ in hurt, dirt, Bert. Equally, one letter or letter cluster can be pronounced in many different ways, such as 'ough' in 'cough', 'rough', 'though' (Wyse and Goswami, 2008). The complexity and irregularity of English phonology and English spelling mean that direct phonetic teaching is only a small, if important, part of equipping children with the complex skills they need to become effective readers.

How, then, can early educators support young children's literacy learning through activities which interest them and which cut across cultures and across media? In the following sections, I present a few examples from recent classroom-based practice, to show just a few ways that early literacy development can be supported through playful activities with traditional and 'new' media.

Literacy learning as diverse

Due to the increase in economic and political migration over past decades, early years settings in England now provide for children from many different national, ethnic, religious and linguistic backgrounds. In a recent study I have been involved in, we investigated how young children from a range of social and ethnic backgrounds in an inner-city school blend and mix their diverse home literacy practices with the schooled versions of literacy they encounter in nursery and reception classes. In this study, we observed how Make-Believe Arts, a London-based theatre and education company, introduced Vivian Gusin Paley's storytelling and story acting programme (Paley, 1990) into the setting (Cremin *et al.*, 2013). This programme, known as 'The Helicopter Technique', involves individual children telling their stories to an adult who scribes them verbatim. There is a 'rule' that the stories can only be one page long, so the process of storytelling and scribing takes only a few minutes. Later the same day the stories are acted out by the storyteller and his or her peers on an improvised 'stage' in the classroom, which is marked out with masking tape and is large enough for all the children and the teacher(s) to sit around on the floor.

Over time, the storytelling activity became a regular feature of classroom practice, so all the children were soon familiar with the format and had many opportunities to explore different stories or to re-work stories. This was a particularly rich activity for children to develop their self expression, their language and the effective use of narrative devices, where they could incorporate ideas from different aspects of their literary experience in their home, school and community networks. Its inclusive approach meant it was effective for all children, including those with learning and/or behavioural challenges and those who were learning English as an additional language. Some children's stories focused on their home experiences, on family or friendships, others on popular culture or traditional tales, while others created stories that combined real characters and plots with imaginary worlds.

For example, over the eight weeks of our observations, five-year-old Yakubu developed a story that featured characters and settings associated with popular fiction, traditional fairytales and from his own personal experience. Early on in the programme, he told the following story, which was scribed by his teacher:

> *There was a power ranger and then there was a knight. And then there was a princess and then there was a castle. There was a dragon and then there was a penguin. He died. And then there was an egg. And then there was a ladybug. There was another castle and it was in the forest.*

As the weeks passed, Yakubu re-worked this story, always retaining the core themes of castles and forests, while increasing his use of dramatic and descriptive devices. The example below is the third story we observed him telling, approximately three weeks after the first story above:

> *Once upon a time there was a big castle and then somebody was walking through the forest and then there was a ladybird and there was a big ginormous giraffe and he floated in a magic book and then there was a magic carpet that took books and then there was a bad fairy that turned the wolf into a house.*

We can see evidence here of Yakubu's developing narrative style and increasingly complex use of language, including adding mystery ('somebody'), creative and amusing descriptors ('ginormous'), increasingly evocative language ('floated in a magic book'), familiar villains ('bad fairy', 'wolf') and supernatural powers ('turned the wolf into a house'). This rapid progression in Yakubu's use of highly effective narrative devices shows how the Helicopter Technique can enhance children's language use through the telling of stories that have personal significance.

Literacy learning as multi-modal

Children's use of verbal language played a central role in the Helicopter Technique, as discussed above, but we also saw how the children's language was accompanied or replaced by other modes of communication, such as gestures, postures, facial expression and movement. During the storytelling and story acting sessions, the children expressed themselves through a range of embodied modes (action, gesture, facial expression), which contributed to practitioners' appreciation of their understandings. In this respect, the technique offered all children, including those from diverse linguistic backgrounds and children with particular learning needs, the opportunity for non-verbal modes of communication to be valued (DfE, 2012b: 21).

Young children's multi-modal literacy learning was also an aspect of an ethnographic video study I conducted with colleagues about the communicative experiences of young children with learning difficulties who attended both mainstream and special early education settings (Flewitt *et al.*, 2009). One of the children we observed in this study, four-year-old Mandy, spent two mornings every week at an inclusive, suburban Sure Start Children's Centre (a 30-minute drive from home), and two mornings at a rural and local preschool playgroup (a five-minute drive from home). The Children's Centre had a 50 per cent quota for children identified with special needs, and offered access to on-site specialists and therapy resources. Here, particular attention was paid to Mandy's physical development. In the preschool playgroup, Mandy was included in a wider range of activities, including one-to-one, small group and whole group literacy activities. For example, the lead practitioner, Jackie, included Mandy in whole group book reading sessions using a combination of subtle yet highly effective strategies. First, she ensured that Mandy was sitting close to her in a supportive chair, which enabled her both to see the book easily and to be included in the circle of children on the mat. By holding the book up and showing the book to all the children, Jackie clearly signalled that this was the artefact that was to be the focus of everyone's attention. As Jackie began to read, she frequently used pointing actions and her own gaze direction to signal different parts of the book including the book title, illustrations, the written words, and so on. These actions indicated that she wasn't just talking, but that she was reading. Jackie also used her body orientation and gaze to gain and retain Mandy's attention, saying her name quietly, touching her gently on the arm to regain her attention, smiling at her reassuringly from time to time – always vigilant as she read to the whole group that all the children were attentive, including Mandy. When Mandy's gaze was fixed on the book, and her interest clearly aroused, Jackie asked her questions, such as 'ooh cake, you like cake don't you?' When Mandy's attention strayed to a toy she was holding, Jackie leaned forward and gently took the toy from Mandy's hand, interpreting her lack of resistance and fixed gaze as a sign of acquiescence, and congratulating her with a smile and gentle 'Good girl' before returning to face the full circle of children. These sensitively orchestrated actions lasted just a few seconds, and were almost imperceptible in the whole group book reading activity, yet they resulted in Mandy's attention being maintained on the book reading experience, and to her responses being celebrated by adults and her peers as making valuable contributions to the activity. Overall, we found that when adults had high expectations of children's communicative competence, and valued and mirrored their silent modes of expression, all children responded enthusiastically and were included in a wide range of literacy practices which they then began to adopt in their own practices.

Harnessing the learning potential of new technologies

In another recent study, I investigated with colleagues at the Open University the potential of touch-screen technologies for early literacy and for inclusive educational practice (Flewitt *et al.*, in press). In this study, we lent iPads to a Children's Centre nursery (three- to four-year-olds), a primary school Reception class (four- to five-year-olds) and a Special School (seven- to eighteen-year-olds). We observed their use in practice, conducted pre and post interviews with staff in each setting about their potential educational value, and asked parents in each setting to complete short questionnaires about home uses of new technologies. Our analysis revealed the iPads were incorporated differently into practice within the three settings, reflecting their differing teaching and learning practices. Although staff and parents expressed some concerns about children's over-reliance on new technologies, across the settings, iPad activities were found to increase children's motivation, attention and concentration. Pre-reading children were able to 'read' on-screen icons and images, which gave them the independence to access and begin to use carefully selected word-based apps. They also linked well with National Curriculum guidelines and offered rich opportunities for collaborative interaction, independent learning, communication and creative work. Furthermore, staff welcomed the opportunities the iPad afforded to make links between children's home and school lives and to prepare children for a future where they would need high levels of technological competence and skills. We also worked with the children using the iPads app *Our Story*, a freely available picture-based story-telling app that is based on sound research evidence about effective strategies for the development of children's narrative through personalized stories. The children and adults greatly enjoyed using this as a tool to create personalized stories. Overall, we found that new digital devices such as the iPad offer the potential for the mediation of knowledge and power, using everyday events as story anchors to co-create collaborative stories.

Conclusion

In this chapter, I have outlined how the term 'literacy' has been interpreted differently across the ages, always reflecting different social and historical understandings of what literacy is for, and what young children are able to learn. Different understandings of what literacy is continue to underpin current debates about how young children's literacy learning can best be supported at home and in early education. As a result, early literacy has become a highly contested and dichotomized field. The revised EYFS places a particular emphasis on the teaching of synthetic phonics to support early reading, yet research evidence for the efficacy of this approach is weak. There is a risk that practitioners' anxiety about putting into practice the current curriculum targets set for young children's phonic awareness may erode their confidence to interpret the literacy curriculum in playful ways that engage children's interests and create spaces for children's self-expression. I have presented a few examples from practice that offer scope to nurture all children's love for expressing themselves through diverse modes and in diverse media which reflect the wealth of knowledge and practices they bring with them to nursery and to school.

Points for reflection and discussion

1. Do children in your setting have easy and open access to a range of high-quality literacy resources that they can use freely to initiate activities involving handwritten, printed and screen-based texts?
2. Do children in your setting have time and relaxed opportunities to make use of these resources, and are staff able and confident enough to encourage children to build on their literacy-related interests across media?

References and further reading

Cremin, T., Swann, J., Flewitt, R.S., Faulkner, D. and Kucirkova, N. (2013) *Evaluation Report of MakeBelieve Arts Helicopter Technique of Storytelling and Story Acting*. The Open University. Available at: http://www.makebelievearts.co.uk/Helicopter (accessed 17 June 2013).

Department for Education (DfE) (2012a) *Early Years Foundation Stage*. Available at: https://www.education.gov.uk/schools/teachingandlearning/assessment/EYFS/ (accessed 25 February 2012).

Department for Education (DfE) (2012b) *Development Matters in the Early Years Foundation Stage (EYFS)*. London: Early Education/DfE.

Department for Education (DfE) (2013) *Publications Archive*. Available at: https://www.education.gov.uk/publications/standard/publicationDetail/Page1/QCDA/09/4355 (accessed 25 February 2013).

Dombey, H. (2010) *Teaching Reading: What the evidence says*. Royston: UKLA.

Ehri, L., Nunes, S.R., Stahl, S.A. and Willows, D.M. (2001) Systematic phonics instruction help students learn to read: Evidence from the National Reading Panel's meta-analysis, *Review of Education*, 71(3): 393–447.

Flewitt, R.S. (2010) *Multimodal Literacies in the Early Years*. Available at: http:// www.open.ac.uk/blogs/multimodalliteracies (accessed 25 February 2013).

Flewitt, R.S. (2013) Multimodal perspectives on early childhood literacies, in J. Larson and J. Marsh (eds.) *The Sage Handbook of Early Childhood Literacy*, 2nd edn. London: Sage.

Flewitt, R.S., Nind, M. and Payler, J. (2009) 'If she's left with books she'll just eat them': Considering inclusive multimodal literacy practices, *Journal of Early Childhood Literacy*, 9(2): 211–33.

Flewitt, R.S., Messer, D. and Kucirkova, N. (in press) New directions for early literacy in a digital age: the iPad.

Gillen, J. and Hall, N. (2013) The emergence of early childhood literacy, in J. Larson and J. Marsh (eds.) *The Sage Handbook of Early Childhood Literacy*, 2nd edn. London: Sage.

Gregory, E., Long, S. and Volk, D. (2004) *Many Pathways to Literacy: Young children learning with siblings, grandparents, peers and communities*. London: RoutledgeFalmer.

Hall, K. (1998) Critical literacy and the case for it in the early years of school, *Language, Culture and Curriculum*, 11(2): 183–94.

Heath, S.B. (1983) *Ways with Words: Language, life, and work in communities and classrooms*. New York: Oxford University Press.

Kenner, C. (2005) Bilingual families as literacy eco-systems, *Early Years: An International Journal of Research and Development*, 25(3): 283–98.

Larson, J. and Marsh, J. (eds.) (2012) *The Sage Handbook of Early Childhood Literacy*, 2nd edn. London: Sage.

Michael, I. (1984) Early evidence for whole word methods, in G. Brooks and A.K. Pugh (eds.) *Studies in the History of Reading*. Reading: Centre for the Teaching of Reading, University of Reading.

Moll, L.C., Amanti, C., Neff, D. and Gonzalez, N. (1992) Funds of knowledge for teaching: Using a qualitative approach to connect homes and classrooms – theory into practice, *Qualitative Issues in Educational Research*, 31(2): 132–41.

National Early Literacy Panel (NELP) (2008) *Developing Early Literacy: Report of the National Early Literacy Panel*. Washington, DC: National Institute for Literacy. Available at: http://lincs.ed.gov/publications/pdf/NELPReport09.pdf (accessed 25 February 2013).

Nieto, S. (1999) *The Light in Their Eyes: Creating multicultural learning communities*. New York: Teachers College Press.

Olson, D. and Torrance, N. (eds.) (2009) *The Cambridge Handbook of Literacy*. New York: Cambridge University Press.

Paley, V.G. (1990) *The Boy Who Would Be a Helicopter: The uses of storytelling in the classroom*. Cambridge, MA: Harvard University Press.

Patrick, G. (1899) Should children under 10 learn to read and write?, *Popular Science Monthly*, 54: 382–92.

Plowman L., Stephen, C. and McPake, J. (2010) Supporting young children's learning with technology at home and in preschool, *Research Papers in Education*, 25(1): 93–113.

Rose, J. (2009) *Independent Review of the Primary Curriculum: Final Report*. London: DCSF. Available at: http://www.educationengland.org.uk/documents/pdfs/2009-IRPC-final-report.pdf (accessed 25 February 2013).

Roskos, K. and Christie, J. (2001) Examining the play–literacy interface: A critical review and future directions, *Journal of Early Childhood Literacy*, 1(1): 59–89.

Smith, F. (1971) *Understanding Reading: A psycholinguistic analysis of reading and learning to read.* New York: Holt, Rinehart & Winston.

Street, B. (1984) *Literacy in Theory and Practice.* Cambridge: Cambridge University Press.

Wyse, D. and Goswami, U. (2008) Synthetic phonics and the teaching of reading, *British Educational Research Journal*, 34(6): 691–710.

Wyse, D. and Styles, M. (2007) Synthetic phonics and the teaching of reading: The debate surrounding England's Rose Report, *Literacy*, 47(1): 35–42.

10 The teaching and learning of mathematics: a simple matter of 1, 2, 3?

Anne D. Cockburn

Abstract

In this chapter, we will explore some of the fundamental mathematical concepts it is important for young children to acquire; examine why they are more complex than one might imagine; and consider the consequences if we fail to provide future generations with a firm mathematical foundation.

Introduction

Watch a typical three-year-old such as Arthur (Photograph 10.1) playing for any length of time and it quickly becomes apparent that a considerable amount of mathematical experimentation and learning is involved. As the sand is poured from one container to another, for example, or tables are arranged for a teddies' tea party, or how judgements are made as to how big a leap is required to jump over a puddle successfully. When discussing young children, Linder *et al.* (2011: 30) noted that:

> They instinctively compare quantities, observe and make patterns, navigate through different kinds of spaces, and problem-solve in their play interactions with objects and with peers in the classroom.

So given such enthusiasm and engagement, surely the early years practitioner's task is very simple. Indeed, in the past, I have heard people say something along the lines of, 'I don't like maths much but I can count, add and take away so where's the problem? I can easily teach young children a few basic sums.' As I will discuss in this chapter, this statement is rather disturbing for a number of reasons, not least because the thinking it reflects is still remarkably prevalent among many across a wide spectrum of society. If you have any doubts on this just ask a few friends and older acquaintances unconnected with the world of education.

As someone interested in mathematics education, I think there is much to commend in the Early Years Foundation Stage (EYFS) documents. For example, they advocate a very hands-on approach with plenty of practical activities and experimentation:

Photograph 10.1 A typical three-year-old.

Three characteristics of effective teaching and learning are:

- **playing and exploring** – children investigate and experience things, and 'have a go';
- **active learning** – children concentrate and keep on trying if they encounter difficulties, and enjoy achievements; and
- **creating and thinking critically** – children have and develop their own ideas, make links between ideas, and develop strategies for doing things.

(DfE, 2012: 7)

Such experiences are ideal opportunities to foster young children's mathematical skills and understanding. It is reassuring to see that there is no demand to introduce formal recording of mathematical calculations, which can result in many problems and misconceptions in later life (Cockburn, 1999). As you read this chapter, however, I would encourage you to reflect on the Early Learning Goal for Numbers (ELG 11):

Numbers: Children count reliably with numbers from one to 20, place them in order and say which number is one more or one less than a given number. Using quantities and objects, they add and subtract two single-digit numbers and count on or back to find the answer. They solve problems, including doubling, halving and sharing.

(Standards and Testing Agency, 2013: 28)

Counting: a simple matter of 1, 2, 3?

How would you feel about having zero teeth? An odd question perhaps for a book such as this, but it is one of fundamental importance. Zero matters! All too often, however, the seemingly insignificant symbol '0' is dismissed as simply meaning nothing. The consequences of such a misconception can create considerable confusion and difficulties in later life.

Returning to ELG 11 for numbers, there is no requirement that zero needs to be mentioned and, indeed, it is true that, unlike mathematicians, early years specialists have little call to work with rational or irrational numbers for example. Sometimes we will venture into numbers beyond 10 but rarely, if ever, do we touch on topics such as negative numbers, decimals or fractions. At this point, I can almost see some readers beginning to sweat but, have no fear, I am not about to launch into a complicated discussion of advanced mathematical concepts! If we are to teach mathematics to young children effectively and responsibly, however, we need to be aware that in the past the concept of zero has been misrepresented with significant long-term consequences. In essence, '0' represents the absence of something – not nothing. Some might consider this to be a pedantic distinction but think again of the trauma associated with an absence of teeth or the joy of the absence of an overload of tedious tasks to complete.

It may not be until the upper primary and lower secondary years that a child's misconception of zero becomes apparent when, for example, they read '502' as 'fifty two' or write the number of days in a year as '30056'. Take a few moments to think about further examples when zero – as opposed to nothing – might be critical. Does zero ever come up in your conversations with the children? Should it in your view? [See Cockburn and Littler (2008) for a more detailed account of zero and its misconceptions.] Later in the chapter, early years' teachers describe how it might be done. [To learn about counting more generally, I can recommend Haylock and Cockburn (2013).]

A few brief words on addition

Fostering young children's understanding of addition is not something that need concern you unduly but, remember, adding is not always simply a question of adding two – or even, three or four – groups of objects such as four teddies plus 2 teddies ($4 + 2 = \square$), and so on. Sometimes adding only involves one object. The daffodils you are growing might be 4 cm one week and they grow a further 2 cm the next. This, again, may be represented as $4 + 2 = \square$. It is important to present children with examples of both types of problem so that they develop a broad understanding of the concept. Please note, however, I am not advocating that you should insist on three- and four-year-olds formally recording their calculations using 4, +, 2 and = as I have done for you. I am far more of an advocate of emergent mathematics discussed by Worthington (2007). What I am suggesting is presenting children with lots of practical opportunities to discover the number of items resulting when you combine two groups together *and*, for example, the height, weight or volume of something that has grown.

Check back to ELG 11 at the start of this chapter: does it cover both of the approaches I have described? If it does I would suggest that it is implicit rather than explicit for, as it stands, it could be taken as referring to only the second of my examples where, in effect, you could count on how much the daffodil has grown. More specifically – and perhaps due to the need for a concise ELG statement – it does not articulate the stages many young children go through as they learn to add, starting most commonly with *counting all* rather than *counting on* (Montague-Smith, 1997).

Subtraction: a case of taking away?

Yes, subtraction can be a case of taking away but, crucially, it is considerably more than this. Introducing subtraction as taking away – or, to give it its more formal title, *partitioning* – is very common for entirely understandable reasons. It is easy to demonstrate and a part of everyday life: Sam has six biscuits, for example. If he eats two of them, how many are left ($6 - 2 = \square$)? I might draw such a situation thus:

But what about when Sam has six biscuits and I have two? Formally, this would also be represented as $6 - 2 = \square$ but the accompanying picture would be quite different and might look like:

In other words, *no* taking away is involved. Referring back to ELG 11 again, one wonders how children could count back to find the answer on this occasion.

As I write the weather is very cold outside. It has been reaching about 6°C in the daytime but at night it goes down to –2°C. What is the difference in the temperatures? If you are unsure, think of a thermometer and the number of degrees between +6 and –2. Again *no* taking away is involved. Haylock and Cockburn (2013) discuss a range of different types of subtraction including some I have not mentioned above.

Adding to subtraction

A wide range of research studies (e.g. Behr *et al.*, 1980; Falkner *et al.*, 1999; Freiman and Lee, 2004; Parslow-Williams and Cockburn, 2008; Marchini *et al.*, 2009) illustrate that a significant number of secondary students and adults have difficulties with the mathematical concept of equality. For example, some would argue that a statement such as '6 = 4 + 2' is impossible, as the equals sign signifies that an action is required. Rest assured, I am not suggesting that you present young children with pages of written calculations to consider. What I am proposing, however, is that you provide them with practical activities and stories that involve the reversal of addition and subtraction situations. Thus you might have a situation where six children from Family A and two children from Family B go out for the day (how many altogether?) and then, after the trip, all the children from Family A go home by car but those from Family B walk (how many children walk?). I am sure you can think of some more elegant examples that match the children's interests and demonstrate how numbers can be built up using addition and later separated through subtraction. You might then reflect on situations where a story might begin with subtraction and later result in addition.

Again you may wonder why it is important for early years practitioners to bother about such matters. There are various ways in which to respond but, in this case, the particularly important one is that, once something has been learnt, it can be very difficult to unlearn it. Several examples come to mind and I am sure you can think of others that are more pertinent for you. For those of you who touch type, imagine the chaos if the positioning of the letters on the keyboard was radically altered and upper and lower case letters were intermingled. In time you would get used to the change I am sure, but it would take quite a bit of re-thinking.

Much closer to home for me is the fact that I was exclusively taught subtraction as taking away. Later I learnt the rule that 'two minuses make a plus', but it was not until I was embarrassingly old that I appreciated why, or indeed that, subtraction could involve comparison. Had I as a three- and four-year-old compared and contrasted the number of toys or biscuits I had with my friends or discussed differences in our heights, I might have reached considerably higher mathematical heights. As it was I was considerably luckier than many others, which brings me to my next – and most crucial – section.

Attitudes towards mathematics

As a young child I loved mathematics and, at the risk of sounding conceited, I was good at it. It gave me great pleasure to work through pages and pages of 'sums' and be rewarded with lots of ticks and gold stars. I suspect my love of the subject was also much enhanced by my teachers' enthusiasm: in my early years of schooling I was fortunate in having educators who wanted to facilitate and encourage my thirst for learning. They might not have appreciated the importance of zero or the value of introducing a range of approaches to subtraction, but they enabled my confidence to grow and my curiosity to develop and thrive. They were excellent at building up my 'self-confidence and self-awareness' (DfE, 2012: 8). It was not until mid-way through secondary school that I encountered a teacher who was undoubtedly a good mathematician but who was not such an effective educator. Lessons had one of two formats: the first was her whizzing through a new concept on the board followed by the class working through examples in our books. The other type of lesson was much the same as the first without the introduction. Initially, it was fine and I did well in my first formal external examinations but then I got further and further behind and only just passed my final mathematics exam at school. It was not that the teacher was unhelpful. She did her best and was always willing to help if I was stuck. The problem was that she could not seem to understand that I could not understand, as it was all so easy for her!

I am lucky, for these legacies have not only left me with a love of the subject but a determination to try and help others exceed my mathematical knowledge and understanding. Many – and indeed, almost certainly, a significant number of those reading this chapter – have not been so fortunate. What an indictment of our society when Williams (2008: 3) concluded that, 'the United Kingdom is still one of the few advanced nations where it is socially acceptable – fashionable even – to profess an inability to cope with the subject'.

Before I proceed, I wish to make it absolutely clear that I am not about to blame or criticize past, present or future educators. Indeed, I want to emphasize that my aim is to *understand* behaviour rather than to pass judgement on dedicated practitioners as they endeavour to give of their best day in and day out. I am a firm believer of William James's (1899: 13–14) view that:

> The worst thing that can happen to a good teacher is to get a bad conscience about her profession…our teachers are overworked already…A bad conscience increases the weight of every other burden…

Throughout my career I have been extremely impressed by the commitment and quality of the early years teachers I have encountered. One of the factors that has impressed me most has been their almost universal desire to ensure that each and every one of the children in their care realizes their full potential.

It is likely that your feelings about mathematics were formed at an early age and may well have been a combination of your teachers' attitudes, your parents' response to the subject and your own success…or lack of it! People's anxiety and even hatred of the subject has been well documented (e.g. Nardi and Steward, 2003; Jordan *et al.*, 2006) and Margaret Brown and her colleagues (2008) even went so far as to write a paper entitled, '"I would rather die": reasons given by 16-year-olds for not continuing their study of mathematics.'. The challenge for us is that it is hard to change deep-seated attitudes but the encouraging news is that it can be done.

Recently, I asked successful head teachers whether they perceived there to be an issue with their early years practitioners and mathematics and, if there was, how they managed it. Bob (not his real name) was in no doubt, 'a lot of them come in with their own baggage, don't they?' (Cockburn, 2012: 592–3). This was echoed by Hannah, who, describing the attitudes of her staff said: 'I still think as a culture we don't do maths terribly well. So easily people say, "I'm not very good"' (pp. 672–3). Hannah remarked, 'The more self-critical people are generally, the better I find them as teachers' (Cockburn, 2012: 24–5). Accordingly, she tends to work to people's strengths:

> There's all that sense of 'we're not very good'…the two teachers who are really good in school, they are both passionate about literature so what we are trying to say is, 'well, what is it you do, in teaching literacy, that we can transfer to teaching mathematics?'

(Cockburn, 2012: 672–6)

Take a minute to reflect on how you work best with the children in your care. What do you enjoy most? When do you think they make the most progress? What lessons can you transfer from such situations to those with a more mathematical focus? (Or, if you love mathematics but are not so keen on language, vice versa?)

Another head teacher, Jean, explained that her early years colleagues found planning rather arid and tedious but she observed:

> I think the key thing about them is that on pedagogy they are very, very strong and if we sit down and... look at it... with a pedagogical focus... they can go 'yes, actually, you're right'... Whereas if I started from saying like 'I'm not happy with your planning – do it like this', they would probably say 'no, I don't think I want to do it like that'. But if you can say, 'Look, this is the outcome. This is how... how is that child learning within this?', they will go 'yeah, yes, I can see what you are saying'.
>
> (Cockburn, 2012: 184–90)

Jean was also keen to point out, however, that, changing practitioners' attitudes was not enough, for 'If we don't work with the parents, there is no way we can get those children because it just isn't important' (Cockburn, 2012: 475–6). I could say a lot more about that. Where you work it might not be an issue but, if you think back to the creation of your own attitudes, it may be.

One thing in our favour in terms of young children's attitudes towards mathematics is that, in the early years, many of them have very little idea what it is. This is illustrated by a powerful exchange from over twenty years ago. If you are sceptical about it because of the date, I suggest you ask your children the same question as this kindergarten teacher:

Teacher:	Why do we do these numbers?
Michelle:	So that we can spell things.
Teacher:	Spell things with numbers?
Antoinette:	So we can count properly.
Teacher:	What kind of things do we need to count?
Antoinette:	You need to count the numbers.
Simon:	We need to draw the numbers.
Teacher:	Why do we need to draw the numbers?
Lisa:	So we can copy them.
Teacher:	But why do we need the numbers at all?
Lisa:	So we can colour them in.

(adapted from Desforges and Cockburn, 1987: 100)

BUT – and this is crucial – although the children may be unaware of the different areas of the curriculum, their attitudes towards learning will undoubtedly be developing. Moreover, some of their parents may not appreciate the educational value of early years education and may be a little too free with comments such as, 'I was never very good with numbers at school'!

How do you know what you don't know?

This is a very pertinent question! Sadly, the answer is not necessarily simply to check what is being asked of you in official documents. Here are three strategies I, and others, have found helpful in the past.

> *Sandy*: I think it is important that zero is displayed alongside the other numbers in the classroom in a wide variety of ways.
>
> *Annabelle*: Yes, I agree. I have all kinds of numbers around the classroom: phone numbers (pretend of course!), house numbers, birthday and date charts, number lines...
>
> *Sandy*: Someone suggested that I have a zero to ten 'washing line' with shirts on it labelled '0' to '10' but I think that's confusing, as should one count the shirts or focus on the numbers? Instead, I hang string bags from a number line. The first one – that is hanging from zero – is empty, the next one contains one cube, the next two, and so on.
>
> *Annabelle*: I really like that idea! At the moment I have a vertical number line with '0' at floor level rising up to '10', but I am now wondering if that might create problems when we come to negative numbers later.
>
> *Ruth*: I worry about showing empty palms to represent zero, as they could be seen as showing 10 fingers. I much prefer showing my fists for zero and then raising one finger for one, two for two, and so on.
>
> *Annabelle*: In the past we always counted up from 1 to 10 but down from 10 to 0. I'm now going to try counting up from 0. It may be unconventional but it is worth a try!
>
> *Ruth*: I quite like the standpoint of the same approach for each digit. I have always given my children a card with a number on it and asked them to get the same number of cubes as shown on the card. Now I could include a card with '0' on it and make sure that there is a table with nothing on it in the room and ask the children to show me zero and they've actually got to show me something. Of course, they might not point to the table but if they pointed to a space on the carpet or showed their fists that would be fine.
> (Cockburn and Parslow-Williams, 2008: 9–10)

> You focus on your own group and forget what they are going on to. I've done year 3, 2, 1 and R and so you get an idea of what the children are moving towards... [but] some of the children have misconceptions and still have them 5 years on.
> (Ivan, in Parslow-Williams and Cockburn, 2008: 30)

Here is an example of early years practitioners discussing zero:

> This whole project has made me very aware of zero: how important it is and it has affected the way in which I teach but it has also reinforced some of the good things I do in terms of the visual and the practical. It makes me aware

of the importance of working on zero right from day 1 and it's important to get it right otherwise it can have dire effects in year 2. I wasn't really aware of what a problem it was getting it wrong until I talked to people here. The children have got to see the practical/physical side of zero.

(Cockburn and Parslow-Williams, 2008: 15)

Implications for practice

In 1899, William James wrote that, in order to be successful, teachers should:

1. capture the child's interest;
2. build on what they know;
3. teach and assess for understanding;
4. provide plenty of oral and practical experience;
5. adopt a varied approach;
6. foster children's confidence in their mathematical abilities.

I agree entirely! Most of the early years practitioners I have encountered seem to be particularly gifted in the first, fourth and sixth of these. It is only recently, in my view, that researchers in mathematics education have really become aware of the skills involved in (3) and, hence to some extent (2). Deborah Ball and her colleagues have observed that the most successful teachers are those who not only have a sound understanding of mathematics but also the ability to break it down in order to facilitate a child's learning when they experience difficulties (Ball *et al.*, 2008). The second of these, as I described above, was a skill my secondary maths teacher was so obviously lacking.

On the matter of adopting a varied approach in early years mathematics education, it is worth looking at Figure 10.1 developed by Haylock (Haylock and

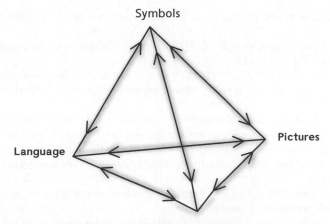

Figure 10.1 For someone to optimize their understanding of a concept, they need to consider/play with/explore it through language, concrete experiences, pictures and symbols, thus developing a network of cognitive connections (from Haylock and Cockburn, 2013).

Cockburn, 2013). In essence, his argument is that, in order to optimize someone's understanding of a concept, they need to consider/play with/explore it through language, concrete experiences, pictures and symbols thus developing a network of cognitive connections. As indicated above, I would not interpret 'symbols' to mean '+', '=', and so on in early years settings.

Conclusion

To conclude, facilitating a young child's mathematical journey is not an easy task but, if done with due care and attention, the dividends are immense!

Points for reflection and discussion

1. Reflect on what you have had difficulty with when you were at school. Did you find, for example, you had problems with decimals? Why does 'adding 0' when you multiply 2.6 by 10 not work? Or, algebra might have been a mystery for you. Perhaps your understanding of equality or subtraction was limited . . .
2. Discuss with colleagues areas you have found challenging in the past and share your ideas more generally.
3. Talk to colleagues further up the educational ladder. For example, in one study teachers from across the four to eleven age range discussed mathematical concepts together.

References and further reading

Ball, D.L., Thames, M.H. and Phelps, G. (2008) Content knowledge for teaching: What makes it special?, *Journal of Teacher Education*, 59(5): 389–407.

Behr, M., Erlwanger, S. and Nichols, E. (1980). How children view the equals sign, *Mathematics Teaching*, 92: 13–15.

Brown, M., Brown, P. and Bibby, T. (2008) 'I would rather die': Reasons given by 16-year-olds for not continuing their study of mathematics, *Research in Mathematics Education*, 10(1): 3–18.

Cockburn, A.D. (1999) *Teaching Mathematics with Insight*. London: Falmer Press.

Cockburn, A.D. (2012) 'To generalize or not to generalize, that is the question' (with apologies to Hamlet and William Shakespeare), in B. Maj-Tatis and K. Tatis (eds.) *Generalization in Mathematics at all Educational Levels*. Rzeszów: Wydawnictwo Uniwersytetu Rzeszowskiego.

Cockburn, A.D. and Littler, G. (eds.) (2008) *Mathematical Misconceptions: A guide for primary teachers*. London: Sage.

Cockburn, A.D. and Parslow-Williams, P. (2008) Zero: Understanding an apparently paradoxical number, in A.D. Cockburn and G. Littler (eds.) *Mathematical Misconceptions*. London: Sage.

Department for Education (DfE) (2012) *Statutory Framework for the Early Years Foundation Stage: Setting the standards for learning, development and care for children from birth to five*. Available at: http://www.foundationyears.org.uk/wp-content/uploads/2012/07/EYFS-Statutory-Framework-2012.pdf.

Desforges, C. and Cockburn, A. (1987) *Understanding the Mathematics Teacher*. Lewes: Falmer Press.

Falkner, K.P., Levi, L. and Carpenter, T.P. (1999) Children's understanding of equality: A foundation for algebra, *Teaching Children Mathematics*, 6(4): 232–6.

Freiman, V. and Lee, L. (2004) Tracking primary students' understanding of the equality sign, in M. Hoines and A. Fuglestad (eds.) *Proceedings of the 28th Conference of the International Group for the Psychology of Mathematics Education*, Vol. 2, pp. 415–22. Bergen: Bergen University College.

Haylock, D.W. and Cockburn, A.D. (2013) *Understanding Mathematics for Young Children*, **5th edn. London: Sage.**

James, W. (1899) *Talks to Teachers*. New York: Holt.

Jordan, N., Kaplan, D., Ola'h, L. and Locuniak, M. (2006) Number sense growth in kindergarten: A longitudinal investigation of children at risk for mathematics difficulties, *Child Development*, 77(1): 153–75.

Linder, S.M., Powers-Costello, B. and Stegelin, D.A. (2011) Mathematics in early childhood: Research-based rationale and practical strategies, *Early Childhood Education Journal*, **39: 29–37.**

Marchini, C., Cockburn, A., Parslow-Williams, P. and Vighi, P. (2009) Equality relation and structural properties – a vertical study, in *Proceedings of the Sixth Conference of European Research in Mathematics Education*, pp. 569–78. Paris: Institut National de Recherche Pédagogique. Available at: www.inrp.fr/editions/cerme6 (accessed 23 January 2013).

Montague-Smith, A. (1997) *Mathematics in Nursery Education*. London: David Fulton.

Nardi, E. and Steward, S. (2003). Is mathematics T.I.R.E.D? A profile of quiet disaffection in the secondary mathematics classroom, *British Educational Research Journal*, 29(3): 345–66.

Parslow-Williams, P. and Cockburn, A.D. (2008) Equality, in A.D. Cockburn and G. Littler (eds.) *Mathematical Misconceptions: A Guide for primary teachers*. London: Sage.

Standards and Testing Agency (2013) *Early Years Foundation Stage Handbook*. Runcorn: Department for Education.

Williams, P. (2008) *Independent Review of Mathematics Teaching in Early Years Settings and Primary Schools*. London: Department for Children, Schools and Families.

Worthington, M. (2007) Multi-modality, play and children's mark-making in maths, in J. Moyles (ed.) *Early Years Foundations: Meeting the challenge*. Maidenhead: Open University Press.

11 Understanding the world, including ICT

Karen Phethean and Helen Clarke

Abstract

Young children are curious and playful explorers and enquirers on exciting voyages of discovery. Within their highly sensory worlds, children encounter amazing things every day. As they journey they interact with people, communities and the physical world with whom they collaborate and communicate to make sense of their experiences. Skills such as observation and questioning facilitate development of deep level understanding and capture moments of thinking, possibilities and connections. To navigate this world of enquiry, children use a range of tools to express and communicate their amazement in these encounters. In such interactions, partnerships and ideas emerge and grow within environments of trust and respect where children's voices are heard and valued. This in turn nurtures strong learning dispositions of curiosity and perseverance for children to become active and confident enquirers from birth. This chapter explores and celebrates the unique capabilities of young children as they encounter and engage in the world around them. We invite those involved in partnerships with children to recognize and use the boundless opportunities to learn together and to consider applying their own differing pedagogical approaches within such a statutory framework.

Introduction

The young child is the first great researcher. Children are born searching for and, therefore, researching the meaning of life, the meaning of the self in relation to others and to the world. Children are born searching for the meaning of their existence...the meaning of the conventions, customs and habits we have, and of the rules and the answers we provide.

(Rinaldi, 2003: 2)

In this chapter, we consider how the Statutory Framework for the Early Years Foundation Stage (EYFS) (DfE, 2012a) supports children in developing an understanding of the world around them and their interaction with that world. This is identified in the EYFS framework as a specific area – 'Understanding the World'. The EYFS identifies that this 'involves **guiding** children to make sense of their physical world and their community through opportunities to explore, observe and find out about people, places, technology and the environment' (DfE, 2012a: 5; original emphasis). A key issue we raise is the way in which the EYFS framework places *learning* about the world as the responsibility of the adult rather than the child. While the framework recognizes many fundamental aspirations for children's learning in this area, an important omission is the lack of recognition of children as *owners* of their learning; that learning should be initiated and developed by the child, arising from the child's ideas, interests and needs.

Practitioners operating within this statutory framework in England are also required to support and uphold the human rights framework enshrined within the United Nations Convention on the Rights of the Child (UNCRC) (United Nations, 1989). The right to an education (article 28) and the goals of that education (article 29) are enshrined within the other articles whose language embodies that of ownership, agency and identity. Enabling children to gain an understanding of the world requires adults to help them recognize their integral role in the world – active agents not only in constructing understanding but in their interactions with that world. Acting on behalf of children, adults put together frameworks intended to guide children's learning about their world so they become *responsible* adults of the future. The EYFS framework presents one such adult role of mastery and dominance in delivery and in assessment. However, we must be careful to avoid interpreting that world on children's behalf, in a rather deficit view of their capabilities. Instead, we might facilitate each *individual's* interpretation of their world, scaffolding their journey towards dispositions, skills and an accepted body of knowledge that explains that world. We need to be led by rather than lead the children to allow the world to reveal itself fully to them, and for children to reveal their understanding to us. The relationship between adult and child is democratic when both are confronting problems that are meaningful to them; adults who listen to learners acknowledge how much they learn in return (Kaplan, 2000).

Pedagogical approaches

The EYFS framework recognizes that children's developing understanding of the world around them occurs through play, acknowledged widely within pedagogical literature and research (Moyles, 2008; Brock *et al.*, 2009; Brooker and Edwards, 2010). That play is the natural medium of expression (Sutterby and Frost, 2006: 309; Schaffer and Drewes, 2010: 3) has long been recognized. The review of the EYFS curriculum (Tickell, 2011) advocates play as a means of supporting children's learning in the early years. The framework identifies the 'confusion about what learning through play actually means, and what the implications of this are for the role of adults' (Tickell, 2011: 28). It resolves this tension by adopting a socio-constructivist approach to learning throughout the recommendations:

3.35 In considering these issues, I considered what supporting children's learning and development should actually mean in practice. A definition I found very helpful describes this support as *the difference between what a child can do on their own, and what they can do when guided by someone else – either an adult or a more able child.*[12] This simple concept captures many of the valuable interactions between an adult and a child, and is the type of relationship that the requirements of the EYFS are intended to support. When considered from this perspective, all of the interactions between a child and parents, carers, early years practitioners, other adults or other children, could be described as learning or teaching interactions. The purpose of the EYFS is to ensure that when these types of interaction take place between children and early years practitioners, practitioners recognize these and can consciously build upon them. I believe it is right that all early years practitioners are, in this way, expected to guide children's learning and development.

> (Tickell, 2011: 29; Note 12 refers to Tickell's citation
> to Vygotsky's, 1978, classic work, *Mind and Society*)

This acknowledgement of the constructivist approach to learning is reinforced in the reference to Rabelais at the start of Section 3, 'Equipped for life, ready for school' where 'A child is not a vase to be filled, but a candle to be lit' (Rabelais, in Tickell, 2011: 19). Piaget (1959) recognized that children are not empty vessels to be filled with knowledge, but active learners who engage to construct their own theories of the world. The EYFS framework acknowledges the values that support pedagogical approaches in which children are encouraged to interact both with those around them and with their environment using social and cultural tools to facilitate that understanding, and in which their 'natural medium of expression' – their play – is a key part in that learning. The independent review of early education and childcare qualifications (Nutbrown, 2012) reinforces the value of play in learning, noting the implications of this for providers:

> ...that an understanding of the importance of play in children's lives and learning – both guided exploratory play through a well-planned environment, and play which allows children to explore their world for themselves – is part of fully understanding child development and fostering independent and enquiring minds. It is necessary, therefore, that adults understand their roles in providing for play, including when they should participate to extend and support learning, and when they should observe and not interfere.
>
> (Nutbrown, 2012: 20)

An initial digest of the statement above and that of the EYFS framework relating to play may consider the rationale to be similar. However, there are subtle differences, such as turns of phrase in the EYFS framework that lead back to the 'adult mastery model' proposed earlier in this chapter, compared with the more child-centred 'partnership model' of the independent review (Nutbrown, 2012). Nutbrown acknowledges that adults need to be aware as to when it is appropriate for them to engage in the child's world of play; implicit in this is the idea that the child is the owner of that play. The EYFS framework section (para. 1.9), while acknowledging that children may initiate play, again shows an adult mastery model:

> Each area of learning and development must be implemented through planned, purposeful play and through a mix of adult-led and child-initiated activity. Play is essential for children's development, building their confidence as they learn to explore, to think about problems, and relate to others. Children learn by leading their own play, and by taking part in play which is guided by adults. There is an ongoing judgement to be made by practitioners about the balance between activities led by children, and activities led or guided by adults. Practitioners must respond to each child's emerging needs and interests, guiding their development through warm, positive interaction. As children grow older, and as their development allows, it is expected that the balance will gradually shift towards more activities led by adults, to help children prepare for more formal learning, ready for Year 1.
>
> (DfE, 2012a: 6)

It is clear that play must be planned (by adults), purposeful (an adult's purpose?) and that 'an ongoing judgement' (by adults) must be made as to when children might lead their play or when an adult should intervene. As children get older (five to six years) play, or their 'natural medium of expression', should be replaced (by adults) with more 'formal learning' (as identified by adults). Children do indeed 'learn by leading their own play' (DfE, 2012a: 6); however, from a constructivist perspective it is not 'guided by adults' (DfE, 2012a: 6) but should involve *sharing* with peers and adults to help them gain an understanding of their world. Practitioners supporting children in gaining an understanding of the world should recognize that 'when you liberate and channel the energy and enthusiasm of young children they can be amazing explorers of their worlds. When you observe that energy and enthusiasm, you will in turn, also recognise opportunities to develop as a practitioner' (Fletcher *et al.*, 2009). Learning becomes a *shared* experience with shared *ownership* of learning.

Using and applying – Making meaning

Figure 11.1 is one representation of the complexity of making meaning, which identifies three characteristics of effective learning: 'playing and exploring', 'active learning' and 'creating and thinking critically'. These elements are represented here as convergent and, when combined or 'funnelled' in the diagram, as narrow in scope.

Figure 11.2 is an alternative representation of the complexity of making meaning. We encourage practitioners to look again at the three elements: 'playing and exploring', 'active learning' and 'creating and thinking critically'. This time these elements are represented as divergent, wide open possibilities.

The following discussion considers these three elements in more detail, each with a specific slant: 'playing and exploring' – as curiosity; 'active learning' – as involvement; and 'creating and thinking critically' – as imagination.

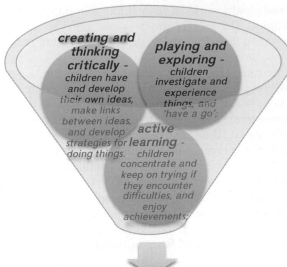

Making meaning

Figure 11.1 Learning characteristics taken from EYFS Statutory Framework 1.10 (DfE, 2012: 7).

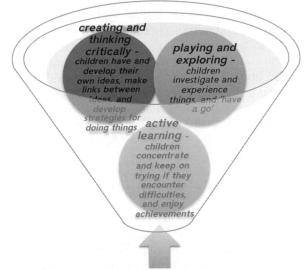

Making meaning

Figure 11.2 Learning characteristics taken from EYFS Statutory Framework, 1.10 (DfE, 2012: 7). Note the change from an 'input–output' approach in Fig. 11.1 to a more 'open' divergent approach in this representation. Here, children's opportunities for making meaning from the EYFS learning characteristics are seen to interact and merge – 'tossed together' in endless unique opportunities for individuals to make their own meaning and sense of the world around them.

Curiosity and emerging ideas

'Development Matters', the non-statutory guidance (Early Education, 2012), describes 'playing and exploring' as a characteristic of effective learning, where children's open-ended, hands-on experiences result from innate curiosity about the world. The EYFS suggests that the more developed a child becomes the more emphasis should be placed on adult-led activities. Yet, young children are expert enquirers and the complexity of their ideas increases rather than diminishes. Katz (2003: 17) reminds us that 'for sustained, continuous interactions to occur, the interactors must have something to interact about...something that matters to them, that is of interest and concern to them' (original emphasis). The early years should be taken up by a great deal of first-hand experiences of the world; 'mindful rather than mindless' (Katz, 2003: 17) interactions with people, places, phenomena and technology. Thus, 'treating children's questions with the care they deserve' allows 'authentic curiosity' to develop into 'emergent objectives' (Ovens, 2004: 18–19). Such ownership is demonstrated by Cox and Noble (Fletcher *et al.*, 2009), in that the children are supported to follow through their enquiries. Chak (2007), too, makes the link between curiosity, adult response and potential intellectual development; indeed, adults need to be curious *with* children and model genuine curiosity (Tovey, 2007).

Photograph 11.1 shows a young child at ease with his world; the horizon is wide and possibilities for exploration of place and phenomena are endless.

Photograph 11.1 A young child at ease with his world.

Involvement and learning dispositions

Development Matters (Early Education, 2012) describes 'active learning' as another characteristic of effective learning, where children concentrate and keep on trying if they encounter difficulties. Full involvement and fascination in a task suggests an intensity of attention and stresses the importance of endeavour. Such focused fascination invites children to become involved with people, places, phenomena and technology. Laevers (1994) proposes experiential education where involvement in a task, a central feature in a learning environment, acts as a measure of deep learning and is thus an indicator of quality. Involvement is recognized by concentration and persistence; characterized by motivation, fascination, and intensity at a sensory and cognitive level; and occurs when the task matches the capabilities of the learner. Laevers' Experiential Education Theory (1995) advocates maximum freedom for the children, opportunities to explore, and a relationship between child and adult that is sensitive to the emotional needs of the child. Involvement is a crucial first step to interaction and development of understanding, skills and attitudes towards the world – its people, places and processes. We suggest that taking involvement as a point of reference empowers practitioners to make innovations that are valued as child-oriented and fruitful. Fostering involvement is central to planning challenging experiences for young children. It offers children a level of control over the learning process as they follow their own lines of enquiry about the world.

Photograph 11.2 shows a young boy exploring in the sand. Here the context is informal and outdoors – he explores, he is involved, he uses tools and he has

Photograph 11.2 A young boy exploring the sand.

much to communicate to others. He works at the edge of his personal capabilities (Bianchi and Feasey, 2011) and we wait to be invited into this interaction.

Imagination, positive attitudes and diverse capabilities

Development Matters (Early Education, 2012) also describes creating and thinking critically as a characteristic of effective learning, where children develop their own ideas, make links between ideas and develop creative strategies for doing things. We encourage practitioners to reflect on notions of their own and children's creativity. 'Observant teachers recognise capabilities dormant in the child's imagination and use them to develop understanding'; indeed, 'teachers support children in divergent thinking and value imaginative ideas' (Oliver, 2006: 49). Gallas (1994: 78) stresses the centrality of imagination in children's learning. Indeed, 'for children, who have not abandoned the universe of the imagination, who are still filled with wonder and awe, finding ways to study the world that incorporate transcendent modes of thinking becomes an imperative'.

The tenets of practice in early years settings, such as sensory learning and role play, are well suited to tapping into this spiritual domain. For example, Steiner's (1964) active use of fantasy and imagination are strategies on which practitioners continue to build their teaching today.

The complexity of young children's thought and communication about their experiences in the world suggests a rich landscape of representation beyond immediate speech. Bruner (2006) proposed ways children use to represent the world: 'enactive' denoting procedural action routines; 'iconic' where images serve as prototypes for events; and 'symbolic' where systems of symbols are created and used. Modes such as acting, drawing, modelling, dancing and singing (Gallas, 1994; Anning and Ring, 1999; Pahl, 1999) allow children to share their developing ideas. Adults must make efforts to understand children's attempts at making meaning and value what children bring to their meaning-making and composing activities in a complex world (Pahl, 1999).

Assessment: capturing complex understandings

A key aspect of the EYFS framework is that of assessment for all children from birth to five years supported by an assessment handbook for the EYFS Profile (DfE, 2012b) in which guidance for summative assessment of a child's 'school readiness' (DfE, 2012a: 2) is provided. While recognizing that assessment is ongoing, the approach is very much one of *convergent* assessment where 'the important thing is to find out *if* the learner knows, understands or can do a predetermined thing' (Torrance and Pryor, 2001: 153) and rooted in normative, summative assessment. This is in opposition to *divergent* assessment, which is about finding out '*what* the learner knows, understands and can do' and is focused on 'the learner's understanding rather than the agendas of the assessor' (Torrance and Pryor, 2001: 154) and upholds a constructivist approach to learning.

A divergent approach to assessment reflects a learner's individual interests and needs. It sees learners as following individual paths of exploration, delight and discovery, sometimes shared and sometimes alone, some paths longer and some shorter than others. This philosophy is illustrated in the Deuleuzian concept of rhizomatic growth (Ryan and Amorim, 2005; Gough, 2006), in which 'the children may be the learners, but they are also the teachers; the teachers may teach, but they are on a learning path too…Thus it is that the paths of learning and self-discovery converge and diverge' (Phethean and Clarke, 2011: 41). In this divergent approach, the learner is intrinsically involved in the learning process: those involved can reflect upon the learning that has taken place and so identify the next steps on that path or paths. Learning and its progression is not necessarily sequential:

> …progression implies progress, and progress suggests a journey. Conceptual progress might be considered as a journey through a landscape of developing ideas and it is a journey travelled by learners. It is, of course, a lifelong journey.
>
> (Kibble, 2006: 198)

While the EYFS framework (DfE, 2012a) is geared towards setting the standards for learning, development and care for children from birth to five and heads towards statutory summative assessment in the EYFS Profile (DfE, 2012b), practitioners should regard this within the bigger picture of the socio-constructivist framework underpinning it. That is, an approach in which it is formative and ongoing assessment where the learners are involved in sharing their learning path with those they meet along that journey. The EYFS Profile handbook states that it 'has been developed to support practitioners in making accurate judgements about each child's attainment' (DfE, 2012b: 5) but we would again encourage practitioners to move away from the 'mastery model' to the model of partnership – listening to and involving children in identifying what they feel confident in doing and understanding. We must find ways of listening to children:

> All children are intelligent, different from each other and unpredictable. If we know how to listen to them, children can give back to us the pleasure of amazement, of marvel, of doubt…the pleasure of the 'why'.
>
> (Rinaldi, 2003: 3)

In so doing, we will reveal the true capabilities of children as they make sense of subtle interactions between people, explore place and space, find patterns in the complex processes of the natural world, and choose technologies to capture communication and expression. Learning is collaboration, developed through finding out and exploring.

Conclusion

Overall, the EYFS specific area 'Understanding the World' (DfE, 2012a) has positive aspirations for children's development. It promotes a perspective that children learn through experience and playful interactions. However, our caution is that there is an underlying thread, of adults owning these interactions with the world, of leading and assessing those interactions rather than the children taking responsibility. There is neither clear acknowledgement of the children's role in meaning-making, nor recognition of the richness of children's ideas. We encourage practitioners to avoid assumptions that mask the experiences and voices of children.

As practitioners consider 'Understanding the World', we encourage them to reflect on what type of teachers they strive to be and adapt any perceived confines of the framework to their own context. Children's early understanding of the world – their first steps in a developing literacy of people (identity), place (and environment) and phenomena (natural and manmade, living and non-living) and the cultural tools of technology (including ICT) – prepare them for informed decision-making about the world and their interactions with it. Attitudes and dispositions, skills, knowledge and understandings lead to meaning-making. Any curriculum hides the complexity of learning and its idiosyncratic, playful, social and joyful 'messiness'. Flexibility and openness are essential to respecting children's meaning-making. Von Glasersfeld (1995) adopts a more radical constructivism where a child's response to the world is accepted as a 'good one for the moment'; one that holds meaning for the child in that situation.

We encourage practitioners to respond positively to the challenges of the EYFS 'Understanding the World' in emergent, creative, multimodal and playful ways; to question the assumptions in the framework that children learn in linear, normative and target-driven ways; to ask what the framework means for individual approaches; to make priorities, and follow the children's lead as they take pleasure in finding things out about the world – its people, places, and technologies – in a divergent model, where the child leads vibrant co-construction of knowing and becoming, along paths of curiosity, involvement and imagination.

Points for reflection and discussion

1. What is your pedagogical approach to supporting children's learning and how is this reflected in your interactions with children?
2. What are the tensions arising for you in your practice between your pedagogical approach and curriculum documents?
3. How do you support children in reflecting upon their learning? How might you develop this further?

References and further reading

Anning, A. and Ring, K. (1999) *The influence of the socio-cultural context on young children's meaning making.* Paper presented at the British Educational Research Association Conference, University of Sussex at Brighton, 2–5 September.
Bianchi, L. and Feasey, R. (2011) *Science Beyond the Classroom Boundaries for 3–7 Year Olds.* Maidenhead: Open University Press.

Brock, A., Dodds, S., Jarvis, P. and Olusoga, Y. (2009) *Perspectives on Play: Learning through life*. Harlow: Pearson Educational.

Brooker, L. and Edwards, S. (eds.) (2010) *Engaging Play*. Maidenhead: Open University Press.

Bruner, J.S. (2006) The course of cognitive growth, in *In Search of Pedagogy, Vol. 1: The selected works of Jerome S. Bruner*. Abingdon: Routledge.

Chak, A. (2007) Teachers' and parents' conceptions of children's curiosity and exploration, *International Journal of Early Years Education*, 15(2): 141–59.

Department for Education (DfE) (2012a) *Statutory Framework for the Early Years Foundation Stage: Setting the standards for learning, development and care for children from birth to five*. Available at: http://www.foundationyears.org.uk/wp-content/uploads/2012/07/EYFS-Statutory-Framework-2012.pdf.

Department for Education (DfE) (2012b) *Early Years Foundation Stage Profile 2013*. Available at: http://media.education.gov.uk/assets/files/pdf/2/2013_EYFS_handbook.pdf (accessed 16 February 2013).

Early Education (2012) *Development Matters in the Early Years Foundation Stage*. Available at: http://www.foundationyears.org.uk/wp-content/uploads/2012/03/Development-Matters-FINAL-PRINT-AMENDED.pdf (accessed 16 February 2013).

Fletcher, L., Ryan, C., Phethean, K. and Clarke, C. (2009) *Fostering Curiosity in the Early Years*. AstraZeneca Science Teaching Trust/University of Winchester Continuing Professional Development Unit. Available at: http://www.azteach-science.co.uk/resources/continuing-professional-development/fostering-curiosity-in-early-years-science.aspx (accessed 23 February 2013).

Gallas, K. (1994) *The Languages of Learning: How children talk, write, dance, draw and sing their understanding of the world*. Columbia, NY: Teachers College Press.

Gough, N. (2006) Shaking the tree, making a rhizome: Towards a nomadic geophilosophy of science education, *Educational Philosophy and Theory*, 38(5): 625–45.

Kaplan, A. (2000) Teacher and student: Designing democratic relationship, *Journal of Curriculum Studies*, 32(3): 377–402.

Katz, L. (2003) Engaging children's hearts and minds, *Early Years*, 35: 15–22.

Kibble, R. (2006) Teaching for progression in conceptual understanding, in W. Harlen (ed.) *ASE Guide to Primary Science*. Hatfield: Association for Science Education.

Laevers, F. (ed.) (1994) *Defining and Assessing Quality in Early Childhood Education*. Leuven: Leuven University Press.

Laevers, F. (1995) *An Exploration of the Concept of Involvement as an Indicator for Quality in Early Childhood Care and Education*. Consortium of Institutions for Development and Research in Education in Europe. Dundee: Scottish Curriculum Council.

Moyles, J. (ed.) (2008) *The Excellence of Play*, 2nd edn. Maidenhead: Open University Press.

Nutbrown, C. (2012) *Foundations for Quality: The independent review of early education and childcare qualifications: Final Report*. Available at: https://www.education.gov.uk/publications/eOrderingDownload/Foundations%20for%20quality%20-%20Nutbrown%20final%20report.pdf (accessed 2 February 2013).

Oliver, A. (2006) *Creative Teaching: Science in the early years and primary classroom*. London: David Fulton.

Ovens, P. (2004) A 'SANE' way to encourage creativity, *Primary Science Review*, 81: 17–20.

Pahl, K. (1999) *Transformations: Children's meaning making in a nursery*. Stoke-on Trent: Trentham Books.

Phethean, K. and Clarke, H. (2011) Tutor your footsteps are the path…*Science Teacher Education*, 60: 37–45.

Piaget, J. (1959) *The Language and Thought of the Child.* London: Routledge & Kegan Paul.

Rinaldi, C. (2003) The teacher as researcher, *Innovations in Early Education: The International Reggio Exchange,* 10(2). Available at: http://www.reggioalliance.org/downloads/researcher:rinaldi.pdf (accessed 26 February 2013).

Ryan, C. and Amorim, A.C. (2005) Deleuze, action research and rhizomatic growth, *Educational Action Research,* 13(4): 581–93.

Schaffer, C.E. and Drewes, A.A. (2010) The therapeutic powers of play and play-based therapy, in A.A. Drewes and C.E. Schaffer (eds.) *School-based Play Therapy.* New York: Wiley.

Steiner, R. (1964) *The Kingdom of Childhood.* London: Rudolf Steiner Press.

Sutterby, J.A. and Frost, J. (2006) Creating play environments for early childhood: Indoors and out, in B. Spodek and O. Saracho (eds.) *Handbook of Research on the Education of Young Children.* Mahwah, NJ: Lawrence Erlbaum Associates.

Tickell, C. (2011) *The Early Years: Foundations for life, health and learning: An independent report on the Early Years Foundation Stage to Her Majesty's Government.* Available at: http://media.education.gov.uk/MediaFiles/B/1/5/%7BB15EFF0D-A4DF-4294-93A1-1E1B88C13F68%7DTickell%20review.pdf (accessed 25 February 2013).

Torrance, H. and Pryor, J. (2001) Developing formative assessment in the classroom, *British Educational Research Journal,* 27(5): 615–31.

Tovey, H. (2007) *Playing Outdoors: Spaces and places, risk and challenge.* Maidenhead: Open University Press.

United Nations (1989) *United Nations Convention on the Rights of the Child.* Paris: United Nations.

UNICEF (undated) *A Summary of the Rights Under the Convention on the Rights of the Child: Fact Sheet.* UNICEF. Available at: http://www.unicef.org/crc/files/Rights_overview.pdf (accessed 12 February 2013).

Von Glasersfeld, E. (1995) *Radical Constructivism: A way of knowing and learning.* London: Falmer Press.

Vygotsky, L. (1978) *Mind and Society.* Cambridge, MA: Harvard University Press.

12 Expressive arts and design

Suzy Tutchell

Abstract

Throughout this chapter, my focus respects and acknowledges the many possibilities of expressive arts and design of our youngest generation. Disciplines in the arts are multifaceted and are not to be confined to a definitive list within a curriculum that defies potentiality. We must be mindful that creative thought and application take place throughout all areas and moments of learning and are not just confined to expressive arts, a fact recognized in part by the revised Early Years Foundation Stage (EYFS) framework within one of the overarching characteristics of effective learning: creating and thinking critically.

Introduction

Young children's sensorimotor skills and active imaginations cast moments of great ingenuity in the creative experience as they continue, from birth, to discover aspects of their emerging and expressively alert characters. Their ability to work as visual artists, actors, musicians and dancers is unselfconscious and dynamic. They capture the essence of what it means to create artistically, visually and haptically – bringing new imaginative ideas into existence through their playful endeavours. Anning and Ring (2004: 3) marvel at this astounding quality:

> ... young children's flexibility of thinking and their unselfconscious ability to flick from one mode of representation to another ... are capabilities that many artists spend their lives trying to recapture.

A further astounding aspect is that, within their flexible purposing (Eisner, 2002), young children are capable of abstract thinking and expression that tends to be far removed from our everyday adult existence. Infants' uninhibited ability to be curious and actively find out motivates them to construe new ideas, dream up innovative scenarios and express unusual imaginings. This characteristic affords unpredictability, which is the very essence of contemporary artistes – the expressive thinkers of today.

The conundrum for adults who work with young children in various settings is how to value and support the child who expresses with abstract and unhindered thought. This, in itself, is no puzzle: it is when an expectation exists to align children's existence in this golden age of childhood (Coates and Coates, 2006) with a nationally imposed curriculum that contradictions occur. There are phrases, within the Early Years Foundation Stage (EYFS) (DfE, 2012), which positively denote the importance of curiosity, the unusual and choice. Grateful though we are of their inclusion, there remains a suggestion of age and stage; deficit in knowledge of the young child and a lack of recognition of just how astounding creative young infants are from birth.

Craft reminds us always to be wary of placing ceilings on young children's ability by defining them in relation to achievement and attainment:

> ...children's intelligence needs to be considered with great care – it is very personal and not always visible. Achievement deepening can happen over long periods of time and is not always testament to what they 'learn' or 'listen to'.
>
> (Craft, 2002: 66)

Assessment and scale points, though informing us of what has been reached, do not always celebrate the 'can do' of a young child. Instead, such formalization can often lead to premature progression, to the next set of targets rather than crucially regarding the children as citizens of today (Belaguer, 2004). A prescribed curriculum represents a set of principles which we work *with*, not *for*. Neither us, nor a set of printed words should prescribe young children the freedom, space and time to negotiate their own creative rules and regulations.

The creative soul is predisposed to learn in an active and enquiring way within different aspects of engagement and, therefore, similar skill-scapes will be generic to a creative mind working in maths, in literacy, in physical development. All babies and infants are different and so there is no 'one size fits all' as they play. They will continue to find their own intuitive and idiosyncratic patterns as they avidly forage and investigate what life presents to them. 'New babies have the rich potential for becoming creative explorers with the curiosity, desire and inclination to understand the world they are now a part of' (Chilvers, 2012: 6).

It is the very crucial aspect of individual ownership of the arts that is missing from the existing framework and must be clear in our minds as we work with young children from birth so that their creative journeys are personal and individually recognized and not used as a comparative curriculum-based study.

Birth of expression

From birth, human beings have a voracious appetite for seeking out means to express themselves. A baby mimicking a facial gesture, an infant making patterns on a steamed-up window, or a young child jumping in a muddy puddle is as natural to this generation as sleeping, breathing and laughing. An infant's embryonic spirit desires interaction with the many visually and haptically rich encounters that fill their everyday lives. Such encounters during the emergent verbal phase are the concrete foundations for making sense of our curious world. Sensory exploration is the basis for growing aesthetic awareness intrinsic to the expressive characters that develop in each and every child.

Eisner (2002) reminds us that the senses serve as the first avenue to consciousness. To understand this, we need to examine the relationship between babies and toddlers and their interpretation of the brave new world that confronts them from the moment they come into existence.

> What was first a reflex response, a function of instinct, becomes a gradual search for stimulation, differentiation, exploration, and eventually for meaning. Our sensory system becomes a means through which we pursue our own development.
>
> (Eisner, 2002: 2)

As young infants touch material, smell food cooking or hear loud sounds, their small bodies are energized with a multitude of complex known and unknown perceptible encounters. Familiar and unfamiliar enterprises and interactions continue alongside each other, each one informing the other and so a personalized repertoire of understanding starts to emerge.

Senses and the developing brain

This repertoire is a direct consequence of the power of the senses and the connections that are being rapidly and busily made in the brain. Gopnik *et al.* (2001) liken this fast and furious connection of cells to the intricate and complex paths of a telephone wire. They add:

> In the first few months of life, babies already seem to have solved a number of deep philosophical conundrums. They know something about how those objects characteristically move. They know those objects are part of a three-dimensional space. And they know the relationship between information that comes from their different senses.
>
> (Gopnik *et al.*, 2001: 70)

Babies and young infants start to develop a conceptual clarity in the early stages of life by way of their sensory exploits. As they grow, their interactions steer perceived thought to a more concrete stage, and conception of ideas can be generated, as suggested in the following diagram:

A progressive flow of perceptive visual understanding and intent:
Sensorial exploration ⟶ Concrete understandings ⟶ Expressive intent

---

The development of tactile, visual, auditory, spatial and movement perception has an impact on their experiences, as considered in the stages above. By the sixth month, babies are able to reach for an object they see and at about a year can follow rapidly moving objects (Goddard-Blythe, 2004). Their ability to see with understanding has a direct impact on their ability to represent and conceive thoughts and ideas (Duffy, 2006).

Sensory modalities and aesthetic understanding

As infants use their senses to learn and understand, they begin to develop an awareness of aesthetic appreciation. Young children begin to learn how to use their sensory powers in order to select, see, hear, observe, distinguish and feel in the arts. Aesthetic experiences bridge the sensory encounter with an ability to invest further than the original moment of interaction. These states of being can facilitate discovery and examination and enable young children to see and appreciate beauty that surrounds them.

> [Children] can develop their understanding of the world, experience beauty and express their cultural heritage. Such experiences help children to gain self-esteem and create a view of the world that is uniquely their own.
>
> (Duffy, 2010: 25)

A growing perception in aesthetic appreciation encourages children to expand their already natural sense of wonder and this often leads to expressive art making. The power of the experiences is often so all consuming and overwhelming that they are naturally motivated and compelled to respond verbally, visually and physically.

The vivacity of young expression

The 2012 revised EYFS gives little thought to the wondrous animation and vivacity of young infants as defined in this chapter. To value and relish the expressive capacities of a young child during their sensorially based journeys, time, space and awareness are essential. There is a tendency to move children on, to invest time in engagement in order to reach the next stage of development and therefore undernourish the child of 'today'. Our expressive children live in their present-day lives – lives that are very short in the scheme of a whole lifetime and so this precious and enthralling 'era' needs to be nurtured and appreciated to recognize fully the amazingly high levels of thinking of which they are capable.

Dowling (2005) refers to the 'transcendence' of young children's experiences, when their great adventures and explorations enable them to reach out to the limits of their world as part of growing up. Children are very successful at existing in their esoteric and individual encounters. It is a testament to their age that they allow themselves to be distracted by beauty, fun, interest and phenomena. Animated and uninhibited curiosity such as this throws into the ring all the 'whys', 'whats', 'wheres', 'what fors' and requires the young mind and brain to think critically and creatively and to consider and ask questions.

Playing in the expressive arts and design

> I begin with an idea and then it becomes something else.
>
> (Pablo Picasso)

As children come into contact with the objects and fascinations of life, they spend a lot of physical time and energy playing and exploring. Spooning a dollop of gloopy paint on to a surface, moving in time to a beat and mimicking characters in role play are all acts of investigative play which allow the child to find out and define their own relationships with these materials through playful actions.

Such intimate and life-affirming moments confirm the very intense quality of play and its arena, which house the dynamic meeting between the child's inner life (emotions and thoughts) and their external world (Ring, 2006). Expressive play affords young children the chance to enter a transcendent, interpretative space where they can tell themselves about themselves (Wright, 2010).

The rich stratification of creative knowledge enables the child to use their play experiences as firm foundations for understanding themselves as artistes. Cox (2005) refers to this work in progress and continued enquiry as a young child's 'central source of data'. All too often government-led guidance is irreverently ignorant of the rich 'person' that exists from birth, designating advice as to how to inform and extend as if we are born with a deficit of understanding to be filled rather than a 'root' of deep individual knowledge on which to base our experience.

Somatic involvement in child-led expressive play

During expressive exploration, the involvement and idiosyncratic behaviours of the infant's body cohabit a state of immersion as somatic knowledge and understanding develops. Infants' bodies are energized, both physically and mentally as they are consumed in the learning and micro-eureka moments. Such states of mind denote the immense ability young children have to think with their bodies, where physical actions unconsciously and consciously intertwine with cognitive thought (Eglinton, 2003). This richly combined dance emanates a myriad of expressive encounters, some intentional, some coincidental and some spontaneous.

We are reminded of the self-choreographed and visceral sensory rich movement of a child's interaction by Cavazonni's (2012) expression 'the child dances with the light' while they expressively explore. There is a vivid quality to such a somatic moment; symptomatic of mind and body actively playing and creating. It is a beautifully composed metaphor that tells us of what we can 'see' and 'feel' when we engage and trust in children's embodied creative minds.

Roles of adults

Babies learn to become part of the world through interaction with the human beings around them. Learnt gestures, expressions and mannerisms are idiosyncratically owned but their existence came about as much through nurture as nature.

Consider the mother and child who 'tune into each other' (Anning and Ring, 2004). As they exchange facial expressions, participate in interactive rituals and movement games, the child and parent learn something more about each other. Each interpersonal 'melody exchange' (Matthews, 2003: 26) ensures another layering of shared understanding. This dyadic experience is set within the secure and familiar home environment. The transition from home to setting requires young children to familiarize themselves with a whole new set of expressive-rich aspects of the setting.

The very rich intersubjective activities of mother and child (Trevarthen and Aitken, 2001) have formed a solid and firm schematic root of cognition for the young infant that will be tested, built upon and extended by other partnerships, outside home. These interactions will be key to the infant's journey in the expressive arts, rooted in the firm interrelational foundations formed from birth (Matthews, 2003).

'Riding the waves together' – cooperative interactions

During socially bound expressively creative moments, we can 'ride the wave of discovery' with the child, as one practitioner once described it. If we know our children well, and have learnt about them through mutual responsiveness and trust (Reddy, 2010), then we can identify illumination appropriately. As the adult observes, appreciates and advocates the expressive and meandering paths taken by the infant, they both acknowledge and trust the outcome that is owned by the child, if there is an outcome at all. Trust also comes in the form of trusting ourselves not to interfere in order to allow the moment to take shape and find its way.

'Riding the wave' with young children encourages both the infant and the adult to engage in a respected union of interest – their responses to expressive creativity can be discussed, considered and constructed. Positive body language can also display our joining in physically with the adventure. Here the active mirroring of our own creative and explorative movements reflect those of the child painting with a large brush, sculpting clay with both hands or peeling and unwrapping masking tape. Our cooperative and energized hands can demonstrate to a child our interest in the artistic journey undertaken.

In the EYFS (DfE, 2012), 'sharing' is recognized as an aspect of 'positive relationships' and 'being imaginative', as we are advised to 'play along with a child who is beginning to pretend' (Early Education, 2012: 45). What is surprisingly absent, however, throughout the guidance for this area of learning are words such as 'co-explore', 'joint' and 'interact' in order to define what lies at the heart of our adult and child creative engagement and endeavours.

The shared physical exploration produces conjoined moments of tactile and visual discoveries. A shared experience between child and adult gives rise to a growing sense of self-esteem in the child, as their adventure is valued by someone else who, with careful and considered language, can extend the journey to a higher level of thinking. Paired co-existence and co-exploration in art extends both the quality and richness of the process. It is an immensely powerful companionship and one that affects both parties as they reaffirm their interest in one another (Simpson, 2011).

Body language tells many stories of joint non-verbal participation, appreciation and investigation. It is a point of discussion that needs to be had regularly in settings where very young children are engaged in expressive art-and-design-based activities and thus investigate aesthetic awareness. As verbally active adults, we often feel the need to speak, to use words in order to form a dialogue with a very young child whose verbal communication is still emerging. Communication and language are enhanced through speech but the power of silent cooperation can be devalued and ignored. Awareness sensing (Tutchell, 2013) can be defined as a reciprocal exchange in which two protagonists have a silent awareness of one another. Such quiet moments are absent from the EYFS guidance on 'Positive relationships'. Yet the silence is, very importantly, responding to the present time; in those still and silent moments the partnership is actively alert to the possibilities that lie in waiting.

The focused one-to-oneness of a childminder and thirty-month-old child as they interact with two pieces of wood describes such an exchange of cooperation and shared interest. In this scenario, the childminder, with imperceptible awareness of intention, follows the child's every move and inclination of body gesture. The wood's layered surface provokes a tactile response and both child and adult embark on a peeling sequence. Their movements coincide and collide as they both show pleasure and enjoyment through smiles and gestures at the extracted shavings. The quietness of space, company and extended time in the childminder's home leads to this rich, intimate exchange of ideas where concentration of mind, hands and emotions are contemporaneously involved.

The inviting spaces of our environments

'Space' connotes a rich plethora of opportunities, including potential arenas inside and out. Space can be defined as the unlimited and incalculably great three-dimensional expanse in which all material objects are located and all events occur. In the EYFS, however, recommendations for enabling environments in response to expressive arts and design include 'space' only once with regards to an area for movement and dance.

Architectural intelligence urges us to draw on the creative potentiality of this space rather than being restricted by building boundaries, and hindered by the obstacles of unnecessary furniture. Through flexible organization and an open mind to young expressive possibilities, spaces within environments can support and embrace children's achievements.

Theatres of space

Dramas of expressive discovery take place in potential theatres of space (Tutchell, 2013). Such dynamic spaces positively encourage successes and failures within explorations and investigations. Creative dramas are repeated, reviewed, adapted and modified during process driven moments. The spaces also provide dramas that are borne out of the somatically enhanced physical activities of expressive arts and design. We witness escapades that are akin to the fantasy play of child actors. Wright (2010: 172) refers to these wonderfully dramatic moments:

Like film-makers: children can be the cast of one – taking on all the characters which live on their paper – multiple roles. Intertextuality – seeing life through an alternative prism. The use of quasi-human figures, hybrids of nature, offers the child opportunities to polarise between real and fantasy worlds.

Creating and maintaining spaces where expressive-based interaction is multisensory in exploration and vast in discovery relinquishes boundaries of conformity. An aspect of continuous provision is that there will be some familiar features and routine procedures, which are necessary for the status quo and social equilibrium. But spaces that are open-ended or 'whatever you want it to be' spaces (Broadhead, 2012) are places where children can flourish in ways that we might not have thought possible. Accessible resources will also encourage independence and will release the adult from a 'control' of space that deprecates the expressive creativity of a young child.

Our commitment to generating spaces that respond to the 'emotionally expressive' individual are indicative of our recognition of the inevitable and powerful link between the emotional individual and the arts. The two cannot be extricated as one motivates the other; they are intrinsically intertwined in their value for the young infant. Words to define such emotional and expressive entanglement are absent from the 'Expressive arts' of the EYFS and must be redefined by the practitioner to ensure practice is concurrent with young children's feelings, thoughts and emotions during their development in the expressive arts.

Conclusion

The words of Eisner resonate the magic of the arts for us all and help us to remember how we, as adults, relate to this very individual expressive and emotive aspect of life:

> The arts are a means of exploring our own interior landscape. When the arts genuinely move us, we discover what it is that we are capable of experiencing. In this sense, the arts help us discover the contours of our emotional selves. They provide resources for experiencing the range and varieties of our responsive capacities.
>
> (Eisner, 2002: 11)

Points for reflection and discussion

1. What ways are there to encourage, sustain and enjoy young children's positive and preferred expressively rich learning styles?
2. Evaluate the personal qualities you have that will help you to develop warm, interactive relationships with young children in their arts-based explorations.
3. Consider the spaces both you and the children you work with occupy. Do they suggest, support and motivate curiosity-based explorations?

References and further reading

Anning, A. and Ring, K. (2004) *Making Sense of Children's Drawings*. Maidenhead: Open University Press.

Belaguer, I. (2004) Speech delivered at the *Crossing Boundaries Conference*, Reggio Emilia, Italy, February.

Broadhead, P. (2012) Speech delivered at the *How Children Learn Conference*, Aston University, Birmingham, September.

Cavazonni, P. (2012) Speech delivered at '*What is a Child*', University of Winchester, November.

Chilvers, D. (2012) What does 'creating and thinking critically' mean?, *Early Years Update*, 95: 5–7.

Coates, E. and Coates, A. (2006) Young children talking and drawing, *International Journal of Early Years Education*, 14(3): 221–41.

Cox, S. (2005) Intention and meaning in young children's drawing, *International Journal of Art and Design Education*, 24(2): 115–25.

Craft, A. (2002) *Creativity and Early Years Education*. London: Continuum.

Department for Education (DfE) (2012) *Statutory Framework for the Early Years Foundation Stage: Setting the standards for learning, development and care for children from birth to five*. Available at: http://www.foundationyears.org.uk/wp-content/uploads/2012/07/EYFS-Statutory-Framework-2012.pdf.

Dowling, M. (2005) *Young Children's Personal, Social and Emotional Development*. London: Paul Chapman.

Duffy, B. (2006) *Supporting Creativity and Imagination in the Early Years*, 2nd edn. Maidenhead: Open University Press.

Duffy, B. (2010) Using creativity and creative learning to enrich the lives of young children at the Thomas Coram Centre, in C. Timms (ed.) *Born Creative*. London: Demos.

Early Education (2012) *Development Matters in the Early Years Foundation Stage*. London: BAECE.

Eglinton, K.A. (2003) *Art in the Early Years*. Abingdon: Routledge.

Eisner, E.W. (2002) *The Arts and the Creation of Mind*. New Haven, CT: Yale University Press.

Goddard-Blythe, S. (2004) *Well Balanced Child*. Stroud: Hawthorn Press.

Gopnik, A., Meltzoff, A. and Kuhl, P. (2001) *How Babies Think*. London: Orion Books.

Matthews, J. (2003) *Drawing and Painting: Children and visual representation*. London: Paul Chapman.

Reddy, V. (2010) *How Infants Know Minds*. Cambridge, MA: Harvard University Press.

Ring, K. (2006) What mothers do: Everyday routines and rituals and their impact upon young children's use of drawing for meaning making, *International Journal of Early Years Education*, 14(1): 63–84.

Simpson, K. (2011) The unfolding self, in R. House (ed.) *Too Much, Too Soon*. Stroud: Hawthorn Press.

Trevarthen, C. and Aitken, K.J. (2001) Infant intersubjectivity: Research, theory, and clinical applications, *Journal of Child Psychology and Psychiatry*, 42(2): 3–48.

Tutchell, S. (2013) *Young Children as Artists: Art and design in the early years and Key Stage 1*. Abingdon: Routledge.

Wright, S. (2010) *Understanding Creativity in Early Childhood*. London: Sage.

PART 3
Partnership working

13 The pressures of leading early years services in a changing world

Caroline Leeson

Abstract

This chapter debates the rise of new models of early years leadership, funding and perceptions of the provision of welfare services across the sector. Through an exploration of the increased attention being given to early years leadership by governments, practitioners and academics, the chapter identifies the discourses that have developed and debates their helpfulness to the provision of services to children and their families. In particular, there is a focus on the policy shift in emphasis away from leading a learning community towards leading a business to improve service delivery and outcomes in adverse circumstances using entrepreneurial skills and aptitudes. A critique is offered of what leaders of early years services might learn from the literature on entrepreneurial leadership.

Introduction

Historically, there was very little interest in how leadership is expressed in early years settings – early manifestations of provision were often the village playgroup run by a committee of local parents (usually mothers) or the occasional state-run nursery often attached to a school and administered by the head teacher. Consequently, early years leaders were commonly regarded as 'caring, capable women in the service of the nation' (Woodrow and Busch, 2008: 89). Thus, a highly feminized concept of early years work, workers and leaders (Hard and O'Gorman, 2007) developed that was at odds with masculine models of leadership taken from the business sector and focusing on hierarchy, control and performance management (Graham and Jarvis, 2011).

A further factor was the perception of self as a leader. Rodd (2006) explored this phenomenon finding that early years leaders were unlikely to see themselves as leaders, preferring to define themselves as women serving and supporting other women. Consequently, this position contributed to the identification of early years work as low level, low paid and undervalued work that is only performed by women and is merely an extension of their role as mothers (Taggart, 2011).

Subsequently, concerns were raised that these women lacked business skills and would be unable to develop services to meet the burgeoning demands of politicians and the public (Campbell-Barr, 2009). Increased demand for high-quality day care to enable women to return to the workplace, coupled with key reports in the 1990s into the importance of early years services in enhancing the development of children's learning, led to considerable development in the provision of services to young children and their families. As a consequence of public and political expectations of what constitutes a quality environment for optimizing the potential of young children (Early Years Foundation Stage; DfE, 2012), we have seen an increased regulatory focus on the practice of early years leaders and workers with questions raised regarding quality and leadership (Leeson *et al.*, 2012; Osgood, 2012).

Ideological perspectives on the provision of a mixed economy of early childhood education and care (ECEC) required identification of effective measures of quality, leading to the introduction of standards of practice (CWDC, 2006; DfES, 2007) and training programmes for existing and aspiring early years workers. As early years services increased in number, and both parents and the state became ever more vociferous in their expectations, issues of leadership and quality became central to determining both the value and worth of the individual setting and the collective (Campbell-Barr, 2009). Educational leadership models offered inspiration for early years leaders but were found wanting in the unique context of early childhood, with its historical concentration on relationships, personal empowerment and community nourishment (Leeson, 2010).

The subsequent discourse on what a unique early years model of leadership might look like led to the development of specific leadership training programmes, including the National Professional Qualification in Integrated Centre Leadership (NCSL, 2004) and the development of the National Standards for Leaders of SureStart Children's Centres (DfES, 2007). What became known as the new leadership paradigm (Northouse, 2010) espoused theories that placed relationships at the centre of leadership activities offering early years leaders the guidance they needed towards the leadership they espoused (Leeson *et al.*, 2012).

Currently, leadership is again in the spotlight, maybe as never before, as the English government looks to further raise the quality of services and outcomes while, at the same time, seeking significant cost-cutting measures for preschool day care. In England and Wales, we have seen the publication of two substantial documents, the Nutbrown Review (Nutbrown, 2012) and the subsequent government consultation paper, More Great Childcare (DfE, 2013), signal changes for the sector in terms of qualification, quality and regulation. What is clearly discernible within both these documents is a significant shift in concepts of quality, professionalism and the business nature of childcare. Garvey and Lancaster (2011: 129) argue that quality in early years is best described by two of Garvin's five typologies of quality: user-based and value-based. What can be seen in this document is a shift towards a different two: product-based and manufacturing-based. This is a very telling shift from relational, contextual community work towards a concentration on the product (successful measured quality outcomes that are externally applied) and its ingredients (building, staff qualifications and services provided). Such a shift makes much more explicit the commodification of early years care and education and the acceptance that the relationship between families and settings will therefore become even more formalized in terms of purchaser and provider (Taggart, 2011). Although this has already been debated and predicted (Osgood, 2006, 2012), the boldness of the current moves is quite shocking to behold as the government seems to have embraced the rhetoric of enterprise, accountability and competition with its only alternative being laziness, untrustworthiness and lack of ambition (Osgood, 2011).

The positioning of the child as investment can also be clearly seen as a strong feature of the discourse within the latter of these documents as well as a significant increase in top-down frameworks of surveillance and control that assume quality cannot exist unless settings are severely policed and rigorously checked (Moss, 2007). There is little debate as to why this must be, why it is assumed that settings and staff are not naturally driven to provide a good quality experience for children in their communities and an acceptance of the assumption that this justifies an externally provided regulatory system. Osgood (2011) argues that the government seems to regard evidence of self-regulation as unprofessional and anti-market and, therefore, to be denigrated and discouraged in favour of top-down regimes.

Combining the policy development which regards young children as 'money in the bank' to be invested wisely and encouraged to grow to be of significant use in the future, with the proliferation of the theoretical perspective of human capital (Campbell-Barr, 2012), means we risk losing all the ground that had been made arguing that the here-and-now experiences of children are more important than what they might become in the future (Moss and Petrie, 2002). There has been a palpable shift away from transformational models of leadership concentrating on personal development towards entrepreneurial styles of leadership where financial priorities are assumed to be the same as the quest for quality and espouse 'masculinist undertones of new managerialism' (Osgood, 2011: 190).

Underpinning this shift is the assumption that the market will support services that are good (and diminish or close those that are not) as well as giving value for money. Furthermore, in this shift social capital is regarded as key in terms of effective resource exchanges between organizations, especially knowledge (Brush et al., 2002). Although social capital can be extremely appealing to ECEC in that it offers the potential to build on the important aspects of developing relationships and sustaining communities, there is a more worrying, darker side to the movement as it may encourage the development of overly strong bonds within and between individuals or groups that create a clique or club from which others are excluded (Forbes and McCartney, 2012). The Australian experience of a shift towards market-based models of practice includes the rise and fall of a private company that initially responded very well to the demand for more, affordable childcare only to collapse raising serious questions regarding 'market failure, corporate governance and fiscal impropriety' (Woodrow, 2010: 31). Leadership had become a commodity, 'McDonaldized' where efficiency, predictability and quantifiability were the centrally stated objectives (Bolden et al., 2011: 113) with leaders expected to follow a centrally specified pattern of behaviour as well as being able to lead anywhere at any time. Such a vision of leadership is anathema to a sector that regards leadership as highly contextualized to the culture and needs of the community in which it is situated. Questions concerning leadership styles and theories become even more important as we see the discourse move from describing early years work as an extended form of mothering towards something that is more measurable in terms of quality, more measured in terms of planning and achievement and therefore becoming more distant in terms of relationships between adults and children. We need effective models of leadership that allow early years leaders to maintain those important relationships and to remain collaborative within their communities while following the demands of social policy to be more efficient and successful.

Comparing theoretical understandings of transformational leadership and entrepreneurial leadership

Transformational theories of leadership have offered early years providers a leadership approach that has moved away from 'masculine' business models such as Total Quality Management (TQM) (Hellsten and Klefjsjo, 2000) with their focus on hierarchy, control and performance management towards more feminine, nurturing styles that have a more comfortable feel for a predominantly female workforce (Brush *et al.*, 2010; Osgood, 2011). There is a growing sense that effective leadership, irrespective of which model, has to be contextualized with regards to gender, community, geography and culture (Fleer, 2003; Tobin, 2005; Coleman and Campbell-Stephens, 2010; Bolden *et al.*, 2011). It does seem that gender matters in terms of the choice of leadership style and this should not be dismissed in the free market ideological stance that the current English government seems to have espoused (Blundel and Lockett, 2011; Duhn, 2011; Thorpe *et al.*, 2012).

Female preference for 'power for' rather than 'power over' (Rodd, 2006: 11) has informed the adoption and subsequent development of transformational models of leadership for the early years sector, including distributed leadership (Harris, 2007; Spillane, 2005), transformational leadership (Bass, 1985; Bass and Avolio, 1993) and authentic leadership (Avolio and Gardner, 2005; Northouse, 2010). Early years leaders are naturally inclined to be inclusive and collective, concerned with the community they serve and focus on the context of their relationships with that community; these models place a strong emphasis on leaders caring for, protecting and supporting their staff and service users and demand the wholehearted engagement of leaders in the emotional domain. Transformative models of leadership require a strong value base with the identification of common goals and a solid ethic of care that underpins their service provision and their decision-making.

More recently, distributed leadership has been embraced within the new leadership paradigm (NCSL, 2004; Spillane, 2005) with its capacity for flexibility and adaptability (Earley and Weindling, 2004), collaboration and interdependence (Aubrey, 2007) regarded as important foundations from which to develop powerful and sustainable learning communities. Distributed leadership sees the sharing of responsibility across the organization and, at all levels, utilizing the strengths and capacity of all members of the workforce (Gronn, 2002) irrespective of position within the organization. All transformative models of leadership regard the development of the workforce, both individually and collectively as a key objective, providing the leaders of the future as well as creating a powerful model of nurturing potential that can be transmitted to the children and their families, changing their behaviour in terms of aspiration and social commitment as a consequence. However, distributed leadership has been criticized for being too amorphous, open to interpretation and thus easily suborned into a business-oriented model that privileges the marketization of care and education over relationships (Harris, 2007; Hartley, 2007; Campbell-Barr, 2009).

Entrepreneurial leadership places a strong emphasis on the identification, creation and exploitation of opportunities to develop a service or product, to generate income and/or reputation and create a powerful entity that is both sustainable and profitable (Gupta et al., 2004). Key attributes of entrepreneurial leadership are the abilities to be creative, strategic and to motivate and/or influence others to follow or to subscribe to the vision and plan being presented; in other words, a manifestation of heroic leadership (Garvey and Lancaster, 2011: 10). Typically, entrepreneurial leaders are seen as prepared to take responsibility for their actions and for being charismatic and powerful in their vision and purpose (Vecchio, 2003). Entrepreneurs are therefore characterized by their perseverance, their independent and competitive spirit and their confidence in taking risks (Bolton and Thompson, 2004: 27–30).

Entrepreneurial leaders are also characterized as having strong internal drivers for personal achievement, autonomy and control that are often manifested through their charismatic and inspirational communications with staff, investors and customers (Kansikas et al., 2012). Success stories that focus on the power of the individual leader have been highlighted within the early years sector over the last few years. The National College website has a store of stories of successful enterprises run by successful individuals, furthering the perception of effective leaders as being heroic, charismatic people who embody strong leadership and create good businesses through their own efforts.

However, what has begun to happen within the literature on entrepreneurial leadership is a discourse on the power and efficacy of the entrepreneurial team as opposed to that of the individual leader (Harper, 2008). It is argued that our idealization of the lone entrepreneur as an exceptional person and the hero of the hour is an oversimplification of the reality of entrepreneurialism that requires multiple opportunities for collaboration and networking to create new business ideas and products (Blundel and Lockett, 2011). An entrepreneurial team needs to have a common bond with shared interests and commitment that facilitates the creative process and sustains the service delivery: otherwise, they risk becoming internally competitive and falling apart. It is claimed that an entrepreneurial team will be more creative than a lone individual as they are able to bounce ideas off each other. Furthermore, they are better placed to withstand uncertainty and develop sustainable services and products that will survive the vagaries of the market and the economic climate (Harper, 2008). We should ask whether the entrepreneurial team might offer a more helpful model of leadership for early years, moving away from the heroic concept of leadership and focusing on the

Table 13.1 Comparison of leadership theories.

Component	Transformational leadership	Entrepreneurial leadership
Vision	Vision is the main component in inspiring followers	Intention is more important than vision. Entrepreneurs use that intention to persuade others to follow
Risk	Risk is a creative potential that should be investigated. However, there needs to be careful consideration of impact of risk on standards	Entrepreneurs are risk takers – seeing opportunities and taking chances
Personal qualities	Energy, enthusiasm and passion that are communicated to others	Personal need for achievement and autonomy encapsulated in energy and enthusiasm
Relationships	Interrelationship with followers is paramount	Good interpersonal relationships assist the activities of the agency
Priority	Concerned with process	Concerned with outcome
Consideration	Importance of personal integrity	Potential to be maverick

relationships within the team, negotiation and shared purposes. Might the entre-preneurial team offer opportunities for ethical and moral challenge that will keep a setting's vision and aims in proper perspective? A closer investigation of the entrepreneurial team suggests that this may indeed be an opportunity to play with the possibilities and encourage others to do so (Duhn, 2011).

A comparison of transformational leadership and entrepreneurial leadership in Table 13.1 draws attention to the considerable similarities that exist. Both theo-ries regard the development of effective teams as crucial to the success of the venture (Bolton and Thompson, 2004; Kansikas *et al.*, 2012) and both recognize the importance of holding a vision of what the service/product should look like as well as the relevance of identifying and maintaining the underpinning values for their consumers or service users. Critically, where the models part company is on their attitudes towards their capacity for taking risks and whether they are more concerned with process (transformational) or outcome (entrepreneurial).

Risk

It could be argued that risk should be regarded as anathema for early years set-tings; after all, the provision of such an important service for children and fami-lies holds serious implications for the future should its delivery be inadequate or wrong in some way. Indeed, the present inspection regime appears to exist to ensure compliance to a narrow band of externally identified objectives and has the power to penalize settings that have engaged in what they regard as risky behaviour (what the setting may have seen as creativity) with harsh penalties, even closure (Moss, 2007). It seems that entrepreneurs are able to engage in far riskier behaviour, challenging themselves and their workforce to 'think outside the box' and come up with innovative and creative ways of building the business. The risk of failure, of potential collapse or damage, is taken account of and accepted as part of the process towards great outcomes. In the entrepreneurial world, businesses fail and emerge in a different iteration with leaders using their skills and drive to create a new enterprise. While this could be regarded as laudable in a business sense, there has to be a debate on whether this is good practice where the experiences of children and families are concerned – there is a great deal of evidence of the cost of poor early years experiences and the requirement to make multiple relationships with different people in a number of settings. Nevertheless, it is no wonder that the British government has moved towards a model of entrepreneurial leadership for early years care and education as a way of enlarging the service, maximizing value for money and transferring responsibility from the public to the private sector.

Process or outcome

There is also evidence of embracing entrepreneurial leadership in the early years as a means of moving from being regarded as passionate mothers towards being viewed as performative professionals, demonstrating competent practice and entrepreneurial skills (Taggart, 2011). However, we should perhaps approach this new phenomenon with caution, as a focus on the entrepreneurial skills of an individual seems to be at odds with a female-dominated context of embracing emotional engagement with a strong ethic of care (Osgood, 2006; Taggart, 2011). A concentration on competition, performativity and rationality 'does not sit comfortably with practitioners, predominantly female' (Osgood, 2011: 190). Is there a tension between process and outcome? Should a balance be struck between these two objectives so that children and their families experience a nurturing process where they are valued and supported in not just their future development, but in their here and now? Are process and outcome necessarily in opposition to each other, or is it possible to develop an intertwined system that privileges both? It would seem that an overwhelmingly outcome-driven approach risks looking too much towards the future without acknowledging the importance of the present. Similarly, an overwhelming focus on nurturing may move into a culture of overprotectionism, diminishing challenge, creativity and personal development.

Relationships

The importance of caring relationships between early years practitioners and the children and families in their care has long been acknowledged (Dahlberg *et al.*, 1999; Elfer and Dearnley, 2007; Campbell-Barr, 2009). Jones and Pound (2008) argue that young children are extremely sensitive to their environment and atmosphere and require a strong sense that those around them actively care for and about them. Good early years settings therefore see their role as one of 'protecting, supporting and engaging empathetically with children' (Osgood, 2011: 113).

Similarly, relationships between leaders and staff have been regarded as essential for the well-being of the entire organization and the modelling of care for all engaged in activity within a setting (Owen, 2000; Garvey and Lancaster, 2011). The engagement and management of personal emotions within the early years setting (Elfer and Dearnley, 2007), what is known as 'emotional labour' (Hochschild, 1983), is a contested but important aspect of effective professional work in the sector. Confusion arises over what the word 'care' actually describes in reference to paid, professional work with the word 'help' (Shakespeare, 2000) or 'support' (Finkelstein, 1991) suggested instead. Sevenhuijsen (2000) sees a distinction between care as an activity – a piece of work for which people are remunerated – and care as a moral orientation, a value-based way of working with people that underpins every action, which has hitherto been embraced within early years (Elfer and Dearnley, 2007).

The literature on entrepreneurial leadership would suggest that a strong ethical stance of care is at odds with its key drivers of exploiting profit and measurable outcomes. Woodrow (2010) cites government figures that showed that, in service providers that are corporate chains, 25 per cent of staff time is spent engaged in relationships with children and families, compared with 54 per cent in community-based provision. The rhetoric from entrepreneurs suggests that this discrepancy is being tackled. Of course any industry needs to make sufficient money to ensure its sustainability and this pertains to early years as well as any other social enterprise. Finding the balance between the many dualisms that exist within the early years sector is key: outcome/process, rational/emotional, localism/globalism prompt critical debates that risk being lost in the current drive for cost-effective services.

Being maverick

Entrepreneurial leaders are classically regarded as maverick – thinking outside the box and taking calculated and/or creative risks to pursue their vision and maximize their profits. Early years literature is similarly littered with people who might be seen as maverick; establishing settings that others had dismissed as impossible or had not even conceived of. Such histories lead very neatly towards the identification of heroes who lead the way and take pioneering steps into the future and there appears to be a western predilection for identifying and praising heroic leaders (Bolden *et al.*, 2011). Nevertheless, there is significant anxiety concerning heroic leadership and the opportunities for the inappropriate manipulation of power (Bolden *et al.*, 2011), the development of unsuitable or unsustainable services and questions surrounding accountability and autonomy (Jones and Pound, 2008).

Conclusion: where now for leadership of early years?

In the early years sector we have seen a systematic, well-researched and well-documented movement from male business models of leadership towards pedagogical models of leadership typified by transformational and distributed models that focus on relationships, communities and contexts. Throughout that time we have engaged in considerable debate about the role of women in these leadership developments and what it means to be a professional while caring for the families with whom we work. What is clearly visible in recent policy documents is a return to those business models with an emphasis on entrepreneurial endeavour and purpose to reach the goal of cheap day care that nevertheless achieves good quality results. We have also seen the present and previous governments express their preference for managerialist models of leadership (Wright, 2011) with an inclination for technical goodness rather than moral goodness (Ciulla, 2002). It is naïve to think that entrepreneurialism has no place in early years; early years leaders have always been creative, flexible and responsive in their endeavours with a keen eye on their community and, consequently, their markets, with preparedness to move with the trends and demands of parents and politicians. Furthermore, the mixed economy of the sector already shows a typology of leaders interested in business principles as well as care (Campbell-Barr, 2009). Nevertheless, there is a lot to be concerned about with the recent shift in conceptualization. An uncritical embrace of entrepreneurialism and the power of market forces means there is no clear appreciation of the problems as well as the benefits and that is dangerous and unwelcome.

The commodification of early childhood education and care that is encapsulated within More Great Childcare (DfE, 2013) makes it easier to apply business principles and lose sight of any moral imperative or ethic of care. Indeed, it is clear from some of the consultation responses that the early years sector does not wish to cross the Rubicon (Neville, 2013; Ransom, 2013); some, however, may be happy to take a considered view on the viability of some aspects of entrepreneurial leadership and blend it, in a unique way, with preferred models of transformative leadership to create a more challenging framework of leadership that does not lose sight of its core purpose of caring for the youngest in our society. Indeed, early years practitioners have a strong heritage of developing their own leadership discourse. We should move away from the overwhelming concerns about money, league table position and the neo-liberal standards and measures being promulgated by politicians and get creative; we have a fantastic opportunity to play with the possibilities and encourage others to join in.

Points for reflection and discussion

1. What is the balance between care and business and how comfortable does it feel to identify that balance?
2. Where are the men in early years care and education and how might they shift the leadership discourse?
3. In a time of austerity, the politics are about thrift and creativity. How does this impact upon the provision of services for young children?
4. How does leadership inform quality and vice versa?

References and further reading

Aubrey, C. (2007) *Leading and Managing in the Early Years*. London: Sage.

Avolio, B.J. and Gardner, W.L. (2005) Authentic leadership development: getting to the roots of positive forms of leadership, *The Leadership Quarterly*, 16: 315–38.

Bass, B. (1985) *Leadership and Performance Beyond Expectation*. New York: Free Press.

Bass, B.M. and Avolio, B.J. (1993) *Transformational Leadership: A response to critiques*. New York: Free Press.

Blundel, R. and Lockett, N. (2011) *Exploring Entrepreneurship: Practices and perspectives*. Oxford: Oxford University Press.

Bolden, R., Hawkins, B., Gosling, J. and Taylor, S. (2011) *Exploring Leadership: Individual, organisational and societal perspectives*. Oxford: Oxford University Press.

Bolton, B. and Thompson, J. (2004) *Entrepreneurs: Talent, temperament, technique*, 2nd edn. Oxford: Butterworth-Heinemann.

Brush, C.G., Carter, N.M., Greene, P.G., Hart, M.M. and Gatewood, E. (2002) The role of social capital and gender in linking financial suppliers and entrepreneurial firms: A framework for future research, *International Journal of Entrepreneurial Finance*, 4(4): 305–23.

Campbell-Barr, V. (2009) Care and business orientations in the delivery of childcare: An exploratory study, *Journal of Early Childhood Research*, 7(1): 76–93.

Campbell-Barr, V. (2012) Early years education and the value for money folklore, *European Early Childhood Education Research Journal*, 20(3): 423–37.

Children's Workforce Development Council (CWDC) (2006) *Early Years Professional: Guidance to the standards for the award of early years professional status*. Leeds: CWDC.

Ciulla, J. (2002) Trust and the future of leadership, in N. Bowie (ed.) *The Blackwell Guide to Business Ethics*. Oxford: Blackwell.

Coleman, M. and Campbell-Stephens, R. (2010) Perceptions of career progress: The experience of black and minority ethnic school leaders, *School Leadership and Management*, 30(1): 35–49.

Dahlberg, G., Moss, P. and Pence, A. (1999) *Beyond Quality in Early Childhood Education and Care: Postmodern perspectives*. London: Routledge.

Department for Education (DfE) (2012) *Statutory Framework for the Early Years Foundation Stage: Setting the standards for learning, development and care for children from birth to five*. Available at: http://www.foundationyears.org.uk/wp-content/uploads/2012/07/EYFS-Statutory-Framework-2012.pdf.

Department for Education (DfE) (2013) *More Great Childcare: Raising quality and giving parents more choice*. London: Stationery Office.

Department for Education and Science (DfES) (2007) *National Standards for Leaders of SureStart Children's Centres*. London: Stationery Office.

Duhn, I. (2011) Towards professionalism/s, in L. Miller and C. Cable (eds.) *Professionalization, Leadership and Management in the Early Years*. London, Sage.

Earley, P. and Weindling, D. (2004) *Understanding School Leadership*. London: Sage.

Elfer, P. and Dearnley, K. (2007) Nurseries and emotional well-being: Evaluating an emotionally containing model of continuing professional development, *Early Years: An International Journal of Research and Development*, 27(3): 267–79.

Finkelstein, V. (1991) Disability: An administrative challenge?, in M. Oliver (ed.) *Social Work: Disabled people and disabling environments*. London: Jessica Kingsley.

Fleer, M. (2003) Early childhood education as an evolving 'community of practice' or as lived 'social reproduction': Researching the 'taken-for-granted', *Contemporary Issues in Early Childhood*, 4(1): 64–79.

Forbes, J. and McCartney, E. (2012) Leadership distribution culturally? Education/speech and language therapy social capital in schools and children's services, *International Journal of Leadership in Education: Theory and Practice*, 15(3): 271–87.

Garvey, D. and Lancaster, A. (2011) *Leadership for Quality in Early Years and Playwork*. London: National Children's Bureau.

Graham, S. and Jarvis, J. (2011) Leadership of uncertainty, in L. Trodd and L. Chivers (eds.) *Interprofessional Working in Practice: Learning and working together for children and families*. Maidenhead: McGraw-Hill.

Gronn, P. (2002) Distributed leadership as a unit of analysis, *Leadership Quarterly*, 13: 423–51.

Gupta, V., MacMillan, I. and Surie, G. (2004) Entrepreneurial leadership: Developing and measuring a cross-cultural construct, *Journal of Business Venturing*, 19: 241–60.

Hard, L.M. and O'Gorman, L.M. (2007) 'Push-Me' or 'Pull-You'? An opportunity for early childhood leadership in the implementation of Queensland's early years curriculum, *Contemporary Issues in Early Childhood*, 8(1): 50–60.

Harper, D. (2008) Towards a theory of entrepreneurial teams, *Journal of Business Venturing*, 23: 613–26.

Harris, A. (2007) Distributed leadership: Conceptual confusion and empirical reticence, *International Journal of Leadership in Education*, 10(3): 315–25.

Hartley, D. (2007) The emergence of distributed leadership in education: Why now?, *British Journal of Educational Studies*, 55(2): 202–14.

Hellsten, U. and Klefjsjo, B. (2000) TQM as a management system consisting of values, techniques and tools, *The TQM Magazine*, 12(4): 238–44.

Hochschild, A.R. (1983) *The Managed Heart: Commercialisation of human feeling*. Berkeley, CA: University of California Press.

Jones, C. and Pound, L. (2008) *Leadership and Management in the Early Years: From principles to practice*. Maidenhead: McGraw-Hill.

Kansikas, J., Laakkonen, A., Sarpo, V. and Kontinen, T. (2012) Entrepreneurial leadership and familiness as resources for strategic entrepreneurship, *International Journal of Entrepreneurial Behaviour and Research*, 18(2): 141–58.

Leeson, C. (2010) Leadership in early childhood settings, in R. Parker-Rees, C. Leeson, J. Willan and J. Savage (eds.) *Early Childhood Studies: An introduction to the study of children's worlds and children's lives*. Exeter: Learning Matters.

Leeson, C., Campbell-Barr, V. and Ho, D. (2012) Leading for quality improvement: A comparative research agenda in early childhood education in England and Hong Kong, *International Journal of Leadership in Education*, 15(2): 221–36.

Moss, P. (2007) Meeting across the paradigmatic divide, *Educational Philosophy and Theory*, 39(3): 229–40.

Moss, P. and Petrie, P. (2002) *From Children's Services to Children's Spaces*. London: RoutledgeFalmer.

National College for School Leadership (NCSL) (2004) *National Professional Qualification in Integrated Centre Leadership*. Nottingham: NCSL.

Neville, S. (2013) *More Great Childcare: An analysis of the government's plans written by childminders*. Available at: http://www.childmindingforum.co.uk (accessed 11 June 2013).

Northouse, P. (2010) *Leadership: Theory and practice*, 5th edn. London: Sage.

Nutbrown, C. (2012) *Foundations for Quality*. Available at: http://www.education.gov.uk/inthenews/inthenews/a00210425/nubrownpn (accessed 11 June 2013).

Osgood, J. (2006) Deconstructing professionalism in early childhood education: Resisting the regulatory gaze, *Contemporary Issues in Early Childhood*, 7(1): 5–15.

Osgood, J. (2011) Contested constructions of professionalism in the nursery, in L. Miller and C. Cable (eds.) *Professionalization, Leadership and Management in the Early Years*. London: Sage.

Osgood, J. (2012) *Narratives from the Nursery: Negotiating the professional iden-tities in early childhood*. **London: Routledge.**

Owen, H. (2000) *In Search of Leaders*. Chichester: Wiley.

Ransom, H. (2013) *More Great Childcare: Survey of NCB early years networks*. London: National Children's Bureau.

Rodd, J. (2006) *Leadership in Early Childhood*. Buckingham: Open University Press.

Sevenhuijsen, S. (2000) Caring in the third way: The relation between obligation, responsibil-ity and care in third way discourse, *Critical Social Policy*, 20(1): 5–37.

Shakespeare, T. (2000) *Help*. Birmingham: Venture Press.

Spillane, J.P. (2005) Distributed leadership, *The Educational Forum*, 69: 143–50.

Taggart, G. (2011) Don't we care? The ethics and emotional labour of early years profes-sionalism, *Early Years: An International Journal of Research and Development*, 31(1): 85–95.

Thorpe, K., Millear, P. and Petriwskyj, A. (2012) Can a childcare practicum encourage degree qualified staff to enter the childcare workforce?, *Contemporary Issues in Early Childhood*, 13(4): 317–27.

Tobin, J. (2005) Quality in early childhood education: An anthropologist's perspective, *Early Education and Development*, 16(4): 421–34.

Vecchio, R. (2003) Entrepreneurship and leadership: Common trends and common threads, *Human Resource Management Review*, 13: 303–27.

Woodrow, C. (2010) Challenging identities: A case for leadership, in L. Miller and C. Cable (eds.) *Professionalization, Leadership and Management in the Early Years*. London: Sage.

Woodrow, C. and Busch, G. (2008) Repositioning early childhood leadership as action and activism, *Early Childhood Education Research Journal*, 16(1): 83–93.

Wright, N. (2011) Between 'bastard' and 'wicked' leadership? School leadership and the emerging policies of the UK Coalition Government, *Journal of Educational Adminis-tration and History*, 43(4): 345–62.

Useful websites

http://www.efacets.co.uk
http://www.education.gov.uk

14 'Parents as partners': the new politics of parenting

Gill Boag-Munroe

Abstract

The Statutory Framework for the Early Years Foundation Stage (EYFS) reflects current policy agendas and research into children's well-being to frame a particular approach to child care that might be seen as tension-laden if not contradictory. The policy of promoting the parent as first educator, deriving from the work of *inter alia* Sylva *et al.* (2004), which aims to lead to improved educational outcomes for children, is in tension with the economic and social policy agenda of encouraging mothers back into the workplace in order to improve economic well-being so as to lift children out of poverty.

The Framework relies on hegemonic concepts such as partnership, 'good' parenting and 'positive' relationships. These concepts are highly subjective and fluid, shifting from practitioner to practitioner and from policy enforcer to policy enforcer. In addition, the concept of partnership may be seen to be in tension with the duties placed by the Framework on the setting, which appear to place practitioners in a more powerful position than the families in the setting. Such a level of inscribed tension and slipperiness suggests that a close questioning of some of the central concepts of the Framework is essential.

Introduction

Although the Statutory Framework for the Early Years Foundation Stage (EYFS) (DfE, 2012) appears to assume that settings have similar profiles (of context, parents and practitioners) and presupposes homogeneity of practice (a generalized 'what works' approach; see, for example, Biesta, 2007, 2010), settings are not, in fact, homogeneous. They are unique and individual, shaped by the families they attract, the context in which they are located, the ethos they wish to foster and the beliefs of the practitioners who work in them. They work with parents whose identities, like those of the practitioners, are framed by gender, class and race. They are bound by rules created not only by external agencies such as government, but by those that settings create for themselves, such rules being potentially in conflict with their aims. It is therefore important for settings to have clear understandings of what might constitute 'good' parenting and 'positive' relationships that are specific to the context in which they work, in order to minimize tension between their rules and their aims. Therefore, it is important that each setting's staff reflect on these central, core ideas and find their own nuanced understandings which are pertinent to their context. The following thoughts might assist practitioners to begin the process of reflection on the three concepts of good parenting, positive relationships and partnership.

Good parenting

The EYFS Framework does not define good parenting: it is simply stated to be one of two pillars supporting the 'foundation children need to make the most of their abilities and talents as they grow up' (DfE, 2012: 2). The descriptor 'good' here might appear redundant: surely, no one sets out to be a 'bad' parent? But one only has to recall the cases of Victoria Climbié, Baby Peter or Khyra Ishaq to understand that not all parents behave in what most adults would understand to be the best interests of their child.

Nonetheless, the concept of 'good' parenting is highly subjective and emotive. To propose it is to propose its opposite and risk pathologizing parents who do not conform to the dominant model. What constitutes good parenting in one context may not be seen to be so in a very different context, nor even to colleagues in the same setting. Each practice therefore may need to determine what, for it, constitutes the 'good' parenting that they wish to foster, or where they are willing to place boundaries between 'good' and 'bad' parenting: the grey areas between the two need sensitive unpicking.

Such an approach may involve challenging the hegemony of long-cherished understandings, in particular that 'different' is 'not good'. For those settings that aim to access parents who are harder to reach or engage, the definition may be wider and more nuanced than for those settings in which vocal middle-class parents dominate. For example, for a white middle-class parent, good parenting might involve playing with children, encouraging singing and music making, engaging in arty and often messy activities in order to develop creativity – in other words, introducing the child to a range of developmental experiences through play. For the parent in a Bangladeshi family, for example, such activities might seem wrong: a child may be expected to be quiet or to mimic adults (Brooker, 2002).

A starting point for discussion might be the five points included in the Every Child Matters agenda (DfES, 2003). A good parent might, in this view, be one who creates a safe, healthy environment in which the child can enjoy and achieve; make a positive contribution and achieve economic well-being. But these qualities were proposed by a powerful white middle class, and are, in themselves, subjective and relative: what constitutes economic well-being, for example, may be perceived differently from family to family, and may in turn be dependent on factors beyond the control of the family. What constitutes enjoyment for one child may be at odds with what the parent believes the child should enjoy. Is the parent who denies, in what he believes is the best interest of the child, the opportunity to participate in a non-harmful and (to the child) enjoyable activity therefore a 'bad' parent?

Desforges and Abouchaar (2003) define good parenting as providing 'a good foundation of skills, values, attitudes and self-concept' (p.7), and providing 'intellectual stimulation...a good self-concept...an enduring model of constructive social and educational aspirations and values relating to personal fulfilment and good citizenship' (p. 85). How far this definition clarifies the position is debatable: once again, 'good' parenting is dependent on understandings of what constitutes 'good' and framed in a discourse that needs careful unpacking. For Pederson (2012), good parenting is about reliability, structure, disciplinary consistence, spending time with children and family life. But as Smith (2010) points out, 'good parenting' is often silhouetted by a deficit model of parenting, rather than being a high-relief concept itself.

There are powerful questions to be asked, then, about what might fall within the setting's parameters of 'good' parenting, and about who decides what constitutes 'good': how far are parents drawn into these important discussions and to what extent are their discourses assimilated?

Positive relationships

Again, the word 'positive' here might seem unnecessary: it is not generally the intention of those practitioners working in early years settings to foster relationships that are anything other than positive. The aim of the setting can usually be summarized as to provide an environment that offers each child security and well-being in which the child can develop and learn. However, what is being intended here is that the addition of the word 'positive' directs practitioners to actively building relationships with parents and, in particular, with those who are reluctant to participate in the setting, so that the relationship is demonstrably beneficial to the parents and children.

'Parents, Early Years and Learning' (PEAL) places relationships at the heart of the work done by early years practitioners (Wheeler et al., 2009). For Wheeler and colleagues (2009: 6), the key features of a positive relationship are fourfold:

  i. respect for each other;
 ii. parents as partners;
iii. supporting learning; and
 iv. appointing a key person to work with each parent.

This is a strong starting point for thinking about how to form positive relationships, but as Evangelou et al. (2008) and Boag-Munroe and Evangelou (2010) show, relationships need time and commitment to develop, particularly with parents who are hard to reach or engage, and while a key person may be vital in this process it is equally important to appoint a person who is willing to persevere and be inventive in reaching out to reluctant or hidden families.

Positive relationships may be evident to people coming into the setting in the way that parents and practitioners interact in the hurly burly of arrivals and departures, or that children are listened to as well as parents or that the setting is designed and decorated to create an identity that is inclusive and welcoming (Georgeson and Boag-Munroe, 2012). Parents will spend time talking with practitioners and recommend the setting to other parents. They will seek advice from practitioners, trusting in their expertise, and they will have the confidence to express any concerns to practitioners.

Wheeler and colleagues suggest that such relationships are respectful, valuing parental knowledge and opinion as much as that of practitioners. Parents are valued and 'active participants in problem solving' (Wheeler *et al.*, 2009: 28). Fitzgerald (2004) and Lindon (2009) argue that positive relationships are built through communication: active listening to and sharing of information with parents. In these ways, positive relationships appear to be little different from partnership, since all these qualities are considered equally in discussions of that concept.

Partnership

Building on findings from the Effective Provision of Pre-school Education (EPPE) Project (Sylva *et al.*, 2004), and drawing on policy agendas to bring parents into closer involvement with their children's education, the EYFS Framework aims to set out the basic duties and responsibilities of providers and practitioners towards parents. In so doing, I argue, it offers a limited model of the partnership it aims to foster.

Partnership within the Framework may be understood as a palimpsest, a document that reflects the historical understandings of the relationships that parents and settings form. It emphasizes the importance of partnership between practitioners and parents. Research by Quinton (2004) and Tunstill *et al.* (2005) suggests that parents want to be active participants in their children's learning, though the literature on parents who are hard to reach or engage (Boag-Munroe and Evangelou, 2010; Boag-Munroe, 2012) points to reasons why assisting children to learn might become a low priority for parents. There are those who, for example, lead such chaotic lifestyles that their children's learning is not always a high priority. There are others who are afraid to engage with services that might assist them in educating their child because of their circumstances: perhaps they are refugees or asylum seekers; or perhaps they have a lifestyle which they do not want to reveal and which means that assisting children to learn is not their first priority. The danger is that such parents are presupposed not to be interested in their children's learning and become stigmatized as a result – a position that will drive these parents further to the margins.

The literature points to variations in understandings according to whether the writer's primary audience appears to be those settings where parents are already engaged and involved, or whether the writer is offering thoughts to settings where the parents might be more difficult or sensitive to engage. Partnership in the EYFS Framework is, it is suggested, the basis on which settings and parents work together for the good of the child and to further the child's development such that children can take best advantage of the learning opportunities available to them.

Definitions of partnership

Partnership is a broad description of a relationship that connotes equality of power and effort. It stands in contrast to other forms of parent–practitioner relationship such as 'involvement' or 'participation' by suggesting a working relationship in which each partner contributes what they are able whether in the form of skills, knowledge, ideas or resources and incorporating ideas of collaboration and agency. Yet in much of the literature relating to partnership in early years, the discussion focuses on aspects of the relationship such as communication and the sharing of information, which, at its simplest, is at the level of practitioners listening to parents and informing them of what the child is doing: a relationship of briefing rather than of real engagement.

For Baldock et al. (2009), partnership is about cooperation, collaboration and coordination, though between services rather than between parent and practitioner. Underdown and Barlow (2012) suggest that partnership involves 'developing the expertise of the parent and working alongside them to promote the best outcomes for themselves and their children'. Following Egan (1990), they go on to suggest that it requires 'the kind of relationship that enables empathy to develop' (Underdown and Barlow, 2012: 54).

Jones (2004) argues that partnership 'is often misunderstood' and the term may be bandied about 'without the full acknowledgment of the needs of parents' (cited in Baldock et al., 2000: 116). Observations made in the course of the National Evaluation of the Early Learning Partnership Project (NEELPP) (Evangelou et al., 2008) point to some settings that work hard to draw parents – particularly tentative parents – into a more equal relationship which might look more like partnership. However, settings, like parents, are not always comfortable with reaching out to parents to draw them into partnership for learning. There may also be parents who simply want to leave their child in a setting and know that they are safe and well cared for: Epstein (1987) calls this model the 'school to home transmission' model of partnership. Other parents may feel that they lack the capacity to participate in the model of partnership proposed by a setting, perhaps because they have limited education or because they have learnt to be in awe of teachers and are thus denied the confidence to participate equally.

Partnership and power

The issue of where power is allocated is an important one and is tending to shift: Feiler (2010: 8) notes that policy relating to parental involvement in children's education in England has introduced a 'more coercive note... for some parents described as hard to reach', than policies in the other home nations.

Partnership suggests an equality of power between partners, yet that is often not the case in early years settings. Whereas some parents may have difficulty in believing that they have power in the relationship, others often act as though they have more power than they actually do. Edwards and Knight (1994: 110) point out that '[o]nce children are in school, teachers as key holders to publicly codified knowledge assume a powerful position *vis-à-vis* parents'. They go on to suggest that, while some parents 'find themselves powerless as their "at risk" children are given mandatory places in day care centres', at the other end of the parent power spectrum are those who 'will be involved

powerfully and actively as members of, for example, management committees'
(ibid.). Ultimately, however:

> The major demarcation in the balance of power that exists between home
> and educational settings lies in the extent to which the professionals con-
> cerned are ultimately responsible for managing the institution. Power will
> lie with those who are responsible.
>
> (Edwards and Knight, 1994: 111)

Eisenstadt (2012: 16) argues that there has been a shift away from a model
of parental engagement in which the 'emphasis to start with was empowerment, involving parents in the design of local programmes and in the management and governance of programmes' (i.e. partnership?) to what she calls 'a
more focussed approach', although this approach is less defined than hinted
at. If policy-makers were focusing on 'supporting parents and supporting
parenting', and on 'progressive universalism', then parents were being positioned not as partners but as people who needed help from experts. Thus, in a
true partnership, parents and practitioners alike are responsible for managing
the institution and, therefore, power is equal. However, the EYFS Framework,
while offering the promise of partnership, then places much of the decision-
making power in the hands of practitioners, leaving less scope for parents'
voices.

Different models of partnership

Models of partnership envisaged in the literature vary from those where the relationship is based largely on information transmission, to those where practitioners and parents form a close bond to work together to assist the child's learning.
Parents and practitioners in this model learn as much as children.

Epstein (1987) posits four models of partnership:

1. The protective model, in which the setting understands itself as the
   expert and is reluctant to allow the 'non-expert' parent to participate in
   practice.
2. The school to home transmission model, in which information is passed
   from setting to home about the child and his or her progress.
3. The curriculum enrichment model, in which parents come in to the setting
   to assist practitioners with tasks such as listening to reading, assisting
   with outdoor activities or school visits.
4. The partnership model, in which parents are fully involved in joint planning and decision-making within the setting.

Literature on parental involvement in settings (e.g. Fitzgerald, 2004; Lindon,
2009) tends to support and foster the second two models through examples that
place communication as the focus of partnership. In both these texts, the school
to home transmission model is dominant, with some consideration being given
to the curriculum enrichment model. However, the partnership model is given

minimal consideration, perhaps because these texts are aimed at those settings that work most closely with the middle-class, well-educated parents who might, as Baeck (2010) argues, threaten the professionalism of practitioners.

It is in those texts (e.g. Wheeler *et al.*, 2009; Feiler, 2010) in which an audience of practitioners working with the less well-educated parents (Baeck, 2010) that Epstein's partnership model is most discussed, and which offers a more subtle understanding of the concept, shading meanings to include relationships in which practitioners move from a position where they guide the parent to one where both parent and practitioner are able to negotiate how work with the child will be done.

A Vygotskyan model of learning partnerships might view the 'learner' (either the parent or the child) as someone who is assisted in their learning by another learner who is further along their learning trajectory in a collaborative relationship in which the learners have equal voice about what is learned and how. Moll and Greenberg (1990) discuss a version of this model as 'funds of knowledge' to be shared in a collaborative way. In this model, practitioners are learners as much as are parents and children: while the practitioner may be further along the trajectory of learning about how to assist learning, the parent is further along the trajectory of learning about the individual child and so each can assist the other to learn.

However, just as there are practitioners who are uncomfortable with the idea of working with parents in partnership, so there are parents who are reluctant to work so closely with practitioners.

Partnership and parents who are harder to reach or engage

Families who remain on the margins of society may do so for a wide variety of reasons (Boag-Munroe and Evangelou, 2010). There are two broad categories of family on the margin: those who are hard to reach because they have problems which render them largely invisible to the rest of society; and those who choose to remain hard to reach or engage for reasons relating to their personal situation and experiences.

Developing partnership with families that are hard to reach or engage may be more problematic. If, as so much of the literature suggests, the greater part of partnership consists in fostering communication, then partnership with those who either can't or won't engage with the setting becomes troublesome. Yet Underdown and Barlow (2012) suggest it is these parents at whom the policy of partnership is most directed. Such a partnership might be a practitioner working alongside a parent in the home or in the setting to assist the parent in learning how to engage in developmental activities with their child. It is one in which the parent shares knowledge of the child – likes, dislikes and needs – and the practitioner shares knowledge of child development and age-appropriate activities which might meet the child's needs. Although I have framed this as a one-to-one relationship with parents, the NEELPP (Evangelou *et al.*, 2008) offered very successful models of practitioners working with groups in which group knowledge was shared.

Reaching out to parents who might benefit from such a model requires time, patience and resilience (Evangelou *et al.*, 2008; Wheeler *et al.*, 2009; Boag-Munroe and Evangelou, 2010; Feiler, 2010), although few political initiatives have been allocated sufficient funding to allow practitioners to spend the necessary time with these families, suggesting policies which are espoused rather than in-use (Argyris and Schön, 1974). It is perhaps easier for politicians to frame policy which meets the needs and demands of the middle (more political? more vocal?) classes and which can be demonstrated to be put into practice in middle-class settings, than to frame policy which requires time and funding to achieve results with marginalized and stigmatized families.

Families who live in fear of authority may have had negative experiences of working with agencies that are notionally there to protect them: for example, asylum seekers or refugees who may have little English through which to express their needs. Communication with these families is, therefore, not as simple as the texts offering advice on partnership tend to assume: it has to be achieved through coordinated services which first lead practitioners to the families and then provide assistance with communication (i.e. translators). There is tension here between, on the one hand, government policy on asylum seekers and refugees and how they are managed on arrival in the country, and, on the other, policy relating to childcare and education (Arnot and Pinson, 2005).

Other families who live in fear of authority may be less visible: they may have criminal records, or fear being traced through their involvement in 'officialdom' – parents who have violent partners, or who are fleeing associations with other violent people, for example. To build partnership with such parents, it is important first to find them and then build a relationship of trust so that they can be drawn in to participate in the setting. Partnership with such families is developed with time and patience, and may not necessarily be achieved initially within the setting.

Fear of authority is not the only fear that inhibits families from engaging with settings, however. Families may fear social stigma because of their lifestyle, requiring reassurance from the setting that they are not being judged on their choices. Other families may be fearful that they will be made to look foolish because they are struggling with literacy, or feel they lack skills and competences in some way. Again, time and patience are essential to building relationships in which each partner feels respected and valued for who they are.

What partnership might be about

Partnership appears to be an elusive concept within the EYFS Framework, functioning rather as a euphemism for, at best, involvement and, at worst, information passing. It imposes a duty on practitioners to transmit information to parents but little responsibility to act on the information given to them by parents. They are simply required to respond to 'observations that parents and carers share', which can mean simply acknowledging what has been shared. The central connotation of partnership – equality of power – is abandoned in favour of an unchallenged notion that practitioners are the experts on the development of the child, while parents appear to be the passive recipients of information. Partnership becomes, in effect, a buzzword of policy-making, designed to distract the eye from the sleight of hand which whisks away what it appears to be giving.

Partnership involves more than communication, although communication must be at the heart of the relationship. It involves practitioners and parents taking the time to get to know each other and to find how they want to share responsibility for the child's education. Parents and practitioners need to find the balance of power that is appropriate for their needs and which gives both partners agency in both action and voice. It is a relationship into which both partners bring their particular knowledge, skills, understandings and resources, which are mutually valued. It is not the simplistic relationship of sharing that some of the literature seems to suggest, but a nuanced, fluid and sensitive relationship that can be adapted to need and circumstance and which is sufficiently robust and resilient to navigate the tensions of daily life with children. Finally, it is a relationship that can move between home and setting (should it want or need to) without being judgemental or stigmatizing, and in which both partners feel safe to test out new things. It might be summarized as a concept that encompasses, in ascending order of engagement, participation, involvement, reciprocity and collaboration.

Conclusion

Definitions of 'good' parenting and 'positive' relationships remain elusive and need to be negotiated and agreed on a setting-by-setting basis according to context. Thoughtful literature which aims to put flesh on the bones of the EYFS Framework points to ways that practitioners might construct relationships with parents in which they make the parent feel like a partner, in whatever sense that relationship is understood by parent and practitioner. The key is that parents *feel* or *believe* that they are in partnership; relationships are seen to operate in the best developmental interests of the child and to hold out the possibility of equality of action and responsibility. Such literature shows how these relationships can be built not only with parents who may already be engaged with the setting, but also with parents who are more reluctant to engage or who have more difficulty in doing so. In turn, the partnership developed through positive relationships can lead to good parenting.

Points for reflection and discussion

1. Discuss in your setting what each of these key concepts might mean to you, and how you might put your understandings into practice.
2. What model of partnership seems most appropriate for your setting, and how will you go about developing it?

References and further reading

Argyris, C. and Schön, D.A. (1974) *Theory in Practice: Increasing professional effectiveness*. San Francisco, CA: Jossey-Bass.

Arnot, M. and Pinson, H. (2005) *The Education of Asylum Seeker and Refugee Children: A study of LEA and school values, policy and practices*. Cambridge: Faculty of Education, University of Cambridge.

Baeck, U.-D.K. (2010) 'We are the professionals': A study of teachers' views on parental involvement in school, *British Journal of Sociology of Education*, 31(3): 323–35.

Baldock, P., Fitzgerald, D. and Kay, J. (2009) *Understanding Early Years Policy*, **2nd edn. London: Sage.**

Biesta, G.J. (2007) Why 'what works' won't work: Evidence-based practice and the democratic deficit of educational research, *Educational Theory*, 57(1): 1–22.

Biesta, G.J.J. (2010) Why 'what works' still won't work: From evidence-based education to value-based education, *Studies in Philosophy and Education*, 29(5): 491–503.

Boag-Munroe, G. (2012) Engaging hard-to-reach families: A view from the literature, in T. Papatheodorou (ed.) *International Debates on Early Childhood Practices and Policies*. London: Routledge.

Boag-Munroe, G. and Evangelou, M. (2010) *From Hard to Reach to How to Reach: A systematic review of the literature on hard-to-reach families*. Research Papers in Education. Available at: http://dx.doi.org/10.1080/02671522.2010.509515 (accessed 8 March 2013).

Brooker, L. (2002) *Starting School: Young children's learning cultures*. Buckingham: Open University Press.

Department for Education (DfE) (2012) *Statutory Framework for the Early Years Foundation Stage: Setting the standards for learning, development and care for children from birth to five*. Available at: http://www.foundationyears.org.uk/wp-content/uploads/2012/07/EYFS-Statutory-Framework-2012.pdf.

Department for Education and Skills (DfES) (2003) *Every Child Matters*, Cm 5860. Norwich: The Stationery Office.

Desforges, C. and Abouchaar, A. (2003) *The Impact of Parental Involvement, Parental Support and Family Education on Pupil Achievement and Adjustment: A literature review*. Nottingham: Department for Education and Skills.

Edwards, A. and Knight, P. (1994) *Effective Early Years Education: Teaching young children*. Buckingham: Open University Press.

Egan, G. (1990) *The Skilled Helper: A systematic approach to effective helping*. Belmont, CA: Brookes/Cole.

Eisenstadt, N. (2012) Poverty, social disadvantage and young children, in L. Miller and D. Hevey (eds.) *Policy Issues in the Early Years*. London: Sage.

Epstein, J. (1987) Parent involvement: What research says to administrators, *Education and Urban Society*, 19(2): 119–36.

Evangelou, M., Sylva, K., Edwards, A. and Smith, T. (2008) *Supporting Parents in Promoting Early Learning: The evaluation of the Early Learning Partnership Project*. Report No. RR039. Nottingham: DCSF Publications.

Feiler, A. (2010) *Engaging 'Hard to Reach' Parents: Teacher–parent collaboration to promote children's learning*. **Chichester: Wiley-Blackwell.**

Fitzgerald, D. (2004) *Parent Partnership in the Early Years*. London: Continuum.

Georgeson, J. and Boag-Munroe, G. (2012) Architecture and the early years environment: How might buildings contribute to the experience of early years staff, children and families?, in T. Papatheodorou (ed.) *International Debates on Early Childhood Practices and Policies*. London: Routledge.

Jones, C.A. (2004) *Supporting Inclusion in the Early Years*. Maidenhead: Open University Press.

Lindon, J. (2009) *Parents as Partners: Positive relationships in the early years*. London: Practical Pre-School Books.

Miller, L. and Hevey, D. (eds.) (2012) *Policy Issues in the Early Years*. **London: Sage.**

Moll, L. and Greenberg, J.B. (1990) Creating zones of possibilities and combining social contexts for instruction, in L. Moll (ed.) *Vygotsky and Education*. Cambridge: Cambridge University Press.

Pederson, D. (2012) The good mother, the good father, and the good parent: Gendered definitions of parenting, *Journal of Feminist Family Therapy*, 24(3): 230–46.

Quinton, D. (2004) *Supporting Parents: Messages from research*. London: Jessica Kingsley.

Smith, M. (2010) Good parenting: Making a difference, *Early Human Development*, 86(11): 689–93.

Sylva, K., Melhuish, E.C., Sammons, P., Siraj-Blatchford, I. and Taggart, B. (2004) The *Effective Provision of Pre-School Education (EPPE) Project. Technical Paper 12: The Final Report: Effective Pre-School Education*. London: DfES/Institute of Education.

Tunstill, J., Allnock, D., Akhurst, S. and Garbers, C. (2005) Sure Start local programmes: Implications of case study data from the National Evaluation of Sure Start, *Children and Society*, 19: 158–71.

Underdown, A. and Barlow, J. (2012) Promoting infant mental health: A public health priority approach, in L. Miller and D. Hevey (eds.) *Policy Issues in the Early Years*. London: Sage.

Wheeler, H. and Connor, J., with additional material by Goodwin, H. (2009) *Parents, Early Years and Learning: Parents as partners in the Early Years Foundation Stage – principles into practice*. **London: National Children's Bureau.**

15 Inter-professional practice and very young children

Anne Rawlings

Abstract

This chapter examines inter-professional practice in the light of challenging and unprecedented changes in national and local policy relating to inter-professional working with children and family services in England. It explores the implications for holistic practice between different disciplines and how addressing the heritages and contexts of a wide range of disciplinary practices can support a deeper shared understanding of inter-professionalism, including embedding appropriate ethics, theories, values and principles.

Inter-professional partnerships currently work within communities of practice that encompass health, welfare, learning and development requirements for children from birth to five within England. The chapter raises critical issues around inter-professional practice requiring creative responses, looking in particular at proposals to monitor the developmental progress of two-year-olds.

Introduction

The last ten years has seen the introduction of challenging and unprecedented changes in policy relating to inter-professional working with children and family services in England and elsewhere in the early years field. The change of government in England in 2010 heralded a shift in focus away from the Every Child Matters agenda (DCSF, 2003) and the dissolution of Children's Trusts, while 'Foundation for Quality' (Nutbrown, 2012) and the review of 'Child Protection: A child-centred system' (Munro, 2011) have affected training and qualifications for those working in the early years. Key government reports such as the Marmot Review (2010), Review on Poverty and Life Chances (Field, 2010) and Early Intervention: The Next Steps (Allen, 2011) have all influenced current policy by emphasizing that, in terms of health, education and care, early experiences do have a profound effect on life chances. As Marmot (2010) suggests, 'What a child experiences during the early years lays down a foundation for the whole of their life (para. 2.6.1), and goes on to recommend that 'providing for families in their children's early years should be seen as the responsibility of a range of agencies' (para. 3.5.1).

The landscape of the early years workforce is also changing rapidly (see also Chapter 5) and is currently set within the context of a challenging economic environment. Reduction in staffing and frequent reorganization of local authorities can give rise to inter-professional issues relating to responsibilities for health and assessments as well as a failure among some in the workforce, as they seek to manage workloads under stressful conditions, to value and prioritize partnership working. Inter-professional practice can be more apparent in Children's Centres where there are a range of different disciplines, including health visitors, family nurse practitioners, outreach workers, social workers and early years practitioners. However, status differentials between different professionals may lead to some members of a multi-professional team having less of a voice. At this point it is worthwhile to consider different ways multi-professionalism and inter-professional practice are referred to in the current workforce landscape.

What is inter-professional working?

There are a number of terms used to describe the practice of working with a range of professionals; these include multi-agency, multi- or inter-disciplinary, integrated working, multi-professional and inter-professional. These terms have different meanings to different professional groups and all have relevance in varying contexts.

Inter-disciplinary practice requires that an individual gains a depth of understanding of two or more disciplines and can access their languages and methodologies. In Europe, for example, the 'social pedagogue' promotes well-being through broadly based educational strategies; the 'animateur' in France practises a related form of intervention by promoting access to leisure, cultural activities and education.

Inter-professional practice requires multi-disciplinary teams to collaborate and create a common language and framework for discovery and innovation in order to provide better outcomes for children, young people and their families/carers. In terms of safeguarding and protecting children and young people, this last aspect is crucial if our different professions are to work together to reduce harm to the most vulnerable in our society.

The document 'Working Together to Safeguard Children' (DfE, 2013) will greatly affect arrangements and guidance for all agencies and how they work together to safeguard and promote the welfare of children. Significant steps have already been made in the light of the Munro Review (2011). Highly publicized cases involving Serious Case Reviews (SCRs) such as Victoria Climbié in 2003 and Peter Connelly in 2009 have resulted in new ways of working and policy implementation to promote the engagement of professionals across different disciplines, sectors and agencies in the children's workforce. The 'professionals' involved with each of the above cases were publically criticized for ineffectual individual and collaborative working (Laming, 2003, 2009) and the resulting legislation introduced a policy shift and directives for all professionals to work together purposefully and productively (DCSF, 2004, 2008). In the five published evaluative reviews of lessons learned from the SCRs undertaken by OfSTED between 2007 and 2011, a continuing pattern of identified ineffectual practice was highlighted which indicated that 'lessons learned' were not being embedded in practice. In addition, most of the biennial reviews into SCRs concentrate on children aged 5 years and upwards (Brandon *et al.*, 2012).

The Working Together to Safeguard Children document (DfE, 2013) is intended to provide a national framework within which agencies and professionals at local level – individually and jointly – draw up and agree on their own ways of working together to safeguard and promote the welfare of children. Using this statutory document as a guide, it is proposed that all local agencies will be able to address potential needs locally for individual children. To do this all professionals will need to understand each other's roles, share information effectively and support early identification and assessment. Local Safeguarding Children Boards (LSCBs) are to monitor the effectiveness of multi-agency training for all professionals in their area.

Communities of practice

Working Together to Safeguard Children (DfE, 2013: 7) states that: 'children are best protected when professionals are clear about what is required of them individually and how they are to work together'. If each discipline is recognized for its skills, knowledge and experience, this should facilitate delivery of services and so improve outcomes for children and their families. A commitment to pursuing a shared learning environment between professionals from different disciplines entails understanding each other's roles and responsibilities in an increasingly complex workforce landscape. Ideally, shared values will be promoted by the development and use of a shared language and deeper understanding of what inter-professional practice is.

The development of such 'communities of practice' (Lave and Wenger, 1998) should enable a deeper engagement, leading to robust, long-lasting and trusting relationships in the workplace. Wenger (2006) summarizes 'communities of practice' (CoP) as:

> . . . groups of people who share a concern or a passion for something they do and learn how to do it better as they interact regularly. This learning that takes place is not necessarily intentional. Three components are required in order to be a CoP: (1) the domain, (2) the community, and (3) the practice.

The domain

In terms of early years, the domain is complex. Field (2010: 37) asserts:

> There is a range of services to support parents and children in those early years. But GPs, midwives, health visitors, hospital services, Children's Centres and private and voluntary sector nurseries together provide fragmented services that are neither well understood nor easily accessed by all of those who might benefit most.

Some members of the community from different disciplines may not always share the same commitment to the domain even though they have a passion for their own area and interact with others regularly. It can take time to embed different understanding of titles, terms, roles and responsibilities, particularly when training normally takes place within different disciplinary areas.

Provision for children from birth to five years can occur in a range of day care and educational settings. The settings may be run as private, voluntary or independent businesses that can vary considerably in size, structure and ethos. Larger settings may have a 'baby room', 'toddler room' and a preschool class. Environments can include a family home or church hall with little or no outdoor provision, a small building within school grounds (often separate from the school) or in a leisure centre. Children's Centres may also provide access to a range of other services such as teen parenting support, baby massage and out-of-hours activities. Independent schools (not including academies or free schools) that meet the eligibility criteria can opt to be exempt from the learning and development requirements of the Early Years Foundation Stage in part or all together (DfE, 2012).

The community: practitioners

Staff working with children on a daily basis across all early years provision can have a variety of qualifications, role titles and responsibilities. Whether the voices of babies, toddlers and young children can be heard depends on the quality, training and expertise of practitioners from a variety of disciplines. The Professional Capabilities Framework for Social Workers (PCF) (College of Social Work, 2012) sets out the profession's expectations of what a social worker should be able to do at each stage of their career and professional development. Staff in early years settings can include owners/managers, pedagogues, early years practitioners with or without the Early Years Professional Status (EYPS), Early Years Teacher (EYT) or Qualified Teacher Status (QTS) (see Chapter 5 for further details). In her consultations with practitioners, Nutbrown (2012) found that there is general dissatisfaction with the lack of parity for early years practitioners with practitioners who hold QTS, in the light of which she recommended that there should be a clearer career pathway for those who work in the early years sector. The proposed Early Years Teacher will be at graduate level and cover working with children from birth to seven; Early Years Educators, on the other hand, will be at Level 3. However, the DfE's eight new National Standards for Primary School Teachers cover three to eleven years and more joint training and learning will be needed to share expertise for the full age range.

The practice: creating communities of practice

The government has set out its vision for the services that should be on offer for parents, children and families in the foundation years (DfE/DWP, 2011) and describes the system needed to make its vision a reality, explaining the role of commissioners, leaders and practitioners working together across the range of services for families in these years.

This will mean: encouraging partnerships between health and early years services, leading to stronger integrated working; clarifying how information-sharing in the foundation years can work better; a continuing important role for local authorities in addressing disadvantage and inequalities by securing sufficient early years provision and championing the needs of vulnerable children and families; clarifying how we measure outcomes in the early years; and promoting the development of an increasingly diverse sector with a strong role for private, voluntary, community and social enterprise organisations.

(DfE/DWP, 2011: 2)

I have worked with a team for the past four years which crosses health, social work and education on a degree that is delivered inter-professionally with a cohort of students from a range of work-based disciplines, and it is clear that the reciprocal learning that has taken place is extensive. The standards that social work practitioners and early years practitioners work towards in the early part of training for their careers have many similarities. Interactive learning argues for a shared, participative approach from all involved. It draws upon multiple perspectives from both within and across different discipline areas as a tool for the development of knowledge, skills and understanding, both about childhood (birth to 19 years and beyond) and about learning and teaching. 'Collaborative practice grows out of collaborative learning between the professions, reinforcing the collaborative competencies required' (CAIPE, 2012).

Ensuring people learn from and about each others' disciplines early, however, is not enough to ensure collaborative practice if they then make decisions within their respective disciplines in the workplace. They also need to engage in continuing professional development where practitioners from all disciplines can work together to learn, research and share expertise if we are to re-conceptualize inter-professional practice. Practitioners from all disciplines need to remain motivated, inspired and have access to a wide range of good practices, images, visions and perspectives. For the past three years, nine higher education (HE) institutions from eight European countries have been analysing, comparing and discussing the existing variety in education and care for children under three years in Europe. The English contribution is by Kingston University early years team, 'Towards Opportunities for Disadvantaged and Diverse Learners on the Early Childhood Road' (The Toddler Project; Sutherland and Styman, 2013) and materials from this project can be used by all practitioners in every discipline to prioritize the development of good practice and develop a common understanding concerning the very young in early years settings.

My experience in joint training across disciplines has highlighted some anomalies. For example, when putting experienced work-based practitioner students at HE Level 6 with social work students at HE Level 7, results revealed that early years practitioners are very knowledgeable about child development, observation and assessment of developmental progress. The social work students, on the other hand, demonstrated greater knowledge of the legal aspects relating to safeguarding and child welfare with less knowledge of developmental stages. The feedback from these on-going sessions shows that the students consider them to be invaluable for sharing expertise and developing a shared language.

I never knew that early years practitioners do so much assessing, recording and reporting. It seems like we [social workers] might be replicating what is already available, particularly when it comes to a safeguarding concern.

(social work student)

Recognition of each discipline's respective knowledge, skills, roles and responsibilities is key to ensuring better outcomes for children and families. One of the many emerging themes from all students is that they want more joint sessions on commonalities of practice such as child protection, child development, developmental learning, child protection and safeguarding. However, these commonalities can be lost if, when in practice, different agencies make decisions within their own disciplines without recourse to practitioners who may well have a more consistent daily knowledge of issues and concerns when working with the same families. This is particularly important when there may be serious concerns about the safety of a child.

Increasingly, in a rapidly changing children's workforce environment that encompasses new emerging roles, all practitioners have to adopt or adapt to new procedures when making decisions. Making decisions together can lead to disagreements as professionals hold on to their principles that can be interpreted or prioritized within their own discipline, knowledge and experience. All practitioners when making decisions about a child or family with whom they are working need time to reflect (together as well as individually) after acting on a decision to determine whether their principles are compatible. If there is no time to reflect, then the question should be asked: 'What can we do to ensure we have time to reflect?' This would make working practices in different disciplines more effective.

When individuals have to make quick decisions, they draw on in-built values and beliefs that they assume will benefit those concerned. Rowson (2006) suggests we generally see ethics as giving us a standpoint from which to decide what is right and wrong and what we ought or ought not to do in challenging situations where crucial decisions have to be made. When professionals make decisions from any discipline, it is important that they can articulate why they made that decision in any particular circumstance. Moreover, as part of professional accountability they need to be able to explain why they felt justified in not carrying out a decision. Rowson (2006: 55) has developed a framework for addressing 'working ethics': the FAIR framework embraces four key values – 'Fairness, Autonomy, Integrity and Results of Practice', which aim at enhancing working environments and reducing potential for harm. Ethical dilemmas will continue to occur in practice, requiring all practitioners to be willing and able to share, debate and seek ethical conclusions. If the energy from this tension is used constructively, it can strengthen an inter-professional learning community and develop a research culture.

Inter-professional practice to support younger children

Recent research by Barlow *et al.* (2012) shows that, in physical abuse cases, the younger the age of the child the greater the risk of serious injury from assaults, and that the impact of serious neglect and trauma on a young brain prevents normal development and can cause enlarged ventricles and atrophy, resulting in fewer neural pathways being available for learning. In these challenging economic times, there has never been a more pressing need for different disciplines to work together effectively to combat the effects of poverty.

> Three-year-olds in households with incomes below about £10,000 are 2.5 times more likely to suffer chronic illness than children in households with incomes above £52,000. Infant mortality is 10% higher for infants in the lower social group than the average.
>
> (Barnados, 2013)

Overwhelming findings from previous Serious Case Reviews (SCRs) indicate that 'two-thirds of SCRs concern children under the age of five (and half are for infants under twelve months)' (Brandon *et al.*, 2012; NSPCC, 2012). This means that services for a large number of these children fall under the private, voluntary, independent (PVI) and third sectors, or are looked after by families/carers/neighbours, which adds to the complexity and emphasizes the need for transparency of information sharing and decision making. The agency most frequently involved with babies is the Health Service, but evidence from our large cohorts of work-based inter-professional practitioners (around 1000) suggests there are currently limited ways of communicating with those working in health, particularly midwives and health visitors.

It is in the early years that the socio-economic gaps in outcomes first appear. Already by age three there are large and systematic differences between children from lower and higher income families and these gaps persist throughout childhood, as later attainment tends to be heavily influenced by early development (Field, 2010: 37). To improve life chances and address gaps in attainment, the Two-Year-Old Pilot Project was introduced in 2006. It was aimed at the most economically disadvantaged children age two years to access up to ten hours of formal childcare per week for 38 weeks. Field's Report identifies the crucial elements for improving life chances: 'Family background, parental education, good parenting and the opportunities for learning and development in those crucial years that together matter more to children than money' (Field, 2010: 5).

The DfE/DWP (2011: 1) states a commitment that the offer of two-year-old funding should involve family support as well as early education. Ross (2013) has noticed a potential failure with the two-year-old funding offer to link family support and early education. It was strongly suggested that those implementing the Pilot should include family support and yet this is not a specific requirement of parents who access the two-year-old funding. Simms (2012: 1, cited in Ross, 2013) reinforces this view: 'Separating child and parent might give them a break from each other but it does not change or progress any issues they may want or need to address.' Early research on the impact of the two-year-old funding has shown that early intervention significantly improves the life chances of young children (Smith *et al.*, 2009).

To enable early identification of a child's developmental needs to support progress, the EYFS Framework (DfE, 2012: 11) states that:

2.3 When a child is aged between two and three, practitioners must review their progress, and provide parents and/or carers with a short written summary of their child's development in the prime areas. This progress check must identify the child's strengths, and any areas where the child's progress is less than expected. If there are significant emerging concerns, or an identified special educational need or disability, practitioners should develop a targeted plan to support the child's future learning and development involving other professionals (for example, the provider's Special Educational Needs Co-ordinator) as appropriate.

This progress check should be provided

. . . in time to inform the Healthy Child Programme health and development review at age two whenever possible (when health visitors gather information on a child's health and development, allowing them to identify any developmental delay and any particular support from which they think the child/family might benefit).

(DfE, 2012: 11)

The 'Know How Guide: The EYFS progress check at two' (DfE/NCB, 2012) gives examples of how different approaches have already been adapted by practitioners to address local issues when providing information to parents. However, training to carry out the checks can be patchy, which can lead to questionable results, and anecdotal evidence from early years practitioners attending professional development courses on working with two-year-olds again suggests that sharing information with health visitors is proving problematic. Clearly barriers to inter-professional working still exist.

Barriers to interprofessional working

Evidence about factors affecting inter-professional working has pointed towards barriers such as a lack of role clarity within and between professions as well as issues over accountability and ambiguity concerning policy implementation. In other words, at strategic and operational level, practitioners have had to change existing working practices. This has, in some cases, resulted in productive opportunities but in other cases this has caused delays, anxieties and ill-advised condemnation that may have resulted in reduced public confidence in the current systems, at a time when referrals are on the increase: 'In 2011–2012 over 600,000 children in England were referred to local authority children's social services by individuals who had concerns about their welfare' (DfE, 2013: 7).

All of the above takes place within a climate of reduced public sector resources, which places huge pressures on local services and front line practitioners. In terms of lessons learned from recent delivery of services in order to reduce poverty, health and education inequalities, it is essential to increase and sustain investment and identify programmes that focus on prevention and that challenge barriers to successful delivery. This includes, for example, recognizing that people may be 'deprived' who live in mixed, suburban and or rural communities in any part of the country, rather than just those in the inner city. Our own tracking evidence indicates that those who work in areas of deprivation mainly have qualifications up to Level 3 only, although Children's Centres are generally located in areas of most need and do have staff who have higher qualifications. However, the broader early years sector consists of the private, voluntary, independent and grant-maintained settings and some may be struggling to stay in business in this difficult financial climate, limiting opportunities for professional development. If we are to move towards a truly inter-professional future, we must provide opportunities for workforce development for the whole sector, through vibrant, dynamic inter-disciplinary forums, where students, lecturers, researchers, professionals and children themselves can work together using equal and interactive learning approaches.

Conclusion

The emerging field of inter-professional practice is still in a state of 'becoming' and until inter-professional learning and teaching are embedded across all disciplines at an early stage of training, progress is likely to be slow. There needs to be a will on the part of all disciplines to work together, share common goals, outcomes and values in order to overcome practice barriers. A common language is essential as well as an integrated approach across data, methodologies, perspectives, theory and concepts from multiple disciplines in order to advance fundamental understanding. Those people who work with young children and families know that to hear all voices effectively needs practitioners who are confident in their knowledge, skills and expertise, and proactive and willing to take onboard others' views. As Rowson (2006: 67) suggests:

> In many situations the way for professionals to seek the best results is by acting with integrity, respecting autonomy and treating people fairly. That way they are likely to be trusted and able to achieve the professional objectives that contribute to the overall well-being of people affected by their work.

Addressing the heritages and contexts of a wide range of disciplinary practices required in inter-professional working environments can be successful if all disciplines can gain a deeper shared understanding of inter-professionalism and embed appropriate ethics, values and principles together. This does require a consistent and committed approach from those who are responsible for providing career ladders that encompass and value each discipline. But if we have a

> ... common desire to be a force for positive change in the way we deliver services to very young children and their families, [this can lead us] towards achieving those transformations as we build on the successes of working together across professional, agency and personal boundaries to the extent that it will be possible to imagine that no such boundaries exist.
> (Duckmanton, 2011: 168)

Points for reflection and discussion

1. How do you share information across disciplines and how might you improve communication?
2. What do you know about the process of Serious Case Reviews (SCRs). As an early years practitioner, how do SCRs impact on your practice?
3. Name a minimum of three things your setting does to ensure parents/carers are fully informed of how the two-year-old checks are carried out and how the results should be shared with other professionals.
4. How do you ensure that progress is captured after the checks and parents/carers and other professionals are kept informed of on-going progress?

References and further reading

Allen, G. (2011) *Early Intervention: The Next Steps: An independent report to Her Majesty's Government.* London: HM Government.

Barlow, J., Fisher, J.D. and Jones, D. (2012) *Systematic Review of Models of Analysing Significant Harm.* Research Report DFE RR199. London: DfE.

Barnados (2013) *Child Poverty Statistics and Facts.* Available at: http://www.barnardos.org.uk/what_we_do/our_projects/child_poverty.htm (accessed 15 June 2013).

Brandon, M., Sidebotham, P., Bailey, S., Belderson, P., Hawley, C. *et al.* (2012) *New Learning from Serious Case Reviews: A two year report for 2009–2011.* Research Report No. 226. London: DfE.

Centre for the Advancement of Interprofessional Education (CAIPE) (2012) *Interprofessional Education in Pre-registration Courses: A CAIPE guide for commissioners and regulators of education.* London: CAIPE.

College of Social Work (2012) *The Professional Capabilities Framework for Social Workers.* London: College of Social Work.

Department for Children, Schools and Families (DCSF) (2003) *Every Child Matters.* London: The Stationery Office.

Department for Children, Schools and Families (DCSF) (2004) *Primary Strategy: Guidance for practitioners in EYFS.* Nottingham: DCSF.

Department for Children, Schools and Families (DCSF) (2008) *The Early Years Foundation Stage: Setting the standards for learning, development and care for children from birth to five.* Nottingham: DCSF.

Department for Education (DfE) (2012) *Statutory Framework for the Early Years Foundation Stage: Setting the standards for learning, development and care for children from birth to five.* Available at: http://www.foundationyears.org.uk/wp-content/uploads/2012/07/EYFS-Statutory-Framework-2012.pdf.

Department for Education (DfE) (2013) *Working Together to Safeguard Children: A guide to interagency working to safeguard and promote the welfare of children.* London: DfE.

Department for Education (DfE)/Department of Work and Pensions (DWP) (2011) *A New Approach to Child Poverty: Tackling the causes of disadvantage and transforming families' lives.* London: DfE/DWP.

Department for Education (DfE)/National Children's Bureau (NCB) (2012) *Know How Guide: The EYFS progress check at two.* London: DfE/NCB.

Duckmanton, J. (2011) The possibilities of an imagined future: Observing critical dilemmas in observing interprofessional and interagency working, in L. Trodd and L. Chivers (eds.) *Interprofessional Working in Practice: Learning and working together for children and families.* Maidenhead: Open University Press.

Field, F. (2010) *The Foundation Years: Preventing poor children becoming poor adults. The Report of the Independent Review on Poverty and Life Chances.* London: The Stationery Office.

Laming, Lord (2003) *Victoria Climbié Report Summary.* London: Department of Health and Home Office.

Laming, Lord (2009) *The Protection of Children in England: A progress report.* London: The Stationery Office.

Lave, J. and Wenger, E. (1998) *Communities of Practice: Learning, meaning, and identity.* Cambridge: Cambridge University Press.

Marmot, M. (2010) *The Marmot Review: Fair society, healthy lives.* London: Marmot Review.

Munro, E. (2011) *Child Protection Final Report: A child centred system.* London: The Stationery Office.

National Society for the Prevention of Cruelty to Children (NSPCC) (2012) *Research, Statistics and Information.* Available at: www.nspcc.org.uk/Inform/research/statistics/statistics_wda48748.html (accessed 14 June 2013).

Nutbrown, C. (2012) *Foundation for Quality: The independent review of early education and childcare qualifications. Final Report.* London: HMSO.

Ross, E. (2013) *Supporting Parents to Successfully Access the Two-Year-Old Funding in Order to Fulfil their Child's Potential.* Unpublished report, Institute for Child Centred Interprofessional Practice (ICCIP), Kingston University.

Rowson, R. (2006) *Working Ethics: How to be fair in a culturally complex world.* London: Jessica Kingsley.

Smith, R., Purdon, S., Schneider, V., La Valle, I., Woolny, I. *et al.* (2009) *Early Education Pilot for Two Year Old Children Evaluation.* Research Report DCSF-RR134. London: DCSF.

Sutherland, H. and Styman, J. (2013) *Towards Opportunities for Disadvantaged and Diverse Learners on the Early Childhood Road (The Toddler Project).* Available at: www.toddlerineurope.eu (accessed 15 June 2013).

Trodd, L. and Chivers, L. (2011) *Interprofessional Working in Practice: Learning and working together for children and families.* Maidenhead: Open University Press.

Wenger, E. (2006) *Communities of Practice: A brief introduction.* Available at: http://www.ewenger.com/theory/communities_of_practice_intro.htm (accessed 20 June 2013).

PART 4
Equality of opportunity

16 School readiness: starting age, cohorts and transitions in the early years

David Whitebread and Sue Bingham

Abstract

This chapter examines the influence of schools upon children as their 'schooling' commences. In particular, we examine the evidence concerning the impact of recent developments in England, whereby children are starting school ever younger and the experience they are being offered is a diet of increasingly formal teaching. This has been accompanied, in policy documents and in public debate concerning early education, by discourses on 'narrowing the gap' between children at the point when they enter school and ensuring that all children are 'ready for school'. We argue that these general trends are not supported by the evidence from studies of young children's development as learners and are likely to be counterproductive.

Introduction

If we wish to improve the quality of early educational provision for all children, particularly those who are disadvantaged in some way, we need to locate the problem not in the children but in inappropriate provision. In particular, we need to look again at a system that requires young children to learn from formal teaching methods before they are able to do so. We need to look at the research evidence concerning young children's development of 'cognitive control' and 'self-regulation', abilities that enable them to learn in more deliberate and formal ways, and we need to look at how early educational experiences can support this development.

In most of Europe, as indeed in the USA and Australasia, no child is regarded as 'ready for school' – in other words, ready for formal teaching and learning – until they are at least six (and in some cases seven) years of age. Within England, however, the government has introduced formal curricula at ever-earlier points in school and, within its recent publication of curriculum frameworks and related guidance, has prescribed that children should be 'made ready' for school by the age of five. Indeed, in practice, children as young as four years of age in the UK are currently being introduced to formal aspects of literacy and number and, by five years of age, are being required to spend most of their school day undertaking tasks under the direction of the teacher.

In this chapter, we review briefly how this situation has arisen and the evidence concerning the damaging consequences of an inappropriately early introduction of formal, teacher-directed learning. We also examine the particular consequences for children in the UK who are relatively disadvantaged due to their socio-economic situation and who are relatively young upon entry into school.

Age of entry to school: international comparisons and a brief history

There is now abundant evidence concerning the long-term consequences for children's development as learners of the age at which they are required to make the transition from the informal environments of the home and play-based preschool provision into formal schooling. Starting school involves children responding to changes in identity, roles and relationships as they become a 'pupil', and learning the social rules and values associated with being in an 'institution'. Transitions between preschool systems into primary school pose difficulties for young children when they encounter contrasting or widely differing expectations, approaches and values in the new environment. Table 16.1 indicates the typical age at which children start school in a range of countries, compared with the statutory school starting age and how long they spend on average in early childhood education and care (ECEC) provision beforehand.

According to Bertram and Pascal (2002: 9), the historic reason for the comparatively early admission to primary education in the UK is related to 'the pressures

Table 16.1 Expected number of years of early childhood and primary education for children aged up to 6 years (Eurostat Database, 2000).

Country	Typical starting age ECEC (years)	Expected length of time in ECEC (years)	Primary school typical starting age	Primary school compulsory starting age
England	3	0.6	4	5
USA	3	2.0	6	5–7
New Zealand	2	2.3	5	6
Finland	3–6	1.5	7	7
Denmark	3	3.1	7	7
Sweden	3	2.6	6–7	7
Norway	3	2.8	6	6
Belgium	2.5	3.4	6	6
France	2	3.4	6	6

of a political compromise agreed in the House of Commons in the 1860s and has no judicious basis in educational theory'.

Confusion arises as to what actually constitutes the 'start' of school in England. The statutory age for children to start school in England is at the start of the school term following the child's fifth birthday (DCSF, 2009). In practice, however, most children have been admitted in the term, half year, or year in which they became five. In response to the recommendations on improving attainment of summer-born children made in the Review of the Primary Curriculum (Rose, 2009), the Admissions Code was revised in 2011 to require admissions authorities to make a full-time reception place available for all children from the *September* after their fourth birthday. Hence the trend to adopt an annual admissions policy has become embedded, although parents retain the right to defer their child's entry to school until the term after their fifth birthday. Parents continue to be able to access their free entitlement for their children in other early years settings up until compulsory school age. In practice, therefore, in England, school commences in Reception classes comprising children whose ages range from just over four to over five years.

The use of the phrase 'ready for school' in documents such as the Early Years Foundation Stage (EYFS) (Tickell, 2011) reveals that many policy makers in England hold that the Reception year is the start of school. Yet contradictions abound where the Reception year is also described in policy and curriculum documents as still being within the Foundation Stage, theoretically functioning as a 'transition' year for the child, in which they are prepared gradually, using appropriate teaching methods, for entry into Year 1. Certainly, and partly as a consequence of this confusion, many Reception teachers are pressurized to begin formal teaching to prepare the children for the formal learning content and approaches now common in Year 1.

The irony of the evidence: play approaches enhance academic achievement more than formal approaches in the early years

It is perhaps counter-intuitive that delaying formal schooling will enhance children's development as learners but there is no serious evidence to support the 'earlier is better' position and a very significant body of evidence to support the alternative view.

In a comparison of three preschool models, namely child-initiated, academically directed or a 'combination' approach, Marcon (2002) studied children who began school at age four to examine the influence of the different preschool models upon later school success. The study examined report card grades, retention rates and special educational need diagnoses of 160 children at the end of their fifth year in school as they prepared to leave their primary school and 183 children at the end of their sixth year in school as they started in secondary school. Findings showed that by the end of the fifth year in school, there were no significant differences in academic performance attributable to the different types of preschool models, but by the end of their sixth year in school, children whose preschool model had been academically directed achieved significantly lower marks than children who had attended child-initiated preschool programmes. Findings regarding later school success were significantly poorer for academically directed preschool children; fewer were retained during the primary school years, and they were least successful in making the transition to secondary school. Children's later school success appears to have been enhanced by more active, child-initiated early learning experiences.

The introduction of formal learning approaches to literacy flies in the face of research evidence emanating from several projects. In one large national study, Suggate (2007) compared the reading abilities of children in New Zealand who did not start formal reading instruction until they were seven with children who started at age five. He found that by age eleven there was no difference in reading ability between these two groups. Several other recent national studies echo these findings (Turnbull, 2006; Dollase, 2007). In Suggate's (2009) more recent international study, he suggests no significant association between reading achievement and school entry age: an earlier beginning to formal reading instruction does not appear to result in later higher reading achievement.

Suggate *et al.* (2013) revealed some evidence that children who start formal instruction in reading earlier develop less positive attitudes to reading, and, by the age of eleven, show poorer text comprehension than those children who start later. This parallels the results of the longitudinal High/Scope Perry Pre-School Project (Schweinhart *et al.*, 2005) in which researchers found that, although direct instruction methods of teaching seemed to bring some children initial advantages in terms of their early reading and numeracy competencies, the High/Scope children who had been in 'child-initiated' learning environments showed significantly more positive results over the long term. By age fifteen, the direct instruction group participants were showing signs of having become 'disaffected' with learning, presenting more psychological and social problems than other groups and reading only half as many books.

A growing number of studies suggest that early play experiences enhance young children's self-regulation and that self-regulation is related to academic achievement (Ponitz *et al.*, 2009). Children who attend preschools based predominantly upon models emphasizing play rather than academic outcomes have been found to achieve higher scores on measures of self-regulation (Hyson *et al.*, 2007). Barnett *et al.* (2006) evaluated the effectiveness of the Tools of the Mind play-based curriculum by means of a randomized trial and revealed that, not only were individual children's executive functions enhanced, but also overall classroom quality improved as a result of this enhanced self-regulation by the participating children. Several explanations have been proposed, including the fact that, in play, children practise regulating their own behaviour in many different ways.

The dangers of 'too much, too early'

A number of studies have also pointed to more generally disturbing consequences of early and inappropriate formal instruction. The longitudinal results of the High/Scope Perry Pre-School Project (Schweinhart *et al.*, 2005), for example, revealed disturbing long-term effects of early direct instruction upon individuals' social and psychological frames of mind. Although direct instruction methods of teaching seemed to bring some children initial advantages in terms of their early reading and numeracy competencies, the High/Scope children who had been in 'child-initiated' learning environments showed significantly more positive results over the long term. By age twenty-three, those who had attended play-based preschools were eight times less likely to need treatment for psychological or emotional disturbances and three times less likely to be arrested for committing a crime.

It seems that social problems arise when policy and curriculum directives fail to recognize that early education should be about the whole child; direct instruction does not *cause* social problems, but it seems that depriving children of the opportunity to develop socially is an unintended side effect.

In parallel, several researchers (e.g. Blaustein, 2005) have highlighted the risks to developmental growth that occur through implementing early childhood programmes based on a directed academic curriculum, often replacing essential hands-on learning activities with skill-based performance and rote-learning tasks. Blaustein (2005: 3) argues that in emphasizing rote-learning tasks, a young child is conditioned to concentrate on a very specific skill and use 'lower' parts of the brain, and the insufficiently developed cerebral cortex, to learn that skill. The child is forced to use parts of the brain that are immature and, although the child may be able to practise and acquire the skill, the normal growth and development of the brain may be distorted by such practice (Healy, 2004: 64), since the child will continue to use the lower part of the brain trained to perform the task even when the frontal cortex becomes more developed and suited to the task.

The diversity of early childhood experiences and the emergence of disadvantaged cohorts

Numerous indicators highlight the substantial differences in early childhood experiences across children in England, differences that affect their initial development and which persist as children age, influencing dispositions towards learning as well as the range of skills they will be ready to employ upon arrival in school. Healthy child development may be supported by a variety of factors during the early years or, conversely, the desired outcomes for a child may be compromised whether temporarily or on a more long-lasting basis. Such factors include, for example, the nature of early relationships with parents and other caregivers, the extent of cognitive stimulation, and access to adequate nutrition, health care, and other resources such as a safe home and neighbourhood environment. However, there is now extensive evidence that high-quality early years provision, which follows a holistic 'social constructivist' model, providing young children with informal, playful social and learning experiences, can make a significant contribution to ameliorating the effects of these various kinds of relative disadvantage.

Poverty

Poverty affects a sizeable proportion of young children in the UK; the number living in low-income households in the UK reached 3.9 million in 2008–2009

(DWP, 2010). Living in certain areas where high percentages of the population have income below the poverty line limits healthy development for many children. Extensive research evidence has linked economic disadvantage to parental stress, low responsiveness in parent–child interactions and a range of poor cognitive and social-emotional outcomes in young children, including inadequate language acquisition, self-regulation, and confidence to interact or express their needs (Dearing et al., 2006). Moreover, children from low-income or less educated families may be doubly disadvantaged since they are also less likely to be enrolled in early education settings (Meyers et al., 2004).

International research shows that early intervention contributes significantly to putting children from low-income families on the route to development and achievement in life. Evidence from programmes such as the Family–Nurse Partnership (Barnes et al., 2010), Parent–Child Interaction Therapy (Zisser and Eyberg, 2010) and Community Mothers (McGuire-Schwartz, 2007) have revealed that if appropriately related to health, employment and social services, early childhood services can effectively enhance parenting skills, community-building and maternal employment and decrease family poverty (Brooks-Gunn, 2003; Lynch, 2004). Evidence from Sylva et al. (2004) suggests that investing in good quality preschool provision can be seen as an effective means of achieving targets concerning social exclusion and breaking cycles of disadvantage.

Summer-born children in Reception classes

A major review by Sykes et al. (2009) suggests that summer-born children in Reception classes may be an unacknowledged cohort facing disadvantage upon entry into school, in that they are both young (possibly just having had their fourth birthday) and the youngest in their class when they start school. They may not have reached the level of cognitive competence required to tackle a curriculum designed for five-year-olds or formal teaching methods. They may not be ready for the social and emotional adjustments required to cope with the demands of a school day, factors that may cause stress and anxiety. Furthermore, concerns about 'teacher expectancy effects', where children are possibly being unfairly viewed as 'falling behind' have been raised relating to summer-born children in particular (Sykes et al., 2009), who do not achieve the writing goals by Year 1 and, on average, perform at a lower level than older children in their year group – as revealed in the EYFS Profile scores for 2009, for example (DfE, 2010), which showed that the writing goals were generally more challenging than other goals, especially for boys, with 62 per cent able to hold a pencil and use it to write letters by the end of the EYFS, compared with 79 per cent of girls. There is evidence to suggest that 'birth date' effects may be the result of lower levels of maturity in the physical, cognitive, social and emotional domains in the summer-born children, relative to those who are more than a year older at the start of school.

A further study by Bell and Daniels (1990) revealed that summer-born children are disadvantaged academically and socially. For example, comparisons of August- and September-born children revealed that 25 per cent of the former (who were the youngest in their year group) had lower academic attainment at Key Stage 1 and, in the longer term, 20 per cent were less likely to go to university. Gledhill and colleagues' (2002) large study with a sample of 8000 children aged five to fifteen, revealed that summer-born children with the same level of ability as non-summer-born children are approximately 50 per cent more likely to be diagnosed as having special educational needs.

By contrast, there is some evidence that starting formal education later helps to reduce birth date effects. Bedard and Dhuey (2006, in Sykes *et al.*, 2009: 4) suggest that:

> Birth date effects appear to be greatly reduced in countries where formal education begins at a later age. There needs to be a careful consideration of what is best for all children in the early years of schooling, based on solid evidence from psychological research.

An alternative, evidence-based approach: social constructivism

At the centre of much widely respected early years provision, such as those of Reggio Emilia (Rinaldi, 2006), Experiential Education (Laevers, 2003), High/Scope (Hohmann *et al.*, 2008) and much early years provision in Central Europe and Scandinavia, for example, lies the notion and methods of social constructivism (Vygotsky, 1978). This philosophy places equal value upon care, upbringing and learning and focuses upon the interests, experiences and choices of young children within social contexts. Such an approach is regarded as being 'pedagogy', a broader concept than 'curriculum' in that it also encompasses the physical, emotional and social environments of young children.

The cognitive neuroscience and psychological evidence of recent decades shows clearly that all children, at all ages, are ready to learn. So the significant question is not *whether* a child is ready to learn, but rather *what* a child is ready to learn and what sort of teaching methodologies will best support the child's learning. Practitioners working in a social constructivist tradition recognize that what a child learns influences how they develop and that a child's capacity to think and understand stems from their interactions with others, predominantly through spoken language.

At its heart lies the goal of children developing as independent, intrinsically motivated, powerful learners. Essentially, the teaching methods used in formal instruction require that a child is able to control their cognitive processes, or achieve what is labelled in the psychological literature as 'self-regulation' (i.e. over time, the child becomes able to regulate their own social, emotional and cognitive functions rather then relying on adult support). Before these fundamental psychological abilities develop within the child, they are not able to learn through the teaching methodologies associated with the formal instruction approaches. The neuroscientific and psychological evidence suggests that for most children, these abilities are sufficiently developed to learn through formal teaching and learning methods by around the ages of six or seven (see Whitebread, 2012). Adopting a play-based and process-based pedagogy supports the development of psychologically fundamental processes during early development, including:

- working memory (the ability to hold increasing amounts of information in mind while it is being processed or acted upon);

- control of attention and 'inhibitory' or 'effortful' control (the ability to pro-actively guide behaviour according to an internal goal or plan, rather than behaving reactively to external events);
- language and expressive abilities;

all of which underpin the child's developing capacities for self-regulation (Martin-Korpi, 2005).

Clearly, the goals of such a pedagogy are not so much content-related but process-related; there is an emphasis upon learning skills and acquiring disposi-tions that will be useful to the child in their lifelong learning. Real or 'mastery' learning involves deep understanding, as opposed to 'performance' learning, which is simply aimed at passing tests or examinations. Thus, in many coun-tries the focus is on supporting young children to achieve broad developmen-tal goals in the areas of socio-emotional understanding, personal and social skills, physical and motor skills, and artistic and cultural development. The chil-dren become knowledgeable about basic science, number and literacy notions through experiencing real-life, naturally occurring events and activities rather than undergoing curriculum approaches with defined, pre-determined subject content. The overall outcome is that through acquiring the general knowledge that helps children make sense of their experience and increases their self-esteem and confidence as learners, children become 'ready' for further learning challenges and have the cognitive controls to enable them to benefit from more formal teaching methodologies.

Within early years provision that is not attuned to the 'natural', informal, experiential ways in which young children learn, it is often the case that teach-ers believe that it is their role to make sure that children do things correctly, to convey to the children that they should do as they are told and to use controls in an attempt to make sure that they do. The teacher may resort to coercive strate-gies such as the promise of rewards or threat of sanctions and overtly controlling language.

On the other hand, teachers who use teaching methodologies appropriate for the natural learning capabilities of young children bring about classrooms that nurture and involve young children's psychological needs, personal interests and values. Such teachers believe it is important for children to initiate behaviours, to learn from both their successes and their failures, and to try to solve problems for themselves. In such autonomy-supportive contexts, teachers empathize with the child's perspective, allow opportunities for self-initiation and choice, provide a meaningful rationale if choice is constrained, refrain from the use of pressures and contingencies to motivate behaviour, and provide timely positive feedback (Hardre and Reeve, 2003; Gurland and Grolnick, 2005).

Reception and Year 1 classrooms into which young children enter at the start of school, offer a range of resources and activities, teachers and other adults to relate to, and a 'curriculum' to guide the classroom activity. When these interac-tions go well, the classroom functions as a support system for children to sat-isfy their needs, explore interests, refine skills, internalize values and develop socially. In these conditions, children's classroom behaviours reflect their needs, interests and values and they show strong motivation, active engagement and meaningful learning (Ryan and Deci, 2000, 2004; Reeve, 2002).

Conclusion

'Readiness for school' implies preparing a child to reach a fixed standard of physical, intellectual and social development that prepares them to meet school requirements and assimilate formal curricula, typically embracing specific cognitive and linguistic skills. This perception of 'readiness' is seen in English early years education policy, which endorses the preparation of children for 'starting school' based on the premise that the National Curriculum in Year 1 is 'set' and children must be prepared to fit into it.

Many educationalists have a different perspective on early years learning to that of policy makers. Psychological understandings about children's learning have been deepening and educationalists have been designing pedagogies based upon increasingly sophisticated empirical research but government policy decisions have encroached directly upon classroom practice.

Since the mid-1990s, there has been a growing perception on the part of many educationalists that a 'deficit model' exists in the early years schooling system within England. They hold that the primary school curriculum and testing system is inordinately focused on a narrow range of cognitive skills, placing unreasonable – and inappropriate – demands upon the children within Key Stage 1 at the expense of other social and emotional learning. Although a cognitive-heavy diet is arguably short-sighted at any stage of schooling, it is particularly inappropriate for young children's education, at a time when investment in social and emotional learning is essential to pave the way for future development. Early years educators understand the importance of developing young children's capacities to make meaning from their experiences and to acquire language. Researchers suggest that play-based methods should be a central ingredient in early learning, enabling children to practise gross and fine motor skills, imitate adult behaviours, process emotional episodes and learn about their world. Both free play and guided play are crucial for the development of academic skills and both types feature within most early childhood pedagogies around the world and are consistent with a social pedagogy model.

The 'readiness for school' model offers the security to education ministries of children entering primary school already prepared to read and write and being able to conform to many classroom routines. This 'schoolifying' of the early childhood years (OECD, 2006: 63) is not, however, supported by the research evidence and is very likely to be damaging, particularly for the most deprived and youngest of our children. Educationalists within the social constructivist approach base their practices on the evidence that it is primarily through children's increased cognitive control and self-regulatory abilities, and the pursuit of more holistic aims, including concern for children's emotional and social development, that deep 'mastery' learning occurs, and children's development as learners is supported.

Many early years educationalists suggest that what children need from their early schooling is the opportunity to continue their learning through informal pedagogies – ideally up until the age of seven – in an environment that offers rich stimulation and sensitive, supportive adults who know best how to provide for their emotional and cognitive needs. Rather than being focused upon testing and assessment, early years education should provide a secure foundation for lifelong learning and should effectively draw out young children's full potential as learners and citizens. In summary, rather than making children ready for school, what we need to do is to make schools ready for children.

Points for reflection and discussion

1. What is meant by the transition from informal to formal learning and why is this particularly significant for young children's development as learners within school contexts?
2. What are the key points that would distinguish an 'earlier is better' approach from a 'social pedagogy' approach to early childhood education?
3. Why might children from disadvantaged backgrounds be particularly adversely affected by a 'school readiness' approach?
4. Why are summer-born children likely to do worse at school than autumn-born children, and what can we do to provide more effectively for the needs of the youngest children in each age cohort?
5. How can we develop the nature of educational provision in the early years of primary schooling to provide more effectively for the needs of young children?

References and further reading

Alexander, R.J. (ed.) (2010) *Children, Their World, Their Education: Final report and recommendations of the Cambridge Primary Review*. Abingdon: Routledge.

Anning, A. (1998) Appropriateness or effectiveness in the early childhood curriculum in the UK: Some research evidence, *International Journal of Early Years Education*, 6(3): 299–314.

Barnes, J., Ball, M., Meadows, B., Howden, B., Jackson, A. *et al.* (2010) *The Family–Nurse Partnership Programme in England*. London: Institute for the Study of Children, Families and Social Issues.

Barnett, W.S., Yarosz, D.J., Thomas, J. and Hornbeck, A. (2006) *Educational Effectiveness of a Vygotskian Approach to Preschool Education: A randomized trial*. Rutgers, NJ: National Institute for Early Education Research.

Bedard, K. and Dhuey, E. (2006) The persistence of early childhood maturity: International evidence of long-run age effects, *Quarterly Journal of Economics*, 121(4): 1437–1472.

Bell, J.F. and Daniels, S. (1990) Are summer-born children disadvantaged? The birthdate effect in education, *Oxford Review of Education*, 16(1): 67–80.

Bertram, T. and Pascal, C. (2002) *Early Years Education: An international perspective*. London: Qualifications and Curriculum Authority.

Blaustein, M. (2005) See! Hear! Touch! The basics of learning readiness, *Journal of the National Association for the Education of Young Children*, 41(1): 45–7.

Brooks-Gunn, J. (2003) Do you believe in magic? What we can expect from early childhood intervention programs, *Social Policy Report*, 17(1): 3–7.

Dearing, E., Berry, D. and Zaslow, M. (2006) Poverty during early childhood, in K. McCartney and D. Phillips (eds.) *Blackwell Handbook of Early Childhood Development*. Oxford: Blackwell.

Department for Children, Schools and Families (DCSF) (2009) *Deprivation and Education: The evidence on pupils in England, Foundation Stage to Key Stage 4*. London: DCSF.

Department for Education (DfE) (2010) *Achievement of Children in the EYFSP*. DfE Research Report No. 34. London: DfE.

Department for Work and Pensions (DWP) (2010) *Households Below Average Income* (HBAI) 1994/95-2009/10. London: DWP.

Dollase, R. (2007) Bildung im Kindergarten und Früheinschulung: Ein Fall von Ignoranz und Forschungsamnesie [Learning in kindergarten and preschool: A case of ignorance and forgotten results], *Zeitschrift für Pädagogische Psychologie*, 21: 5–10.

Gledhill, J., Ford, T. and Goodman, R. (2002) Does season of birth matter?, *Research in Education*, 68: 41–7.

Gurland, S.T. and Grolnick, W.S. (2005) Perceived threat, controlling parenting and children's achievement orientations, *Motivation and Emotion*, 29: 103–21.

Hardre, P.L. and Reeve, J. (2003) A motivational model of rural students' intentions to persist in versus drop out of high school, *Journal of Educational Psychology*, 95(2): 347–56.

Healy, J.M. (2004) *Your Child's Growing Mind*. New York: Broadway Books.

Hohmann, M., Weikart, D. and Epstein, A.S. (2008) *Educating Young Children*, 3rd edn. Ypsilanti, MI: High/Scope Press.

Hyson, M., Copple, C. and Jones, J. (2007) Early childhood development and education, in *Handbook of Child Psychology*. New York: Wiley.

Laevers, F. (2003) Experiential education: Making care and education more effective through well-being and involvement, in F. Laevers and L. Heylen (eds.) *Involvement of Children and Teacher Style. Insights from an International study on experiential education*. Studia Pedagogica No. 35. Leuven: Leuven University Press.

Lynch, R. (2004) *Exceptional Returns: Economic, fiscal, and social benefits of investment in early childhood development*. Washington, DC: Economic Policy Institute.

Marcon, R.A (2002) Moving up the grades: Relationship between pre-school model and later school success, *Early Childhood Research and Practice*, 4(1): 517–30.

Martin-Korpi, B. (2005) The foundation for lifelong learning, *Children in Europe*, Issue 9, September, Edinburgh.

McGuire-Schwartz, M. (2007) Community mothers: Relationships between family and social support and mother–child bonds. Multicultural perspectives in Ireland and the United States, *Journal of Poverty and Children*, 13(2): 133–56.

Meyers, M., Rosenbaum, D., Ruhm, C. and Waldfogel, J. (2004) Inequality in early childhood education and care: What do we know?, in K. Neckerman (ed.) *Social Inequality*. New York: Russell Sage Foundation.

Organization for Economic Cooperation and Development (OECD) (2006) *Starting Strong II: Early Childhood Education and Care*. Paris: OECD.

Ponitz, C.C., McClelland, M.M., Matthews, J.S. and Morrison, F.J. (2009) A structured observation of behavioral self-regulation and its contribution to kindergarten outcomes, *Developmental Psychology*, 45: 605–19.

Reeve, J. (2002) Self-determination theory applied to educational settings, in E.L. Deci and R.M. Ryan (eds.) *Handbook of Self-determination Research*. Rochester, NY: University of Rochester Press.

Rinaldi, C. (2006) *In Dialogue with Reggio Emilia: Listening, researching and learning*. London: Routledge.

Rose, J. (2009) *Independent Review of the Primary Curriculum: Final Report*. Nottingham: DfES.

Ryan, R.M. and Deci, E.L. (2000) Self-determination theory and the facilitation of intrinsic motivation, social development and well-being, *American Psychologist*, 55: 68–78.

Ryan, R.M. and Deci, E.L. (2004) The 'what' and the 'why' of goal pursuits: Human needs and the self determination of behaviour, *Psychological Inquiry*, 11: 227–68.

Schweinhart, L.J., Montie, J., Xiang, Z., Barnett, W.S., Belfield, C.R. and Nores, M. (2005) *Lifetime Effects: The HighScope Perry Preschool Study through age 40*. Monographs of the HighScope Educational Research Foundation No. 14. Ypsilanti, MI: High/Scope Press.

Suggate, S.P. (2007) Research into early reading instruction and Luke effects in the development of reading, *Journal for Waldorf/Rudolf Steiner Education*, 11(2): 17–20.

Suggate, S.P. (2009) School entry age and reading achievement in the 2006 Programme for International Student Assessment (PISA), *International Journal of Educational Research*, 48: 151–61.

Suggate, S.P., Schaughency, E.A. and Reese, E. (2013) Children learning to read later catch up to children reading earlier, *Early Childhood Research Quarterly*, 28(1): 33–48.

Sykes, E., Bell, J. and Rodeiro, C. (2009) *Birthdate Effects: A review of the literature from 1990-on*. Cambridge: Cambridge Assessment. Available at: http://www.cambridge-assessment.org.uk/images/109784-birthdate-effects-a-review-of-the-literature-from-1990-on.pdf.

Sylva, K., Melhuish, E.C., Sammons, P., Siraj-Blatchford, I. and Taggart, B. (2004) *The Effective Provision of Pre-School Education (EPPE) Project: Technical Paper 12 – The Final Report: Effective Pre-School Education*. London: DfES/Institute of Education.

Tickell, C. (2011) *The Early Years: Foundations for life, health and Learning*. London: DfE.

Turnbull, S. (2006) The rate of learning to read in a Rudolf Steiner school, *Journal for Waldorf/Rudolf Steiner Education*, 8(2): 11–16.

Vygotsky, L.S. (1978) *Mind in Society*. Cambridge, MA: Harvard University Press.

Whitebread, D. (2012) *Developmental Psychology and Early Childhood Education*. London: Sage.

Zisser, A. and Eyberg, S.M. (2010) PCIT: Treating oppositional behavior in children using parent–child interaction therapy, in A.E. Kazdin and J.R. Weisz (eds.) *Evidence-based Psychotherapies for Children and Adolescents*, 2nd edn. New York: Guilford Press.

17 Playing with gender: making space for post-human childhood(s)

Jayne Osgood

Abstract

This chapter invites those in early childhood to (re)engage with critical debates about gendered childhoods in the age of the Early Years Foundation Stage (EYFS). It endeavours to unearth and explore the foundations upon which the curriculum framework is based and what this does to early years practice and childhoods lived in nursery settings. By extending feminist engagements with post-structuralism, neuroscience, post-developmentalism and post-humanism, this chapter seeks to (re)position children as active agents and co-constructors in processes of developing and transgressing gendered identities. It draws attention to the affective, material and sensory worlds of childhood and crucially invites us (adults, researchers, parents, practitioners) to make the familiar strange so as to make space for children to play with the production of themselves as relational to the material, affective assemblages of which they are part.

Introduction

In 2012, 'a unique child' was (re)born. The revised Early Years Foundation Stage (EYFS) Curriculum (DfE, 2012) is founded upon a core principle that each child is 'unique', which, despite being variously undermined and contradicted by normative and normalizing curriculum goals, nevertheless sets a specific tone that acts upon embodied experiences of doing 'child' in contemporary early childhood education and care (ECEC), in particularly limiting ways. The knowledges children have about themselves and the worlds in which they live, alongside the agency they exercise in negotiating them, are rendered invisible and unimportant. Furthermore, attempts by early years educators to engage critically with the cultures of children, and the communities in which they live – and the classed, 'raced', gendered subjective identities that are variously negotiated in nurseries everyday – become fundamentally obscured.

This chapter draws attention to the fact that the revised EYFS curriculum and associated guidance pay little attention to gender. Instead, gender differences are attributed to biological determinism – that is, that girls and boys are fundamentally different; this simplistic and regressive policy move is aided by the concept of the unique child. I will demonstrate the means by which practitioners effectively become excused from dealing with diversity and difference due to the shifts in curriculum that promote individualism and uniqueness.

Children, early years practitioners and nurseries are located within and, in part, shaped by wider societal discourses that promote the idea that gendered childhoods are inevitable and that girls and boys are fundamentally 'hardwired' to behave in particular ways. By troubling the hegemony of neuroscience, or as Fine (2012) urges us to view it 'neurosexism', this chapter invites all those involved in early childhood to (re)engage with gender debates with a critical eye. I draw attention to contemporary research in early childhood settings that identifies the web of discomforting gendered stereotypes and contradictions that circulate and that might remain unchallenged when the 'hardwired' thesis is accepted and become further reinforced in the name of respecting 'uniqueness'.

Gendered identities in early childhood

Debates about gender and the forming identities of young children have long been a feature of academic debate and pedagogical reflection in the field of early childhood education and care. Yet it remains hotly contested and subject to varying degrees of engagement across theoretical, policy and pedagogical terrains. Concerns that gender might 'fall off the agenda' are frequently voiced by feminist scholars unwilling to accept ideas that circulate from the entrenched discourses of biological determinism – that gender binaries are inevitable and, furthermore, that this is irrelevant to the (future) lives of young children. The contribution of post-structuralist feminists writing in the 1990s (such as Bronwyn Davies, Valerie Walkerdine, Glenda MacNaughton, Susan Grieshaber and Gaile Cannella, among many others) has encouraged the field to question and challenge biological determinism and instead to think of gender as *socially constructed*. This counter to hegemonic discourses in early childhood is significant since it offered important ways to challenge orthodox thinking and find alternative ways to conceptualize gender in early childhood education and care. Variously drawing on Butler's (1990, 1993) theorizations of gender, these scholars pointed to the significance of the everyday – routines, performances, interactions – that come to shape gendered behaviours and (re)imprint gendered identities. As a social construct, gender is fluid and shifting and continuously revised/reinstated through social interactions. The gendered boundaries within nursery contexts are closely monitored and maintained by children themselves and their peers, by teachers and practitioners, by family members, and the media (see Davies, 1989; Boldt, 1997; Robinson, 2005) and, I would add, the toy and children's entertainment industries (see Francis, 2010).

As Burman (2008) argues, there are established ideas about the becoming child in early childhood characterized by an entrenched and largely unquestioned adherence to developmentalism. Discourses about child development privilege certain ways of thinking about young children (and gender) and these are embedded in early childhood policy and practice and broadly taken up unquestioningly across different early childhood sectors and settings. Within developmental discourses, children are expected to perform normative behaviours and dispositions against twofold categorizations of what girls and boys do. Where children break free of these binary constraints and perform 'gender variance' (Robinson, 2013), they are treated with suspicion by their peers, teachers, family and society more generally. The concept of forming a gendered identity encompasses multiple relational and reflexive discourses – a form of heteroglossia (Bakhtin, 1994). Rather than viewing children against a set of developmental milestones according to normative ages and stages, critical feminist theorizations of identity allow for children to be considered as agents in the formation of their identities. Following Butler, children's identities can be understood as slippery, fluid and constantly remade through their active (and unconscious) positioning within discourses and the selection of subject positions through gendered performances. This occurs on a minute-by-minute basis, contingent upon time, space and context (Blaise, 2005).

My intention is to take up these conceptualizations and extend them through the application of post-humanist ideas of lived, embodied experience (Braidotti, 2006, 2013; Renold and Mellor, 2013). In extending social constructionist and performative conceptualizations of identity, borrowing from Deleuze and Guattari (2004), I suggest that the 'becoming' child is, in fact, a series of lots of little becomings set within an early childhood that is made up of objects, feelings, sensory encounters, relationships and intentional and unintentional happenings.

For now, though, I want to stay with Butler's concept of identity as performative; as always in process, and the potential it opens up for alternative ways of doing gender; of doing girl and doing boy in the nursery.

Post-developmentist approaches to gendered childhood(s)

Challenges to the dominance of developmentalism in early childhood, such as those offered by Walkerdine (1993), Burman (2008) and Blaise (2010), represent a paradigm shift to *post*-developmentalist approaches to early childhood policy, teaching and research. Such a shift poses a potential threat and source of discomfort since it requires policy makers, practitioners and researchers to question and unsettle accepted ways of being and doing early childhood. Post-developmentalism invites an engagement with complexity and a challenge to simplistic binaries that deny opportunities to be curious about childhood and difference. As Blaise (2013) stresses, the focus in current approaches to early childhood policy, pedagogy and research is on how to 'know' and 'fix' the child. This is acutely evident in the EYFS curriculum, which galvanizes and reinscribes reductionist and simplistic conceptualizations of young childhoods. As a statutory framework, the EYFS in many significant ways acts to limit and contain both childhood and pedagogical practice. It is shaped by developmental theories of childhood with a focus on ages and stages and, therefore, individual progress is understood as a central aspect of early human development.

This policy shift provides authority to commonsense understandings of young childhood(s) shaped by normalized expectations to 'do' childhood in particularly narrow ways. This is evidenced through features of the EYFS such as the recently introduced assessments for two-year-olds, as the guidance indicates:

The progress check has been introduced to enable early identification of development needs so that any additional support can be put into place as early as possible.

(DfE, 2012: 4)

Within this quote is precisely the 'know' and 'fix' preoccupation of developmentalism identified by Blaise. Guidance on how to implement the EYFS is offered by Early Education (2012) in a document entitled 'Development Matters', which was produced for the Department for Education to accompany the statutory framework. This document also offers an insight into the prevailing discourses that shape EYFS and the expectations of practitioners to implement it in particular ways. Development Matters is an interesting shift from Every Child Matters (DfES, 2003), in that the emphasis has become 'normative development' rather than 'every child'. The guidance claims to support settings throughout the EYFS to 'make best-fit judgements about whether a child is showing typical development for their age, may be at risk of delay or is ahead for their age' (Early Education, 2012: 3). While liberal reference is made to the principle of 'the unique child', there appears to be an inherent contradiction in this framework of developmental progress against normative measures that leave little space to be unique. How can childhoods be unique when they are routinely contained and measured through curriculum and assessment with an emphasis on school-readiness and what the child *will become*? Space is denied to be unique; uniqueness becomes regulated, contained and limited to that which is valued through EYFS discourse.

The tensions and contradictions within the EYFS are a consequence of the continued predominance of developmentalism and tokenistic gestures towards recognizing that this approach is fraught with limitations. This is evident in Development Matters (Early Education, 2012), which frequently cites a caveat to the effect that the EYFS should not be used as a checklist, should not be applied dogmatically, that there is overlap in age/stages and therefore practitioners should exercise professional judgement. Yet the EYFS can be questioned on the basis of the undermining effect it has on practitioner autonomy and professional judgement (House *et al.*, 2012). As I have argued elsewhere, early childhood practitioners are left feeling ontologically and professionally insecure in the face of seemingly relentless policy, workforce and curriculum reform (Osgood, 2012). Yet the statutory nature of the EYFS leaves practitioners with scant opportunity to question or challenge the seeming contradictions and disjuncture between childhoods lived and the expectations of the EYFS.

It is significant that research from the field of neuroscience provides the 'evidence' base that is claimed to inform curriculum development in early childhood care and education. Not least because it reinstates the 'know and fix' discourse but also because it is seductive to the field of early childhood:

We know that there are specific changes that occur in a child's brain in the earliest years of its life that have a disproportionate impact on that child's fate; on that child's capacity to make the right choices and avoid the wrong temptations.

(Gove, 2011)

Gillies (2013) highlighted the means by which the Conservative-led coalition government has presented a selective re-telling of neuroscience in order to support early childhood policy. Citing 'brain science' is offered as a 'persuasive fiction' (Strathern, 1987) readily taken up by practitioners (and policy makers and parents for that matter). The privileging of scientific 'fact' in early childhood is troubling because it acts to shut down alternative explanations and ideas about how children make sense of their worlds. While neuroscience recognizes the significance of relationships, interactions and emotions, this is in relation to optimum brain development against normative measurement. The presentation of 'scientific evidence' about how children develop underpins much early childhood policy and curriculum guidance and is problematic for the overly deterministic account it offers.

> The sad part of the increased knowledge about baby brain development is that it is clear that the way hardwiring consolidates the connections makes it very hard to undo or 're-wire'.
> (NHS, Parenting Programme – cited by Gillies, 2013: 12)

This determinism in turn engenders a sense of panic among those with a stake in the lives of young children. In effect, the messages taken up from neuroscience in early childhood discourses amount to fatalistic resignation; that is, if we fail to 'know' and 'fix' the child in early childhood, then the destiny of entire generations will be dire. No space is left to engage with diversity, difference, or for children to be understood as agentic, co-constructors of knowledge and culture. This is significant in respect of the negotiation of gendered subjectivities that children invest so heavily in and the means by which adults (practitioners, carers, parents) denigrate and dismiss hegemonic masculinities/femininities as inevitable while simultaneously problematizing gender variance in childhood. Claims that young children are 'hardwired' to take up stereotypical gendered ways of being are prevalent in contemporary early years and parenting discourses. This is widely supported by neuroscience 'evidence'; however, there are some important counter narratives that challenge the deterministic inevitability of stereotypically gendered behaviours among young children. For example, neuroscientist Eliot (2012) challenges claims that gendered differences in childhood are innate and inevitable. Eliot argues that the 'that's just the way they're built' argument is without foundation; rather, she argues that infant brains are malleable and that small differences at birth become amplified over time, as parents, teachers and the culture at large, unwittingly reinforce gender stereotypes. Children exacerbate the differences by rarely straying from their gendered comfort zones. By appreciating how gendered differences emerge, rather than assuming them to be fixed biological facts, Eliot claims that children can be freed from the limitations of gendered expectations. Although an interesting departure from the predominance of brain science that reinforces ideas of fatalistic determinism, Eliot's contributions to the debate nevertheless reinscribe the child within a developmentalist framework.

Another important counter narrative is that offered by Fine (2012), also writing from a neuroscientific position. Fine draws on research from developmental psychology, neuroscience and social psychology to challenge claims of biological determinism. Fine as a cognitive neuroscientist points to the plasticity of the brain to argue that culture profoundly influences identity formation and challenges claims that girls and boys are 'hardwired'. Instead, like Eliot she proclaims the malleability of the human brain. The emergence of alternative narratives from neuroscience is significant, and offers support to the important work undertaken by feminist scholars in the field of early childhood – albeit from a different theoretical vantage point. However, the extent to which these counter discourses are taken up and shape the daily encounters within homes and nurseries remains an important site for consideration.

The messages that children are offered through popular culture and media representations are saturated with normative and hyper-feminized/masculinized accounts of gender from *Disney Princesses* to *Transformers*. There are commentators who fervently oppose the deliberate strategies employed by global, commercial toy manufacturers, film industries, clothing retailers and so on, as amounting to a toxic pollution of childhood (Palmer, 2007). There is a paralleled backlash through social media groups made up of mothers who feel that they are targeted through advertising and merchandising. For example, *Pink Stinks* in the UK and *Toward the Stars* in the US comprise activist mothers united in campaigns to resist gender stereotyping of childhood.

While such resistance is noteworthy, it is reminiscent of MacNaughton's (2000) account of liberal feminist attempts to challenge gender stereotypical behaviours within nursery settings by seeking to regulate, contain and manage the social and material contexts in which children are exposed to wider societal messages about gender. While laudable, such attempts nevertheless raise a set of important questions about worldviews of 'the child' and 'childhoods', since attempts to de-toxify childhood, and the heavy investments to protect childhood innocence (unwittingly) reinforce the 'know and fix' preoccupation of developmentalism. Furthermore, the agentic possibilities for young children to negotiate and make sense of their (gendered) worlds, *for themselves*, are fundamentally denied. Children do not, cannot (and I would argue should not) live in a social, cultural vacuum; engagements with the world of which children are part, the relationships and associations that children form, reject and negotiate, and the daily experimentation that children undertake in sense making provide fertile grounds from which adults can learn. Too readily professional or parental fear of childhood engagement with objects, colours, noises, technologies that might be constructed as in some sense gendered or otherwise taboo shuts down vital possibilities for understanding 'a culture of childhood' (Taylor and Giugni, 2012).

The powerful discursive landscape emerging from the policy, media, parenting and early childhood discourses in many ways implicates practitioners in, often unintentionally, underlining the seeming inevitability of normative gender performances in early childhood. Where practitioners make attempts to challenge gender stereotypes in early childhood it is often with little impact [see, for example, Holland's (2003) study of zero tolerance of war, weapon and superhero play in nurseries in London]. This in turn risks practitioners reverting to the position that young children may indeed be hardwired!

The seeming inevitability of gendered performances in early childhood settings is further compounded by a heightened consumerist culture. In the age of EYFS, nurseries are viewed as providing a service to discerning customers.

Therefore, the risks involved in challenging hegemonic gender behaviours or conversely tolerating/enabling gender variance are great. There is a potential danger that a practitioner becomes known as the 'feminist killjoy' (Ahmed, 2004), since gender has become such a contradictory, marginalized, (a)political and (in)visible issue in early childhood. To engage meaningfully with gendered processes, performances, silences and the potential implications has become a secondary consideration to delivering the (statutory) curriculum. Yet gender (as well as race and class) inequalities remain significant features of contemporary life and the role of the feminist killjoy remains vital in order to challenge and seek to reach theorizations of difference that refuse inevitability discourses.

Post-humanist views of childhood

As outlined above, the concept of the unique child is embedded within the EYFS curriculum and is fraught with inherent contradictions and limitations when framed in developmental, biological deterministic discourses. For practitioners, the implications of a 'unique child' present on-going daily challenges because, in effect, the EYFS curriculum and its focus on individualism and normativity shuts down opportunities to engage with diversity and difference. This is laced with a troubling set of contradictions – where child-centredness is overlooked when a child shows curiosity about difference that nurseries and parents find difficult, such as heteronormativity or conversely gender variance. It also reinscribes childhood innocence discourses and reinstates developmentalism; put simply, the child is understood as too young and too innocent to be troubled by such concerns as ethnicity, class and gender. In effect, a child's curiosity about their multiple identities is denied space. The EYFS and the key concepts underpinning it create a set of moral and pedagogical dilemmas for early years practitioners working with young children. But what might happen if space and opportunities are made available to think differently?

Recent feminist engagements with the work of French philosophers Deleuze and Guattari offer opportunities to think differently about young children and their enactments, performances and resistances in early childhood. For example, Renold and Mellor (2013), Jones (2013), Blaise (2013), Olsson (2009), Lenz Taguchi (2010) and Osgood *et al.* (2013) are among a growing number to have taken up Deleuzo-Guattarian concepts so as to highlight the exciting, generative possibilities available to reconceptualize young childhoods; to mobilize theories that attend to the affective, material and corporeal – and to mundane, habitual, everyday events – that occur in early childhood but that risk being overlooked in the age of EYFS.

Taking up Deleuzo-Guattarian concepts allows space to think about young children as *playing with* gender, beyond investments in getting it right (Davies, 1989) and circulating within and against hegemonic gender discourses. Instead, we are invited to observe the means by which children variously challenge, resist, revel, indulge and transgress gendered ways of being through their interactions with people and things, through verbal, non-verbal, physical, becomings in the routine daily goings on in early childhood settings. Such reframing provides new spaces and freedoms to observe rather than assume that we (adults, childhood experts) know what is best for the (unique) child.

Deleuzo-Guattarian approaches tend towards a microscopic engagement with relational affective assemblages made up of people, sensations, sounds, smells and materials. Nurseries are highly physical, emotional spaces where human interactions are accompanied and in many ways shaped by noise, smell and touch; days are punctuated by rhythm and structure, chaos and serendipity. It is unsurprising, then, that post-humanist theories should hold appeal to feminist researchers working in the field of early childhood. Contemporary engagements with Deleuze and Guattari, such as those offered by Jones (2013) and Renold and Mellor (2013) for example, seek to extend perspectives of subjectivity, to go beyond the individual to include the collective, affective assemblage to other bodies and things so as to provide opportunities to open out the concept of childhood subjectivity. This is particularly useful for (re-)engaging debates about gendered subjectivities in early childhood, since it accepts early childhood as uniquely constituted through complex processes of emergence and subjectification. As Renold and Mellor (2013) remind us, dominant systems of power (class, race, gender, age, and so on) remain – they are the mechanics which provide the 'conditions of possibility' for certain subjectivities to emerge, while others are less possible; in early childhood these conditions are deeply embedded at the molar level of sexed subjectivities – i.e. dominant ideas of what it is to be/do boy/girl; but where gender circulates in a multiplicity of ways at the molecular level, through and across bodies and objects.

Renold and Mellor (2013) provide examples from their research in nursery settings where close examination, through a Deleuzo-Guattarian lens, provides alternative and enriched explanations that add to the nuanced understandings of children as complex gendered becomings. The authors highlight the relationship and interactions of a young boy (Tyler) and girl (Sophie). Their play, when read through the heterosexual matrix (Butler, 2005), is characterized by heteronormative, hyper-feminine and hyper-masculine performances; Tyler and Sophie are seemingly appropriating romantic attachments and binary gendered ways of being (i.e. masculine-loud-physical; feminine-quiet-demure). Yet a microscopic, ethnographic, multisensory mapping of their play reveals a far more complex and multi-layered assemblage at work – where both Tyler and Sophie can be interpreted as playing with gender through various subversive and complicit acts, in a multiplicity of ways, through the enactment with objects (toys: Barbie, Action Man) that simultaneously regulate and rupture molar lines, and where agency is exercised in surprising ways that transgress what might otherwise be read as gendered containment – or heteronormativity.

Jones (2013) takes up the interrelationship between desire, lived performances of bodies and the gendered inscriptions that act to frame and contain 'boy' and 'girl' in early childhood. Like Renold and Mellor (2013) and others working with Deleuze and Guattari in early childhood, Jones focuses on the very minute occurrences within children's enactments – in this case, a group of five-year-old children playing in a make believe Medieval castle. Lucy the fairy princess; Jack the Jester who refuses to dance but who will do magic tricks; Sean and Jonathan participant observers; and Harley who refuses to be prince and instead adorns a princess dress. Through her analysis Jones invites us to take up some post-humanist concepts in order that we might reach new ways of engaging with conceptualizations of gender in early childhood, as she stresses 'thinking beyond or outside customary logic necessitates rejecting linearity' (Jones, 2013: 8). To this end the reader is encouraged to transcend what we think is signified (by Harley performing gender variance through dressing as a princess) and instead heed 'the potency of its expression' (Braidotti, 2002: 199 in Jones 2013: 10). Jones asks: What does *becoming dress* make possible? What are its functions with and connections with other things? What does it transmit? What intensities does it induce or condone or negate?

The nature of analysis Jones undertakes, in seeking to explore gender in early childhood, shares much with the approach taken by Renold and Mellor. Both are endeavouring to urge that we (adults, researchers, parents, practitioners) make the familiar strange, keep focused on the middles of becomings (not the causes or fixed trajectories) so as to avoid dualisms that can act to fix. As Renold and Mellor (2013: 38) conclude:

> Taking Deleuze and Guattari into the nursery has afforded us a way of mapping, seeing and attending to events (things, feelings, sounds, bodies) and has enabled a textured multi-sensory way of knowing.

Practical implications

So what might this mean for early childhood practice? First, it requires an engagement with the idea that the conditions for possibility in the nursery are fundamentally material and sensorial, so that we come to understand that identity is not constituted by corporeal subjects but rather it is generated relationally by objects and senses of all kinds. It involves attention to the material – where stuff is not just stuff but rather the constituent parts of subjectivities (as in Harley's princess dress). Rossholt (2012) stresses that in early years settings, children's bodies are more than simply inscribed by external, societal discourses – children participate in the material production of themselves and others as 'doing bodies'. This allows for a focus on material, affective and discursive practices that are so prevalent in the lives of young children but that readily get overlooked with the curriculum's preoccupation with cognitive development. Taking a post-humanist approach, movement and touch are recognized as important ways of being in the world – although as Deleuze and Guattari (2004) stress, this must be understood as embedded in wider stratified social, political and economic contexts. But this refocusing enables new ways of seeing, feeling, engaging with everyday happenings of childhoods lived in early childhood settings and offers a means to engage afresh with persistent political concerns such as gender inequality. Importantly, it requires that we (adults/apparent knowers) are prepared to be surprised, question our world views and make space to consider 'the rights of children' as children who have rights to explore and transgress.

As Taylor and Giugni (2012) argue, when children are given space to explore the worlds in which they live in enabling ways, they are free to generate knowledge about the people, places and events in which they are immersed – and I would add generate knowledges about themselves. This is to recognize the significance of children's abilities, knowledges, agencies and allows for a broader view of what children can do than that prescribed by a 'curriculum' predicated on school-readiness.

Conclusion

Mobilizing a post-humanist approach to early childhood might open up possibilities to rethink childhood and break free from the confines and constraints of hegemonic discourses and curriculum frameworks that limit and contain – and instead allow children to play with the production of themselves as relational to the material, affective assemblages of which they form part.

Points for discussion and reflection

1. What implications might there be for your practice in making space for children to be active agents and co-constructors in developing and transgressing gendered identities?
2. Do you always respond to children in terms of biological determinism or do you think of gender identity as socially constructed? Are you able to share these views? How would/are they received in your setting?
3. What are the positive and negative effects of media representations and commercialization on children's gendered identities?
4. How far do you feel the revised EYFS curriculum 'galvanises and reinscribes reductionist and simplistic conceptualisations of young childhoods'. What is the evidence for your response?
5. In your observations, how do children exhibit similarities and, conversely, show differences in their gendered behaviours? Have you observed children 'playing with gender through various subversive and complicit acts'? How has this made you feel? What, if anything, do you do about it?

References and further reading

Ahmed, S. (2004) *The Cultural Politics of Emotion*. Edinburgh: Edinburgh University Press.
Bakhtin, M.M. (1994) *The Bakhtin Reader* (P. Morris, ed.). Oxford: Oxford University Press.
Blaise, M. (2005) *Playing it Straight! Uncovering gender discourses in the early childhood classroom*. London: Routledge.
Blaise, M. (2010) Creating postdevelopmental logic for mapping gender and sexuality in early childhood, in S. Edwards and L. Brooker (eds.) *Engaging Play*. Maidenhead: Open University Press.
Blaise, M. (2013) Activating micropolitical practices in the early years: (Re)assembling bodies and participant observations, in R. Coleman and J. Ringrose (eds.) *Deleuze and Research Methodologies*. Edinburgh: Edinburgh University Press.
Boldt, G. (1997) Sexist and heterosexist responses to gender bending, in J. Tobin (ed.) *Making a Place for Pleasure in Early Childhood Education*. New Haven, CT: Yale University Press.
Braidotti, R. (2006) *Transpositions: On nomadic ethics*. Cambridge: Polity Press.
Braidotti, R. (2013) *The Posthuman*. Cambridge: Polity Press.
Burman, E. (2008) *Developments: Child, image, nation*. London: Routledge.

Butler, J. (1990) *Gender Trouble: Feminism and the subversion of identity*. London: Routledge.

Butler, J. (1993) *Bodies that Matter*. London: Routledge.

Butler, J. (2005) *Undoing Gender*. London: Routledge.

Davies, B. (1989) *Frogs and Snails and Feminist Tales: Preschool children and gender*. Sydney, NSW: Allen & Unwin.

Deleuze, G. and Guattari, F. (2004) *A Thousand Plateaus*. London: Althone Press.

Department for Education (DfE) (2012) *Statutory Framework for the Early Years Foundation Stage: Setting the standards for learning, development and care for children from birth to five*. Available at: http://www.foundationyears.org.uk/wp-content/uploads/2012/07/EYFS-Statutory-Framework-2012.pdf.

Department for Education and Skills (DfES) (2003) *Every Child Matters*, Cm 5860. Norwich: The Stationery Office.

Early Education (2012) *Development Matters in the Early Years Foundation Stage*. London: Early Education.

Eliot, L. (2012) *Pink Brain, Blue Brain: How small differences grow into troublesome gaps – and what we can do about it*. London: One World Publications.

Fine, C. (2012) *The Real Science Behind Sex Differences: Delusions of gender*. London: Icon Books.

Francis, D. (2010) Gender, toys and learning, *Oxford Review of Education*, 36(3). 325–44.

Gillies, V. (2013) *From baby brain to conduct disorder: The new determinism in the classroom*, Paper delivered to the Gender and Education Association Conference, 25 April, London Southbank University.

Gove, M. (2011) *Improving the quality and range of education and childcare from birth to 5 years*, Speech 21 November 2011. Available at: https://www.gov.uk/government/speeches/michael-gove-speaks-to-the-london-early-years-foundation-about-the-importance-of-early-years (accessed 7 May 2013).

Holland, P. (2003) *We Don't Play with Guns Here: War, weapon and superhero play in the early years*. Buckingham: Open University Press.

House, R., Osgood, J. and Simpson, K. (2012) The revised EYFS: *Still* 'too much, too young', *Early Years Educator*, 14(2): 18–20.

Jones, L. (2013) Becoming child/becoming dress, *Global Studies in Childhood*. Available at: http://www.wwwords.co.uk/gsch/content/pdfs/3/issue3_3.asp (accessed 14 June 2013).

Lenz Taguchi, H. (2010) *Going Beyond the Theory/Practice Divide in Early Childhood Education: Introducing an intra-active pedagogy*. London: Routledge.

MacNaughton, G. (2000) *Rethinking Gender in Early Childhood Education*. London: Paul Chapman.

Olsson, L.M. (2009) *Movement and Experimentation in Young Children's Learning: Deleuze and Guattari in early childhood education*. London: Routledge.

Osgood, J. (2012) *Narratives from the Nursery: Negotiating professional identities in early childhood*. London: Routledge.

Osgood, J., Albon, D., Allen, K. and Hollingworth, S. (2013) 'Hard to reach' or nomadic resistance? Families 'choosing' not to participate in early childhood services, *Global Studies in Childhood*. Available at: http://www.wwwords.co.uk/gsch/content/pdfs/3/issue3_3.asp (accessed 11 June 2013).

Palmer, S. (2007) *Toxic Childhood: How the modern world is damaging our children and what we can do about it*. London: Orion.

Renold, E. and Mellor, D. (2013) Deleuze and Guattari in the nursery: Towards an ethnographic multi-sensory mapping of gendered bodies and becomings, in R. Coleman and J. Ringrose (eds.) *Deleuze and Research Methodologies*. Edinburgh: Edinburgh University Press.

Robinson, K. (2005) 'Queerying' gender: Heteronormativity in early childhood education, *Australian Journal of Early Childhood*, 30(2): 19–28.

Robinson, K. (2013) *Innocence, Knowledge and the Construction of Childhood: The contradictory nature of sexuality and censorship in children's contemporary lives.* **London: Routledge.**

Rossholt, N. (2012) Food as touch/touching the food: The body in-place and out-of-place in preschool, *Educational Philosophy and Theory*, 44(3): 323–34.

Strathern, M. (1987) Out of contexts: The persuasive fictions of anthropology, *Current Anthropology*, 28: 251–81.

Taylor, A. and Giugni, M. (2012) Common worlds: Reconceptualising inclusion in early childhood communities, *Contemporary Issues in Early Childhood*, **13(2): 108–19.**

Walkerdine, V. (1993) Beyond developmentalism?, *Theory and Psychology*, 3: 451–69.

18 Without foundation: the EYFS Framework and its creation of needs

Jonathan Rix and John Parry

Abstract

This chapter examines the language and underpinning ideas of the Statutory Framework for the Early Years Foundation Stage (EYFS) and its supporting documents. It explores how notions of diversity and difference emerge, in particular the construction of special educational needs and disability. It considers the underlying contradictions that arise, including links to the United Nations Convention on the Rights of the Child. The chapter examines the claims that the framework is not about a staged notion of development, and relates this to its vision of what education is for and how parents should be involved. As well as challenging the norm-based notions of development and assessment underpinning the EYFS, the chapter questions why difference is not threaded through the document but emerges as an occasional add on. It also highlights the challenges that emerge in relation to equitable access to support at a time when there is a shift away from centralized systems towards an increasing diversification of provision. It questions whether the processes the framework encourages practitioners to undertake will result in more effective practice that is genuinely responsive to the learning needs of children and relevant to practitioners.

Introduction: Getting the rights wrong

From the outset, the Statutory Framework for the Early Years Foundation Stage (EYFS) (DfE, 2012) and its supporting materials contain contradictory and competing concepts woven together to create an impression of one thing but offering a very different reality. For example, on page 1 of the Non-Statutory Guidance material intended to support practitioners, 'Development Matters in the Early Years Foundation Stage' (Early Education, 2012), it states:

> Children have a right, spelled out in the *United Nations Convention on the Rights of the Child*, to provision which enables them to develop their personalities, talents and abilities irrespective of ethnicity, culture or religion, home language, family background, learning difficulties, disabilities or gender.

Unfortunately (or perhaps fortunately), children do not have this right within the United Nations Convention on the Rights of the Child (1989). The authors of this material have mixed together Articles 2 and 29 to create their own version. Article 2 is concerned with the application of rights 'without discrimination of any kind, irrespective of the child's or his or her parent's or legal guardian's race, colour, sex, language, religion, political or other opinion, national, ethnic or social origin, property, disability, birth or other status', while Article 29 is where States agree that education shall focus upon 'the development of the child's personality, talents and mental and physical abilities to their fullest potential'.

In weaving these two quite different articles together, the non-statutory guidance gives an impression that 'ethnicity, culture or religion, home language, family background, learning difficulties, disabilities or gender' are in some way a potential constraint upon developing their 'personalities, talents and abilities'. They are to develop these capacities without having regard to any of these identified differences. By implication, these differences must pose some kind of risk to their development, otherwise you could pay attention to them. This, however, in many ways is exactly what you do want to do. Who would want to develop their personalities, talents and abilities irrespective of these other key personal characteristics? In many ways, these key characteristics will be at the very heart of children's personalities, talents and abilities. Now it may well be that the authors of the non-statutory guidance would say that this is not what they meant; however, as with so much within the EYFS Framework and its supporting documentation, its content undermines its own aspirations.

Developing evidence

Early on in the Statutory Framework (section 1.1), it is claimed that:

> The learning and development requirements are informed by the best available evidence on how children learn and reflect the broad range of skills, knowledge and attitudes children need as foundations for good future progress.

What exactly these sources are for this evidence is left vague. However, in the statement accompanying the publication of the framework, the Minister noted that the reformed EYFS was built on the 'independent' advice of Dame Clare Tickell. They do not state of what that advice was independent. By implication, the Minister meant 'of government involvement', but since the EYFS is not written by Tickell but by the Department for Education, any independence she may have had when gathering the information becomes irrelevant when the Department have reinterpreted it for the EYFS Framework.

This is particularly evident in relation to the development statements that populate the non-statutory guidance. Tickell's (2011) report includes a chapter that cites its evidence sources. Of 320 cited sources, only five look at child development. All the rest are considerations of experiences, strategies, debates around central issues, brief summary documents of broad fields or assessments of impact of provision and practice. The five citations related to child development are all to the same document, an 'Early Years Learning and Development Literature Review' (Evangelou *et al.*, 2009) commissioned by the then Department for Children, Schools and Families (DCSF). However, the evidence from this review recommends not viewing children's development in the manner adopted in the non-statutory guidance. It specifically warns against linear notions of development, against the 'stepping stones' of the earlier framework and highlights that 'development proceeds in a web of multiple strands, with different children following different pathways' (Evangelou *et al.*, 2009: 8).[1]

What is particularly noticeable on reading Evangelou and colleagues' fascinating review is how little they identify specific ages or age ranges in which things occur. Their review explores the competing theories about development, offers research descriptions of development processes and how social and cultural factors influence these, but only very occasionally presents age ranges for the emergence of behaviours and only then in a very broad and qualified manner.

Evangelou *et al.* (2009) acknowledge that they are updating the evidence from the original EYFS, collected within the Birth to Three Matters Review (David *et al.*, 2003); evidence that is not cited in the Tickell Review (2011) noted by the Minister. However, in their review, David *et al.* (2003: 25) also recognizes that '[i]n real life, children's development and learning is not compartmentalised but is holistic, with many inter-connections across different areas of experience'. This, they state, is why the Birth to Three Framework used four broad categories based on the American High/Scope bandings.

So what is the evidence to support the development statements within the latest version of the framework, and where do they come from? The 'Curriculum Guidance for the Foundation Stage' (DfEE/QCA, 2000) introduced the Stepping Stones, on which some of the developmental characteristics were identified, but the tabular staged representation of typically developing children within broad developmental bands did not appear until 2008 in a document called 'Practice Guidance for the Early Years Foundation Stage' (DCSF, 2008). However, when it appeared there was no mention of an evidence base. It might be assumed that it was informed by David and colleagues' review in 2003, but it has far more dates and specified ranges than David *et al.* provide. It does not provide the same information, either. For example, David *et al.* cite evidence that jokes and teasing begin at about nine months but, in the framework, understanding of humour is situated at 40–60+ months; and while beginning to organize and categorize objects is 16–26 months in the framework, in the review it is suggested that babies can categorize objects from a much younger age.

One can only assume therefore that the development statements did not emerge from a commissioned review but instead from a working party, like those which produced the monitoring protocol for deaf children and developmental journal for children with Down syndrome (DfES, 2006a, 2006b). However, given that the expert reviews which were commissioned advised against such staged lists and the contentious nature of any statements which are made, it is clear that the dominant descriptive tool within the EYFS, which underpins all subsequent assessment, is problematic. It is particularly problematic in relation to children with additional or special educational needs, given that these needs exist because the child's development appears to fall outside the framework's construction of typical development. Once we recognize that the statements are questionable, we have to accept that our basis for identifying additional needs is also questionable.

A theoretical mess

Another key contradiction to emerge from reading the reviews and the framework is to do with the use of theory. Theory is important because it explains a 'thing' in different ways and, therefore, influences how we see and respond to that 'thing'. The competing theories that underpin ideas about children and notions of development are described and drawn upon within the two earlier reviews but within the Framework they are entwined in such a way as to undermine their usage. There seem to be underlying tensions between three broad theoretical views:

- we are all developing within a social and cultural context that develops in relation to our development (sociocultural perspective);
- we each develop as an individual through interactions with a range of social and environmental factors (interactionist perspective);
- we develop as individuals and our development can be seen in isolation to the things around it (individualist perspective).

It may seem as if we can operate these three views at the same time, but in everyday situations they produce very different practices.

Let's take a child with a label. If we have a child with the label of 'autism' and view them from the first perspective, we will seek out practices that involve working and playing with their peers and will explore how changes we make impact on a range of situations they find themselves in. If we take the second perspective, we will focus upon the individual with autism and we will identify key issues in their surroundings that we wish to work upon. If we take the last perspective, we will focus upon the individual problems that the person is facing and design specific interventions to overcome them. But when we mix activities drawing upon the different perspectives we set up conflicts. This is the situation within the 39 pages of tables that attempt to weave together aspects of these three perspectives. As a consequence, each approach is compromised.

One particular contradiction is around the practice that the Framework encourages. Much of the documentation and most of the evidence in the reviews about practice and participation adopt the sociocultural and interactionist perspectives. Children's learning is recognized as arising out of their social interactions, which also create aspects of the context in which those interactions take place. As a consequence, practitioners are told to facilitate play that emerges from the children. But the assessment process is underpinned by an individualist perspective. If you doubt that the Framework is prioritizing the individualist approach, just look at where the learning outcomes are situated. There are seventeen of them, they are in **bold**, and they are in the Unique Child column.

So let's consider the contradictory position in which this places practitioners. Take a practitioner faced with a child who is not engaging in social activities in the prescribed way. The Framework encourages them to assess that child individually and to create an individual support programme for them. The practitioner is not encouraged to assess the collective situation including the wider social expectations and pressures that constrain their own options and practice. As a consequence, they are separating the individual from the context which they have assessed them as being separate from in order to create individualized interventions that will get them to engage in that context.

Another key problem is that the individualist perspective brings with it a notion of a typically developing individual. This establishes the notion of the norm. It creates an average against which all can be measured. But, of course, if you have an average some people are bound to be above average and others are bound to be below. The norm is a consequence of the choices made by those who created the development statements. These choices create some children as *having* special needs and others as *being* gifted and talented.

The chosen development statements also generate a notion of typical behaviours. They narrow the available developmental pathways and create a limited range of everyday expectations, despite each of us having hugely different everyday experiences. For example, consider the typical notion of communication evident within the Framework. It is premised on speech and literacy. There may be some very skilled communicators, for example using body language or signing, whose capabilities would not be recognized within this Framework. Their communication falls outside the normal range. Inevitably, this marginalizes the importance of such communication skills in the minds of practitioners. But it may be the very lack of these communication skills on behalf of the practitioners that creates huge frustration for children. If this frustration is then evidenced as negative behaviours in relation to other aspects of the Framework, the child will be disabled by the Framework.

As a consequence of this focus upon the chosen norm, diversity becomes an add-on. It appears at random moments, for example in 'Speaking (16–26 months)' it is suggested that children should be supported using a variety of communication strategies, and at 20–60 months it suggests children learning English as an additional language (not all children) will value non-verbal communications and use of their home language. In 'The world (30–50 months)', there is a sudden mention that children with sensory impairment need supplementary experience and information in order that their learning is enhanced. Why should such experiences be supplementary? Why aren't they just a matter of everyday practice? Will these practices be so unusual that typically developing children could not cope with them?

Statements about practice also suggest activities based upon norms, much of which goes against the sociocultural perspective of the pedagogy identified in the reviews. For example, this pedagogy recognizes the uncertainty in the learning situation and the different meanings people apply to the same context. This is completely negated when norm-based advice about how to create an enabling environment is presented. For example, in 'Moving and Handling (22–36 months)' it is suggested:

> Use gloop (cornflour and water) in small trays so that babies can enjoy putting fingers into it and lifting them out.

Who says they will enjoy it? If they do not, does that mean they need to or there is something wrong? Certainly it would encourage some practitioners to conclude that a child's choices about what to touch and what to leave alone reveal something about the quality of their development.

Every move you make . . .

The diagnostic function of the Foundation Stage is given particular focus in Section 2 of the Statutory Framework document, which looks at the principles and practices of assessment. In the introduction to this section, assessment is defined as playing 'an important part in helping parents, carers and practitioners to recognise children's progress, understand their needs, and to plan activities and support' (DfES, 2012: 10). Of course, the 'progress' highlighted here is not progress that is relative to the individual child; it is not that they have worked out their own way of solving a problem or have made something happen that they have not made happen before. It is not progress in terms of the young person being happier in their situation or progress in terms of the people around them becoming more familiar with their subtle ways of communicating. Lack of progress against these measures becomes a 'cause for concern' and flags up the need for remedial action.

Since 'progress' in the Framework is conceived in the context of particular developmental criteria, the process of assessment is fundamentally medicalized within an individualistic perspective. Additionally, 'practitioners must consider whether a child may have a special educational need or disability which requires specialist support' (DfES, 2012: 6). The focus of assessment is to identify the individualistic in-child deficit rather than the environmental, social and cultural factors that may be impacting on the child's learning.

Within this section of the statutory guidance, there is also a fundamental contradiction in the use of the terminology associated with assessment. It is stated that the on-going assessment expected of practitioners is formative. However, the process being described is not formative. If the on-going assessment was formative, it would be fed back to the children so they could reflect on their own learning. The on-going assessment within the Framework is normative and summative. The observations are used to 'build a picture' of the child that can then be set against the developmental framework, to plan and review how things are going and to assess whether there has been progress.

Significantly, summative assessment receives increased priority in the 2012 Foundation Stage materials with the introduction of a second mandatory review of progress. The 'EYFS progress check at age two' has been added to the established 'EYFS Profile', assessment that takes place when the child reaches age five. Its alignment with the 'Healthy Child Programme' of developmental checks on children at the same age by health visitors further exposes the individualistic medicalized perspective that permeates the EYFS (see also Chapter 5).

Supplementary guidance for early years providers on the 'Progress Check' only serves to reinforce its underpinning diagnostic function. For example, the 'Know How Guide' (NCB/DfE, 2012), as well as recommending a holistic approach to the progress review (involving the views of parents, practitioners and the child), identifies the Development Matters framework as representing 'standards' which should be used to 'inform and support assessment judgements' (p. 2). The choice of value-laden language such as 'standards' conveys the very real sense that young children, and perhaps their families, are being judged as part of the process. It is perhaps not surprising that materials emerging from local authorities to support the EYFS progress check require the numerical recording of a child's comparative age and stage in the prime areas of development within the EYFS Framework. Labelling a child of 26 months at the 12-month stage of developing communication and language immediately and all too easily separates that young person from their peers, potentially shifting focus away from the child and on to their newly acquired label. By introducing the 'Progress Check at two' into the EYFS, a tipping point has been created for some children. The balance will shift from being part of a collective learning experience to needing individual plans and possibly specialist support.

Ironically, although the guidance and Statutory Framework highlight the need to involve other outside professionals, their availability is also in question. At a time of service reduction, restructuring and fragmentation, resulting from spending cuts, legislative changes and the aspiration for new forms of provision, specialist support may be harder for settings to access.

The guidance accompanying the EYFS Framework also describes a distinct process for carrying out the progress check with children labelled with 'identified disabilities or special educational need' (NCB/DfE, 2012: 20). Involving other agencies, referring to other checklist materials and seeking expert advice to proceed with the assessment are included in the suggestions. For children placed in this category, parents are regarded as pivotal to the process because of their 'significant expertise in and understanding of their child's development' (NCB/DfE, 2012: 20). In contrast, other parents are cast much more as contributors to their children's progress reviews, who can share their 'in depth knowledge of their child' but also need 'suggestions... in supporting their child at home' (NCB/DfE, 2012: 10–11). Evidently, the EYFS Framework has the potential to impose other layers of differentiation and division within the early years community.

The concluding points in the Assessment section of the Statutory Framework cover the Early Years Foundation Stage Profile (EYFSP), the second summative check that practitioners have to complete. Although the recommendations are that the profile will represent a 'well rounded picture' of a child, the focus is on the individual's 'knowledge, understanding and abilities, their progress against expected levels, and their readiness for Year 1' (p. 11). There is recognition that for some children the profile may not capture the diversity of their skills and abilities. For disabled children there is a suggestion that specialist support may be needed to adapt the profile but the guidance states that these adjustments must be 'reasonable' and 'appropriate'. There is no further definition as to what is considered reasonable and so the question remains as to the consequences for those children whose skills and talents cannot be readily mapped on to the profile. What foundation has their years of early learning built for them?

Whose values?

The language of the EYFS Framework and supporting documents also contains a great deal of unspoken assumptions which individually mean little but taken as a whole undermine the aims claimed for early years and the Framework.

In the introduction, for example, it is suggested that 'Good parenting' will lead to a child making the most of their abilities and talents. This leads to the question, who decides what is good? (see also Chapter 14). It also increases the risk of blame being attached to a parent when their child falls behind on the Framework. A great deal is also made about developing 'working partnerships' with parents. This is part of a thread through the Framework that professionalizes parents. They are key players in preparing the child and ensuring their appropriate development.

Similarly, Section 3 opens with a statement that 'children learn best when they are healthy, safe and secure, when their individual needs are met'. They will of course continue to learn in all life situations, but the notion of 'best' is one that goes unquestioned within the Framework. By implication, best learning is that which moves the child along their pathway further and quicker and is facilitated by responding to individual needs. This implies that less good learning does not move the child along the pathway and ignores individual needs. But frequently both of these things are going to apply. Disabled children may simply not develop in an area designated by the Framework; this then becomes identified as an individual need. Consequently, practitioners may feel encouraged to find a remedy for weakness rather than building on strengths and be more likely to design individualized solutions rather than engage with wider social learning opportunities.

The lack of a focus upon collective needs is also pertinent to the notion of behaviour within the EYFS, which expects behaviour to be 'managed'. This suggests that behaviour emerges from the individual; that it is something children do which practitioners need to control. However, evidence from the sociocultural and interactionist perspectives recognizes that behaviour emerges from the context. For example, OfSTED (2005) reported that a lack of planning and differentiation can lead to behavioural problems for some children and exacerbate the problems for others. However, the Scottish government documentation focuses upon promoting positive behaviour (Dunlop *et al.*, 2008) just as the EYFS promotes good health. Regarding negative behaviour from the individualist perspective has a significant implication because the Framework encourages staff to focus upon specific behaviours as evidence of development. This is evidence which travels with children identified with behavioural difficulties in their records, informing their transition and onward journey through school.

Whose priorities?

The EYFS aims to ensure 'school readiness', providing the foundation for progress. The EYFS therefore is not justified on the basis of now, but on what will come. It is about the future and not the present. This is a very particular view of education and one that does not fit with many of the pedagogical suggestions. It is also at odds with much of the sociocultural and interactionist perspectives that underpin the literature reviews.

This tension is evident in the aspiration that all children make 'good progress' and none are 'left behind'. What are they making progress towards? From what are they being left behind? This completely contradicts the statement that is on every page of the development statements: 'Children develop at their own rates, and in their own ways'. It is evident, too, in the statement about providing a secure foundation on the basis of planning around each individual child and providing them with development opportunities. The children cannot be in charge of their own exploration. The Framework implies that development cannot be left up to them and will not occur without planning, assessment and review. As a consequence, the collective process of learning (which is recognized in the sociocultural and interactionist perspectives) is to be planned using an individualist perspective.

This top-down view of child development and the management of their learning environment is particularly salient in relation to issues of equality of opportunity, anti-discriminatory practice and children's agency. Practitioners are to ensure that every child is included and supported. But included in what, to do what, included by whom, and supported by whom? By implication, they are fitting individuals in with the priorities for the majority.

Whose principles?

A real problem for many practitioners is that many of the individualist statements in the Framework will seem unquestionably true; for example, the first guiding principle that every child is a unique child. But this is a major cultural statement. It could say: all children have overlapping needs that they experience individually and collectively. But it does not. It embeds the notion of the individual within that child, as do the second and third guiding principles. The second asserts that children learn strength and independence 'through positive relationships'. Apart from questioning what makes a relationship positive and whose priorities define this, it is worth asking why we are focusing upon independence and strength above all human characteristics. Given the focus within the EYFS upon socialization, surely interdependence and flexibility might be better options? The third principle also seeks strength, claiming that enabling environments are those that respond to children's individual needs within strong adult partnerships. This creates a room full of individualized children responding to opportunities provided by unified authority. In other circumstances, the phrase 'divide and rule' might be applied. It certainly does not sit comfortably with the sociocultural and interactionist literature cited in the underpinning evidence claimed for the EYFS.

This linking together of multiple individual differences creates other problems. The EYFS states, for example, that children develop and learn in different ways and at different rates. It is absolutely true that children develop in different ways and at different rates, but the notion that they learn in different ways is very debatable. What is meant by this? That different children require qualitatively different pedagogy? That not all children learn with all their available senses and from the experiences they have? The view you take on this will very much depend upon your cultural and theoretical perspective. However, to conflate the two notions is much the same as the conflation of the two articles from the UN Convention. Such a statement is particularly disconcerting, given that it is linked to the inclusion of children with special educational needs and disabilities. By implication the ones who develop differently will learn differently. This is not true.

Conclusion – What the EYFS needs?

The EYFS requires that education and care be tailored to individual needs. The notion of needs has long been debated. Typically needs are assessed and defined by professionals who are judging against the norms that their peers have created, rather than identified by people for themselves. Roaf and Bines (1989) note that an emphasis on *needs* in special education detracts from a proper consideration of the *rights* of those who are being educated. Needs have to be established before provision is made. They have to be identified 'disregarding how those needs are constructed through the assessment process itself' (Armstrong, 1995: 149). Mayall (2006: 13) describes professional beliefs in child development and socializing children that lead to:

> a set of powerful and interlinked beliefs: that adults understand children, that adults can legitimately draw up a list of children's needs…that problems besetting children are individual rather than socio-political.

The EYFS suggests that the more developed the child becomes, the more emphasis will be upon adult-led activities. However, if too few of these development statements are in evidence, this too requires increased adult involvement, with a focus upon a next step in development, aiming to overcome perceived weaknesses. But this brings into play an irony recognized by early years practitioners working with very young children in early intervention: 'We wouldn't be doing this with another child' (Rix and Paige-Smith, 2011: 35).

Special educational needs are by definition beyond the ordinary. The EYFS requires that providers focus upon support for children with 'special educational needs or disabilities'.[2] It requires all children's individual needs be met, but in brackets adds that this includes two groups: 'children who are disabled or have special educational needs'. Why do they need to identify these types of child separately? Why not specifically mention every group who are frequently marginalized? Lots of groups have different social and cultural needs. A great many of us require reasonable adjustments to be made for us at different times of our lives.

Additionality is also evident when the EYFS links effectiveness of inclusive practices to a capacity to promote and value diversity and difference. The function of inclusion within the EYFS is to create recognition that people are different and recognition that this is important. It does not – as it could if it drew on the sociocultural perspective – frame inclusive practices as the creation of teaching and learning opportunities that engage all learners in a unifying curriculum that is situated in cultural diversity and difference.

Special educational needs are both created and marginalized by the EYFS. The seventeen early learning goals and the development statements define what learning should achieve. In so doing, the failure to achieve these goals and meet these statements defines learning difficulties, giftedness and additional needs. As a document it identifies social, cultural and biological norms, presenting them as robust, research-based and rights-based. Practitioners need to find a way through this social construction. Their starting point must be to recognize that this framework is infused with practical and theoretical contradictions, underpinned by political assumptions and priorities, creating scaffolds for some but barriers for many others.

Points for reflection and discussion

1. Do you agree that the EYFS is a theoretical mess? Can one document effectively reflect the many voices and anticipate the many audiences who work within the early years?
2. Could we manage without formally assessing children? Who would be disadvantaged if we did not assess them?
3. Why might the notion of child development interfere with our capacity to support a young person's learning and growing?

Notes

1. Evangelou *et al.* (2009) also conclude that findings from neuroscience that can be applied to the EYFS are sparse. However, on five separate occasions the Tickell Review refers to evidence from neuroscience in absolute terms.
2. The definition of special educational needs at the time of writing already includes mention of disabilities. If a child with disabilities as defined in legislation requires additional support, they are already in the definition of special educational needs; if they do not require additional support, why mention them?

References and further reading

Armstrong, D. (1995) *Power and Partnership in Education*. London: Routledge.

David, T., Goouch, K., Powell, S. and Abbott, L. (2003) *Birth to Three Matters: A review of the literature*. London: DfES.

Department for Children, Schools and Families (DCSF) (2008) *Practice Guidance for the Early Years Foundation Stage*. Nottingham: DCSF Publications.

Department for Education (DfE) (2012) *Statutory Framework for the Early Years Foundation Stage: Setting the standards for learning, development and care for children from birth to five*. Available at: http://www.foundationyears.org.uk/wp-content/uploads/2012/07/EYFS-Statutory-Framework-2012.pdf.

Department for Education and Employment/Qualifications and Curriculum Authority (DfEE/QCA) (2000) *Curriculum Guidance for the Foundation Stage*. London: QCA.

Department for Education and Skills (DfES) (2006a) *Monitoring Protocol for Deaf Babies and Children*. Nottingham: DfES.

Department for Education and Skills (DfES) (2006b) *Developmental Journal for Babies and Children with Down Syndrome*. Nottingham: DfES.

Dunlop, A.-W., Hughes, A., Fee, J. and Marwick, H. (2008) *Positive Behaviour in the Early Years: Perceptions of staff, service providers and parents in managing and promoting positive behaviour in early years and early primary settings*. Glasgow: University of Strathclyde/The Scottish Government.

Early Education (2012) *Development Matters in the Early Years Foundation Stage*. London: Early Education.

Evangelou, M., Sylva, K., Kyriacou, M., Wild, M. and Glenny, G. (2009) *Early Years Learning and Development Literature Review*. DCSF Research Report RR176. Oxford: DCSF.

Hedegaard, M. (2009) Children's development from a cultural-historical approach: Children's activity in everyday local settings as foundation for their development, *Mind, Culture, and Activity*, 16(1): 64–82.

Mayall, B. (2006) Values and assumptions underpinning policy for children and young people in England, *Children's Geographies*, 4(1): 9–17.

National Children's Bureau (NCB)/Department for Education (DfE) (2012) *A Know How Guide: The EYFS progress check at age 2*. Available at: http://www.ncb.org.uk/ey/peer-topeersupport (accessed 10 December 2012).

Office for Standards in Education (OfSTED) (2005) *Managing Challenging Behaviour*. Available at: http://www.ofsted.gov.uk/resources/managing-challenging-behaviour (accessed 10 December 2012).

Rix, J. and Paige-Smith, A. (2011) Exploring barriers to reflection and learning – developing a perspective lens, *Journal of Research in Special Educational Needs*, 11(1): 30–41.

Roaf, C. and Bines, H. (1989) Needs, rights and opportunities in special education, in C. Roaf and H. Bines (eds.) *Needs, Rights and Opportunities: Developing approaches to special education*. London: Falmer.

Rogoff, B. (2003) *The Cultural Nature of Child Development*. New York: Oxford University Press.

Tickell, C. (2011) *The Early Years Foundation Stage (EYFS) Review: Report on the evidence*. Available at: https://www.gov.uk/government/publications/the-early-years-foundation-stage-review-report-on-the-evidence (accessed 24 May 2013).

United Nations (1989) *United Nations Convention on the Rights of the Child*. Geneva: United Nations.

19 International perspectives on Early Years Foundation Stage

Lilian G. Katz

Introduction

As I reflect on years of many diverse international early years experiences, they have somehow provoked many questions about early childhood curriculum and pedagogy, such as: Where are we now? Where should we be going? What can we learn from each other? And many more. In this closing chapter, I want to discuss some hunches and hypotheses that have occurred to me in the course of these diverse and extensive international experiences in the hope that they will at least be thought provoking.

Similarities across countries

While it is clearly the case that there are many differences across countries, I am frequently amazed by the similarities of the issues in early education around the world. One hypothesis is that people who do the same kind of work across very different countries often seem to face similar predicaments and, therefore, understand each other somewhat better than those who have different roles within their own countries. One hypothesis is that our roles may be more powerful determinants of our ideas, ideologies, concerns, beliefs and ways of thinking about our work and experiences than the larger political, social and cultural context in which we work.

Another aspect of similarities across many countries is the low status and comparatively lower income attributed to early years teachers than to those of older children, and also comparatively poor and/or insufficient training that is common to most of them, although not all (Cohen *et al.*, 2006). This factor has several determinants in many countries, the major one being the ratio of teachers to children as it varies with children's ages. The care and education of toddlers, or of three-year-olds, requires more adults per class than would a class of six- or seven-year-olds. Thus the salaries, wages or benefits of their staff become a more serious consideration than we often realize in most countries.

Professional practices in various countries

I have often been asked where, internationally, I see the best practices in early childhood education. I suggest that, in terms of national perspectives, the Scandinavian countries have a long history of being considered exemplary in their country-wide provisions of early care and staff training and support. In more recent times, there is general agreement that Reggio Emilia, in Italy, is a great source of inspiration, insights and ideas related to outstanding practices in the foundation stage.

However, since the launching of the European Union in the early 1990s, there have been many shifts in provisions for preschoolers and many countries are currently undergoing changes in their traditional early years and primary practices (House, 2011) based on increasing early use of standardized testing. Typically one of the effects of increases in testing is increased emphasis on the academic components of the curriculum, in many cases substantially decreasing children's opportunities for spontaneous play, a traditionally prized component of early childhood provisions.

The Scandinavian countries have also had a long history of mixed-age grouping of young children, and in many cases, through the primary school years as well. This practice is common in communities that have too small a population to fill a whole class with one age group. However, when the education of children in mixed-age groups is addressed and implemented carefully and seriously, it has a great deal to offer children and teachers (Katz, 1998). The Scandinavian early childhood environments are meant to create a home-like atmosphere rather than an instructional one and also emphasize outdoor activity, even during periods of what adults in many other countries would consider inhospitable weather.

In New Zealand outdoor activity for all age groups is also emphasized and New Zealand educators have consistently addressed the indigenous culture of the Maori and the goal of becoming a fully bi-cultural nation. Scandinavian countries and New Zealand also take seriously the training of personnel. But we should keep in mind that the Scandinavian countries together have a total of about 20 million population and New Zealand has just about four-and-a-half million. Addressing serious developmental and childcare issues in countries like India and also China, each of which has populations of well over a billion people, are obviously far more complex and challenging.

In Reggio Emilia each class has two fully qualified teachers, a *pedagogista* who offers support for all aspects of their work and an *atelierista* who works with small groups of children in an *atelier* (art studio) helping them to represent their ideas, observations, plans and such like in a wide variety of media. Reggio Emilia also has a long history of providing an exceptional programme of in-service education and support for its staff.

The concept of alignment

Some of the practices that others seem to have learned from the USA are not so beneficial to the education of young children. A major example is what was first referred to as the 'push down' phenomenon, now referred to as 'alignment'. Generally, this concept seems to result in doing earlier and earlier to young children what probably should not be done to them later either!

This kind of shift in early education is now referred to as the *alignment of the curriculum* that is intended to smooth the children's transition from preschool to school. The concept of alignment is one of the main ideas in the recent edition of 'Developmentally Appropriate Practices' (NAEYC, 2008; Crawford *et al.*, 2009).

Recently, the English government introduced legislation requiring four-year-olds to have beginning reading instruction earlier than had been the custom in Britain, primarily a 'school readiness' agenda. The fact that the English language is difficult to learn to read seems to be one of several reasons *not* to start formal instruction in reading so early. However, a good preschool programme can provide informal exposure to knowledge and skills related to reading in meaningful contexts that can be of real benefit to preschool age children (see Katz and Chard, 2000).

Building a good foundation

The concept of alignment arises from the notion of placing and keeping things in a straight line: such a paradigm overlooks the dynamic nature of development and implies the simple addition of elements of knowledge and skills to be extended later. A more useful and appropriate concept is that of building a good foundation in the very early years upon which the rest of a child's development and education can be built and remain secure.

Structural engineers claim that four basic principles must be taken into account in the processes of designing the foundation for a good building, which can equally be applied to early years foundation. These are as follows:

The **first basic principle** is to *base the design of the foundation of a structure on comprehensive information concerning the nature of the soil it will be standing upon.* The structure would have to be designed differently depending on whether the soil is rocky, muddy or sandy. In a similar way, a teacher gathers as much information as possible about the kinds of experiences that each child in the group has or has not already had, and what each child has or has not already learned. The teacher gives time and effort not only to knowing *about* each child, but also to *knowing* each child.

The **second basic principle** of foundation design is to develop a clear concept of the *characteristics of the structure* that is to be placed on the foundation. For example, information about the future building's attributes such as height, weight and horizontal expanse is carefully studied and taken into account during the foundation design processes. Similarly, curriculum developers and teachers should be planning experiences for young children in terms of their broad aims and long-term goals for the children's futures as well as their more immediate specific objectives and needs.

According to this second principle, then, a good foundation in the early years is one that takes into account all domains of development and what we know about developmental processes. The first domain addresses social and emotional development, both of which must be off to the right start during the foundation stage, that is by about the age of six, or it will be very difficult to repair. Other domains to consider include all aspects of cognitive development. A comprehensive foundation would, of course, also include attention to physical, aesthetic, cultural and other fundamental aspects of growth, development and learning.

The foundation of human development is not simply limited to learning the letters of the alphabet, basic punctuation rules or to the mastery of a few discrete skills practised in exercise books. A common activity observed in many countries during the early years is the exercise of the daily calendar ritual. The common inclusion of this 'calendar ritual' in the foundation stage should remind us also to take into account the important distinction between children *knowing* something (e.g. the names of the days of the week) and *understanding* something (e.g. what the calendar really means!).

Another important consideration in designing the structure to be placed on the developmental foundation is the distinction between the short-term and long-term effects of the experiences provided to young children. What may seem effective in the short term (e.g. test scores) might not only be ineffective in the long term, but possibly even harmful. There is already evidence to show that when different preschool curricula are compared in the short term, what appears at first most beneficial does not remain so when those same children are followed up well into the elementary school years (Miller and Bizzell, 1983; Nores *et al.*, 2005).

Principles 3 and 4 follow below.

Developing a curriculum

At this point, it is useful to address the four main questions that have to be answered in relation to any curriculum that refers to *plans for learning* that will ensure a healthy and sound foundation structure for each learner.

Question 1

What should be learned? As suggested above, the aims, goals and objectives in response to this question have to be thought of in terms of both their immediate effects as well as long-term effects, and we do not always know what those might be. It is useful to keep in mind also that *children always learn* – but not necessarily what we want them to learn! Starting children on academic instruction too early may provoke them to learn to reject school! In the English language the verb 'to learn' is a transitive one: we do not just learn, we learn something! Thus the first question really is – learn what? Perhaps also the question of what we hope will *not* be learned by the children should also be asked!

Question 2

When should it be learned? When designing a curriculum for a good foundation this developmental question must also be addressed. We all agree that all of our children should, for example, learn to read and write. But we do not all agree on precisely *when* these important skills are best learned. Answers to this question depend heavily on our understandings of the nature of development, both in the short term and the long term.

Question 3

How is it best learned? Answers to this question depend on a mix of the first two questions. Once an educator has decided what should be learned and when, the pedagogical methods have to be determined.

Question 4

How can we tell how well we have answered the first three questions? Answers to this question involve methods of evaluation and assessment, and often involve the development of required benchmarks, performance standards and measurements of outcomes. Any group involved in making serious decisions about what kind of early childhood education should be provided as a foundation must deal with this last question carefully, and resist the temptation to answer the first three questions in order to satisfy the way the fourth question is often answered, namely, various ways of 'teaching to the tests'.

Standards of experience versus of outcomes

Many countries are deeply concerned with the 'outcomes' of early education, particularly in the form of various types of test results, which can be measured against economic values. The concept of outcomes is based on an industrial analogy in which raw materials are placed on an assembly line and subjected to identical series of processes, as a result of which 'out come' identical bottles or shoes or tyres. It seems more appropriate to address standards not in terms of outcomes, but in terms of the *experiences* we believe young children typically benefit from. I recommend that we think in terms of 'standards of experiences' that all of our young children should have much of the time (Katz, 2013), which might include:

- A feeling of belonging to a group of their peers.
- Being intellectually engaged and absorbed and challenged.
- Being engaged in extended interactions (e.g. conversations, discussions, exchanges of views, arguments, participation in planning).
- Being involved in sustained investigations of aspects of their own environment and experiences worthy of their interest, knowledge and understanding.
- Taking initiative in a range of activities and accepting responsibility for what is accomplished.
- Experiencing the satisfaction that can come from overcoming obstacles and setbacks and solving problems.
- Having confidence in their own intellectual powers and their own questions.
- Helping others to find out things and to understand them better.
- Applying their developing basic literacy and numeracy skills in purposeful ways.
- And so on...

I am suggesting that experiences such as these are likely to have good short- as well as long-term effects on children, and much more likely to do so than 'teaching to the test'. The staff and parents of a preschool provision might best be served if they come together to create their own list of answers to the question, 'What experiences should young children have much of the time?'

What should be learned in the early years?

To return to the first of the questions outlined above, some basic principles are outlined that can be useful when seeking answers to the many questions involved in planning to build a good early years foundation. Answers to the basic questions should be based on a developmental approach by taking into account *both of the basic* dimensions of development: (a) the *normative*, that is, what most children of a given age usually can learn and can do fairly naturally; and (b) the *dynamic* dimension of development – the cyclic nature of many aspects of development.

To return to the question of *what* should our preschoolers learn is often surprisingly difficult. I suggest that it helps to think about the answers in terms of four types of learning as follows:

Knowledge and understanding

Helping the young to acquire knowledge (and I think it is important to add the term 'understanding' here) is the unique if not special function of educational institutions, including preschools. In principle, when young children have frequent experience of being engaged in activities and tasks about things that they really don't understand, they give up the quest for understanding and eventually become bored with school, apparently universally. The long-term effects of frequent experience of behaving *as though* you understand something when you really do not could have negative effects.

Skills

The second answer to the question of *what* should be learned is skills. Skills are different from knowledge and understanding. They can be defined roughly as small units of action that can be fairly easily observed or inferred on the basis of observation. The list of skills to be acquired and strengthened during the early years can be very long depending upon how specific we have to be. But in terms of categories of skills, we must address many social, intellectual and some preliminary academic skills, fine and gross motor skills and such like.

It usually requires some practice to achieve skilfulness – some skills need more practice than others, and some children need more practice than others.

Dispositions

The third answer to the question of what should be learned can be called *dispositions*. These are difficult to define and are perhaps best thought of as habits of mind with intentions and motives. If the processes of acquiring knowledge, understanding and skills are experienced as painful (rather than interesting and satisfying), they may indeed be acquired, but at the expense of the disposition to use them.

To summarize, I suggest that as educators, we surely want children to acquire knowledge, understandings and skills but, *at the same time*, the dispositions to use them. Having the dispositions without the knowledge and skills would be use-less; but the reverse would also be true. Keep in mind that not all dispositions are desirable – for example, the dispositions to be bossy, quarrelsome, critical, exces-sively shy, and so forth are not desirable ones. In addition, dispositions are not likely to be learned from instruction as in a command like, 'Be generous, or else!' But it is possible that dispositions can be damaged by instruction, especially if the instruction is offered too early, too intensely, and is about topics that are too distant from the young child's first-hand experience.

Some of the most important dispositions are probably in-born and stronger in some children than in others. But the dispositions to learn and to make sense of one's own experiences are in-born in all mammals. Similarly, the disposition to become related to others, disposition to cooperate or to protect oneself, are also likely to be universal. In other words, unless a child is growing in a chaotic envi-ronment (which by definition cannot be made sense of), it should be assumed that all children have a disposition to make the best sense they can of their experience.

It is likely also that some dispositions are learned from observation of oth-ers. Can the dispositions we want our children to have be seen by them in our behaviour? For example, it may help children to observe the adults around them engaged in considering alternative solutions to problems from time to time. A teacher might say something like, 'I've been wondering whether it might be bet-ter to have the book shelf over there rather than where it is now.' These kinds of visible thought processes should be genuine instances of considering alternative courses of action. There is far too much phony talk on the part of adults with chil-dren. One other point here is that for dispositions to be strengthened, they must be behaved in real and appropriate situations with sufficient frequency.

Feelings

The fourth answer to the question of what should be learned is *feelings*. Clearly, many capacities for feeling are inborn. Babies do not require lessons in how to feel fear or anxiety or even joy. But many important feelings are learned from experience, such as feelings of confidence, competence, self-esteem, and many others. Feelings cannot be learned from instruction, exhortation or indoctrination, although adults do have a role in helping children to learn appropriate feelings in particular situations. Focusing on children's feelings of confidence and compe-tence and 'feeling good about themselves' is vital.

Distinctions between academic and intellectual goals

In recent years, it has become customary to emphasize the importance of includ-ing academic instruction in programmes for preschool children. There are impor-tant distinctions, however, between academic goals and intellectual goals (*versus cognitive goals*). Academic goals are those concerned with acquiring small dis-crete bits of disembedded information, usually related to pre-literacy skills, and practised in drills, worksheets and other kinds of exercises designed to prepare children for later literacy and numeracy learning. The items learned and practised

require correct answers and typically rely heavily on memorization, the application of formulae versus understanding, and consist largely of giving the teacher
the correct answers for which the children know he or she is waiting. These bits of
information are essential components of skills such as reading and counting and
other academic competencies. The issue is not whether academic skills matter;
rather, the issue is *when* they matter.

Intellectual goals and their related activities, on the other hand, address the
life of the mind in its fullest sense, including a range of aesthetic and moral sen-
sibilities. They also address intellectual dispositions. Indeed, the formal definition
of the concept of *intellectual* emphasizes habits or dispositions such as reasoning, hypothesizing, predicting, and the development and analysis of ideas and the
quest for ever deeper understanding.

To build a good foundation upon which to develop a life-long learner the curriculum for young children must focus on supporting their in-born (intellectual)
dispositions to make the best sense they can of their own experiences and environments. An appropriate curriculum in the early years is one that encourages
and motivates children to seek mastery of basic academic skills (e.g. beginning
writing skills), *in the service of their intellectual pursuits*. In other words, in
the course of their work and play, children should be able to sense that the skills
involved in writing and reading have a purpose that makes an important contribution to their motivation.

There are two more points to emphasize in connection with the importance
of intellectual goals. The first is that it is easy to assume mistakenly that because
some young children have not been exposed to the knowledge and skills associated with 'school readiness', they lack the basic intellectual dispositions such as
to make sense of experience, to analyse, hypothesize, predict, as do their peers of
more affluent backgrounds. Children of very low-income families may not have
been read to or held a pencil at home. But they, too, usually have lively minds.
Indeed, the intellectual challenges many children face in coping with precarious – if
not dangerous – environments are likely to be substantial and often complex.

Second, while intellectual dispositions may be weakened or even damaged by
excessive and premature formal instruction, they are also not likely to be strengthened by many of the trivial, banal activities frequently offered in childcare, pre-
school and kindergarten programmes. When young children engage in projects in
which they conduct investigations of significant objects and events around them
for which they have developed the research questions and by which they themselves find out how things work, what things are made of, what people around
them do that contributes to their well-being, and so forth, their minds are fully
engaged. Furthermore, the usefulness and importance of being able to read, write,
measure and count becomes self-evident (Katz and Chard, 2000; Helm and Katz,
2001). An essential feature of good project work is that it provides children with
contexts in which they are motivated to ask for help in the use of basic skills (e.g.
writing captions for drawings or creating bar graphs) as they work with purpose
on representing the findings of their investigations.

The **third basic principle** of designing foundations is *to anticipate all of the
possible stresses* to which the structure is likely to be subjected. In a similar way,
curriculum developers and teachers strive to lay foundations that can support

long-term goals, such as a robust disposition to go on learning for a lifetime, rather than just to focus on short-term gains indicated through testing.

Educators might also keep in mind what builders know only too well as the **fourth** basic **principle**: that if the foundations of a building are not properly laid at the outset, it can be difficult and expensive to repair later on. One of the most intractable issues in the field of early education and child development is that the relationships between early experience and long-term stress management are difficult to pin down. We can only build a good educational foundation if we provide capable well-trained and well-qualified teachers who have decent working conditions and compensation, and who are strongly and fully supported in other ways. As Barnett (2008: 2) has put it, on the basis of many studies:

> ...far too few young children have access to the quality of education it takes to produce the positive lifetime outcomes that classic long-term studies like the Perry Preschool Project show are possible.

In summary, the real challenge facing us if we want to realize the potential long-term social, intellectual and academic benefits of early educational curricula, as well as the potential financial benefits of preschool education, is that we have much to do to ensure that in England, the USA and elsewhere it is of the best possible quality.

References and further reading

Barnett, W.S. (2008) Taking a hard look at quality, *Preschool Matters*, 6(2): 2.

Cohen, J.E., Bloom, D.E. and Malin, M.B. (eds.) (2006) *Educating All Children: A Global Agenda*. Cambridge, MA: American Academy of Arts and Sciences.

Crawford, G.M., Clifford, R.M., Early, D.M. and Reszka, S.S. (2009) Education for children 3 to 8 years old in the United States, in R.M. Clifford and G.M. Crawford (eds.) *Beginning School: U.S. policies in international perspective*. New York: Teachers College Press.

Helm, J.H. and Katz, L.G. (2001) *Young Investigators: The project approach in the early years*. New York: Teachers College Press.

House, R. (ed.) (2011) *Too Much, Too Soon? Early learning and the erosion of childhood*. Stroud: Hawthorn Press.

Katz, L.G. (1998) *The Benefits of Mixed-Age Grouping*. Champaign, IL: ERIC Clearinghouse on Elementary and Early Childhood Education.

Katz, L.G. (2013) Taking a stand of standards of experience, *Exchange 209*, 35(1): 8–10.

Katz, L.G. and Chard, S.C. (2000) *Engaging Children's Minds: The project approach*. Stamford, CT: Ablex.

Miller, L.B. and Bizzell, R. (1983) Long-term effects of four preschool programs: Sixth, seventh, and eighth grades, *Child Development*, 54(3): 727–41.

National Association for the Education of Young Children (NAEYC) (2008) *Developmentally Appropriate Practices*. New York: NAEYC.

Nores, M., Belfield, C.R., Barnett, W.S. and Schweinhart, L. (2005) Updating the economic impacts of the High/Scope Perry Preschool Program, *Educational Evaluation and Policy Analysis*, 27(3): 245–61.

Author index

Aasen, W. 82
Ahmed, S. 197
Alexander, R. 1, 42, 43
Allen, G. 166
Anning, A. 127, 132, 137
Argyris, C. 162
Armstrong, D. 212
Arnot, M. 162
Arredondo, D. E. 48
Athey, C. 79
Aubrey, C. 146
Avolio, B. J. 146

Baeck, U-D. K. 161
Bakhtin, M. M. 193
Baldock, P. 159
Ball, C. 7
Ball, D. L. 117
Ball, S. 1, 54
Barlow, J. 171
Barnados 172
Barnes, J. 184
Barnett, W. S. 182, 223
Bass, B. M. 146
Bath, C. 35, 46
Bedard, K. 185
Behr, M. 112
Belaguer, I. 133
Bell, J. F. 184
Bernstein, B. 43, 44, 48
Bertram, T. 8, 21, 180
Bianchi, L. 127
Biesta, G.J.J. 155
Bilton, H. 79, 80
Blaise, M. 193, 194, 197
Blakemore, S. 78, 79
Blaustein, M. 183

Blundel, R. 146, 147
Boag-Munroe, G. 157, 158, 161
Bolden, R. 145, 146, 150
Boldt, G. 192
Bolton, R. 147, 148
Bradbury, A. 37
Braidotti, R. 193, 199
Brandon, M. 168
Bresler, L. 21
British Association for Early Childhood
    Education (BAECE) 9
Broadhead, P. 139
Brock, A. 2, 121
Brooker, L. 9, 10, 11, 121, 156
Brooks-Gunn, J. 184
Brown, M. 114
Bruer, T. 78
Bruner, J. S. 47, 127
Brush, C. G. 145, 146
Burman, E. 192, 193
Butler, J. 192, 193, 198

Campbell-Barr, V. 144, 145, 147, 151
Carr, M. 31, 45, 46, 81
Cavazonni, P. 136
Centre for the Advancement of
    Interprofessional Education
    (CAIPE) 170
Chak, A. 125
Children's Workforce Development Council
    (CWDC) 9, 55
Chilvers, D. 133
Ciulla, J. 151
Clandinin, J. D. 1
Clarke, J. 3
Claxton, G. 25, 45, 46, 81
Clay, M. 72

Subject index

LIBRARY, UNIVERSITY OF CHESTER